THE PRAGMATIC ENTENTE

The Pragmatic Entente

ISRAELI-IRANIAN RELATIONS, 1948–1988

SOHRAB SOBHANI

PRAEGER

New York
Westport, Connecticut
London

Library of Congress Cataloging-in-Publication Data

Sobhani, Sohrab.
    The pragmatic entente : Israeli-Iranian relations, 1948–1988 /
Sohrab Sobhani.
        p. cm.
    Bibliography: p.
    Includes index.
    ISBN 0-275-93337-7 (alk. paper)
    1. Israel—Foreign relations—Iran. 2. Iran—Foreign relations—
Israel. I. Title.
DS119.8.I7S65   1989
327.5694055—dc19   89-3557

Library of Congress Catalog Card Number: 89-3557
ISBN: 0-275-93337-7

First published in 1989

Praeger Publishers, One Madison Avenue, New York, NY 10010
A division of Greenwood Press, Inc.

Printed in the United States of America

The paper used in this book complies with the Permanent
Paper Standard issued by the National Information Standards
Organization (Z39.48--1984).

10 9 8 7 6 5 4 3 2 1

To my mother, father, and brother

for their patience

Contents

Acknowledgments

This study was prompted by the recognition that otherwise well-informed scholars and policy makers tend to know less about Israeli-Iranian relations than they do about Arab-Israeli relations or Arab-Iranian relations. Accordingly, I have tried to draw the historical picture in broad outline, while concentrating at greater length on the details of bilateral relations between Iran and Israel.

The manuscript was completed over two years and in that time I incurred several debts. Professor Robert Lieber read this entire manuscript thoroughly and critically. Without his comments, suggestions, and encouragement I could not have completed this project. Professor Avner Yaniv's review of this manuscript and his insights into Israeli foreign policy have been indispensable in shaping the final product. Professors Shireen Hunter and William O'Brien also read and meticulously critiqued the manuscript. Charles Feigenoff's editorial comments were a pleasure to read and contemplate. For their critical and helpful comments on an early draft of the manuscript, I am particularly grateful to Ambassadors Armin Meyer and Mahmood Foroughi. Michael Metrinko was, as always, generous with his time, ideas, and disagreements.

Other who have assisted me in many ways include Iran specialist William Royce; administrators, faculty, and friends at Georgetown University; the gracious scholars at Tel Aviv University's Dayan Center.

Other individuals to whom I owe deep thanks include Richard Helms, Joseph Alpher, Aaron Klieman, Arieh Levin,

Uri Lubrani, Shmuel Segev, Ali Amini, Farhad Kazemi, Shahram Chubin, and former Iranian officials who worked with the late Mohammad Reza Shah Pahlavi. Without their kind support I could not have thought of undertaking this project.

It also is a pleasure to acknowledge the cheerful and indefatigable help of Masoud Chaharbakhshi whose computer genius saved this project on a number of occasions.

Introduction

On February 10, 1979, El-Al's last flight departed for Tel Aviv from Tehran's Mehrabad Airport, and with it three decades of friendship and cooperation between Israel and Iran ended abruptly as Palestinian guerrillas took control of Israel's embassy in Tehran. To many observers Khomeini's arrival meant a total collapse of Israeli-Iranian relations, but within months the Islamic Republic of Iran received 250 retreaded tires for its F-4 fighters and $135 million worth of Hawk antiaircraft missiles, 155 mm. mortars, ammunition, and other weapons from "Little Satan" — the name the Ayatollah Khomeini gave to Israel.[1]

During Israel's formative years, although political and strategic concerns entered into Tel Aviv's calculations, efforts to establish formal diplomatic ties with Iran were motivated primarily by human and ideological considerations of immigration (aliyah). In 1948, as Jews were being persecuted in Iraq, Israeli agents, with the tacit approval of Iranian officials, used Iran as a transit point to relocate Iraqi-Jews to Israel. Hence, as of mid-October 1949, the Israeli Foreign Ministry adopted the goal of establishing formal diplomatic relations with Iran, not only to pierce the wall of regional isolation but also to facilitate the aliyah of Iraqi-Jews via Iran.

While Tehran accorded de facto recognition to the Jewish state in March 1950, Iran's ambivalent stance toward Israel during the period from 1948 through 1953 had less to do with the ambiguous nature of Israeli-Soviet relations, as some scholars have suggested, and more to do with the influence of

Shiite clerics in domestic politics. These traditionalists, who viewed Iran's history in terms of Islamic values, opposed the government's de facto recognition of Israel and resisted closer ties to Israel. By the end of the 1956 Sinai campaign, the central government under the leadership of Iran's young monarch, Mohammad Reza Shah Pahlavi, had consolidated its power. In 1957 the Shah, recognizing the utility of Israel in terms of Iran's economic and security interests, dispatched the director of Savak, General Teymour Bakhtiar, to Israel to investigate areas of mutual cooperation between the two countries. During this period Iran-Arab relations were strained by Nasser's belligerent stance toward Iran's pro-Western foreign policy; to a large extent the Iranian decision to cultivate closer ties to Israel was based on the Iran-Arab Cold War. General Bakhtiar's talks with his Israeli counterparts were very successful, and after a series of meetings between Mossad and Savak officials, the foundation for a working relationship between the two intelligence services was established; henceforth, the major thrust of Israeli-Iranian relations would be handled by Mossad and Savak officials.

By the time of the Iraqi revolution of 1958, Arab radicalism and its major supporter, the Soviet Union, directly threatened the security of both Iran and Israel. In 1958, with the Eisenhower Doctrine failing to turn the tide both of Arab radicalism and of Soviet influence in the region, David Ben Gurion proposed in a letter to the Shah the establishment of a "peripheral pact" between Iran and Israel. The Iranian monarch agreed, and, as one of the first moves in bilateral relations, Iran became Israel's supplier of petroleum after the Soviet Union decided to end oil supplies to Israel.

Between 1958 and 1967, Israeli-Iranian relations flourished. The Shah, eager to modernize Iran, welcomed Israeli expertise in agricultural development and water resources. In 1962, for instance, Tehran commissioned Israel's water planning organization, TAHAL, to provide rural assistance to the earthquake-damaged Qazvin area. Such economic cooperation facilitated the establishment of more extensive political and military ties. Until summer 1960, neither government publicly acknowledged the working relations they had forged. Then in a news conference on June 23, 1960, on the eighth anniversary of the Egyptian Revolution, the Shah spoke of continuing

Iran-Israel links and maintained that Iran would continue its de facto recognition of Israel, much to the annoyance of Nasser, who immediately broke off diplomatic relations with Iran. The deterioration of Iranian-Egyptian relations only drove Tehran and Tel Aviv closer together. For instance, in 1964, Israel's chief of staff, Lieutenant-General Tsvi Tsur, and the director-general of the defense ministry, Asher Ben Nathan, conferred with Iran's chief of staff, General Abdulhussein Hejazi, and senior members of his staff. The results of these two-day talks were far-reaching: further intelligence sharing, Israeli training of Savak officers, Iranian purchase of Uzi submachine guns, and cooperation in aiding Mulla Mustafa Barzani's Kurdish rebels fighting the Iraqi Baathist regime.[2] Collaboration concerning assistance to Kurdish rebels was perhaps the most important gain for both Iran and Israel because they were able to divert Iraqi military capabilities by ensuring that Baghdad was preoccupied by the Kurdish insurrection.

Britain's 1968 announcement of her intention to withdraw forces from the Suez heightened Iran's fear of the Soviet Union and her radical Arab clients thus intensifying Tehran's search for security. Both states cooperated in assisting King Hussein of Jordan to resist and quell the Syrian/PLO attempt to overthrow his Hashemite dynasty. Furthermore, Iran and Israel continued their campaign against Iraq by providing financial and logistical support to the Kurdish rebels. These relations were not confined to security or military issues alone; rather, significant economic projects played a major role in bringing Iran and Israel closer together. In February 1970, a joint venture between the National Iranian Oil Company (NIOC) and the Israeli government was completed at a cost of $136 million. The venture involved building an oil pipeline from the port of Eilat on the Red Sea to Ashkelon on the Mediterranean, with NIOC providing the bulk of the crude that passed through the pipeline. Apart from oil, commercial links between Israel and Iran thrived during this period; Israeli exports to Iran increased from $22 million in 1970 to $33 million in 1971.[3] In short, the convergence of mutual security and economic interests contributed to the momentum of Israeli-Iranian relations, which had improved after 1968 and continued through 1973.

From 1974 through 1978, Iran's enlarged security perimeter, which now included the Persian Gulf, the Gulf of Oman, the Indian Ocean, and Horn of Africa, prompted the Shah to embark on two complementary policies designed to improve Iran's new strategic position in the region: a massive build-up of military capabilities and intensive diplomatic activities intended to cultivate Arab friendship. The first policy would solidify Israeli-Iranian relations and lead to numerous military projects such as the joint production of a missile system capable of carrying nuclear warheads. The second policy, however, would strain these relations because the Shah feared that Israeli "intransigence" in dealing with the Arab states would radicalize the Middle East and jeopardize the stability of Iran's extended security perimeter. In 1975, for example, the Shah's exercise of Iran's "Arab option" led to the signing of a peace agreement with Iraq. This agreement abruptly and effectively ended Israeli access to areas of northern Iraq controlled by the Kurdish rebels. Throughout this period, in his conversations with the Israeli policy makers who came to Tehran to visit him, the Shah stressed that the Arab-Israeli conflict had to be settled off the battlefield because, as he put it, the occupied Arab lands would not guarantee Israel impregnable borders in "these days of long-range planes flying at 80,000 feet and ground-to-ground missiles which go over any obstacle."[4] But despite the detente in Iran-Arab relations, Tehran did not diminish her contacts with Tel Aviv. Commercial relations flourished during this period; between 1973 and 1978, Israeli exports to Iran, including military equipment, jumped from about $33 million to $225 million.[5] More important, the success of the Shah's strategic agenda for Iran rested on the continuation of Israeli-Iranian relations, which had paid handsome dividends for both countries since 1948.

With the fall of the Shah, Israel lost one of its most trusted friends in the region and since 1979 has had to respond to the challenges of one of its most vociferous enemies, Khomeini's Shiite theocracy. However, one circumstantial event, the Iran-Iraq conflict, enhanced the strategic utility of Iran for Israel despite Khomeini's stated goal of "eradicating the Zionist entity." Not only did Iran effectively remove the Iraqi military from any Arab war coalition against the Jewish state; the

Persian Gulf conflict exacerbated the divisions in the Arab world. Syria and Libya supported Iran whereas Egypt, Jordan, Saudi Arabia, and Kuwait backed Iraq. Paradoxically, Israel's covert military links to the Islamic Republic have proven just as helpful, if not more, in alleviating the Arab threat to Israel as were its relations with Iran under the Shah.

THE PROBLEM

One of the most intriguing features of Middle East politics has been the Tehran-Tel Aviv axis. This study describes the main elements of bilateral relations between Iran and Israel, traces the principal trends in the emergence of this connection, and identifies the main factors leading to both continuity and change in Israeli-Iranian relations.

Given the major differences between Israel and Iran in size, population, religion, and historic traditions, how does one explain Israeli-Iranian relations since 1948? Were these relations a reaction on both sides to a relentless attempt by Sunni Arab states and the Soviet Union to dominate the Middle East? Or did Israel cultivate the Tehran-Tel Aviv connection to counter the hostility of its Arab neighbors? Would it be more accurate to describe Israeli-Iranian relations in terms of who rules Iran: secularists who espouse the doctrine of the separation of church and state or traditionalists who advocate the rule of Islam in both domestic and international affairs? Or was the whole enterprise merely a commercial exercise, where in exchange for Iranian oil, Israel provided Iran with economic and military assistance? Finally, was Tehran's association with Tel Aviv an attempt to use Israel's relationship with the United States to promote Iran's economic and military agenda in Washington?

The veil of secrecy surrounding these relations and the lack of declassified documents have made the task of answering these questions difficult. In many respects, these questions have yet to be fully answered.

A survey of the literature on the subject suggests that the story of Israeli-Iranian relations is incomplete. While some scholars have looked at these relations either from an Iranian perspective or from an Israeli point of view, others have focused solely on the broad outlines of Iranian and Israeli foreign policy. For example, Robert Reppa's book, *Israel and Iran: Bilateral Relationships and Effect on the Indian Ocean Basin*, is essentially a comparison of Israeli and Iranian foreign policy regarding the Indian Ocean from the late 1960s to 1973, with minimal investigation of bilateral relations and the reasons behind them. R. K. Ramazani's article in the *Middle East Journal* of autumn 1978, "Iran and the Arab-Israeli Conflict," examines Israeli-Iranian relations from Iran's point of view. However, its major drawback is that it focuses almost exclusively on Israeli-Iranian relations primarily in the context of the United States and the Soviet Union.

One scholarly work that addresses the link between Israel and Iran on the regional level is Avner Yaniv's *Deterrence without the Bomb: The Politics of Israeli Strategy*. While Yaniv's study focuses on the main points of bilateral relations between Iran and Israel, the picture is incomplete because he captures the essence of Israeli-Iranian relations from Israel's vantage point. He argues that "'Israel and Iran seemed to be moving towards an alliance that would add important increments of security to Israel by increasing the burden on the Arabs and thereby forcing them to be more preoccupied with their security."[6]

Unlike Yaniv's work, Marvin G. Weinbaum's article in the 1975 edition of *Orbis* looks at Israeli-Iranian relations in general terms. However, he is particularly good at capturing the ambivalent qualities of the relationship. He explains Iran's cultivation of closer ties to Israel in the context of Tehran's relations with the Arab world: "Set against the competition of Iranian and Arab nationalisms, Iran's impatient quest for military and economic modernization has drawn it to Israel." He then goes on to say, "A revival of historic ties with Iran meanwhile allows the regionally isolated Jewish state to demonstrate benevolent and cooperative intent, and to fill a vital oil need." But despite the clear-cut rationale for the relationship, it was conducted behind closed doors. Weinbaum points out that Iran shied away from publicizing her "discreet entente" with Israel because of domestic appeals to Islamic solidarity. Iran thus resisted an open courtship with Israel, "whose governments have [reluctantly] veiled their Persian connection."[7]

Another Israeli scholar, Aaron Klieman, looks at the durability of the Iran-Israel connection by examining the reasons behind the post-Pahlavi sale of Israeli weapons to the Khomeini regime. He argues that the origins of Israeli-Iranian relations had been positive and rested upon permanent geopolitical foundations. Under the Shah, the strategic interests of the United States, Israel, and Iran essentially paralleled each other. In the 1970s those interests, Klieman points out, centered on resisting Soviet encroachment in the area, frustrating Iraqi expansionism, and bolstering moderate Arab regimes like Egypt and Jordan. Klieman points out that even after the Ayatollah Khomeini came to power "those earlier foundations which made an initial Israeli-Iranian political and military relationship possible [were] not dislodged. A convergence of interests [existed], with each still needing the other."[8]

Finally, Hebrew University professor Uri Bialer has contributed to the literature on Israeli-Iranian relations by taking advantage of declassified documents from the Israeli Foreign Ministry to provide an excellent insight into the early period (1948–1951) of Israeli-Iranian relations. However, he admits that having no access to Iranian documentation makes it difficult to reach definitive conclusions about Iranian motives. Nevertheless, Bialer argues that "it is reasonable to assume that this formative period (1948–1951) in relations with Israel, and the contacts established with Israel's representatives, clarified for Iran the potential significance which ties with Jerusalem implied."[9]

While each of these scholarly works explains a part of the Tehran-Tel Aviv nexus, the overall pattern of Israeli-Iranian relations is left unrevealed. A more comprehensive look can be reached by posing two, mutually reinforcing, questions: why do states as dissimilar as Iran and Israel form alliances, and to what extent are Israel's cultivation of closer ties to Iran and the latter's willingness to cooperate a function of an external variable or a result of internal domestic forces? In short, what makes these two states tick?

Although Israeli-Iranian relations have changed substantially in 40 years, several constants have emerged. They will be the touchstones of this study.

ELEMENTS OF ISRAELI-IRANIAN RELATIONS

The International and Regional Environment

Iran and Israel are components of an inherently anarchical interstate system. This system is unruly because it lacks an overarching authority with a monopoly of legitimate force to judge the grievances of states and compel them to behave peacefully.[10] Because states like Iran and Israel exist in such a chaotic and hostile environment, they feel insecure and "worry about their survival, and the worry conditions their behaviour."[11] Consequently states resort to searching for security. One of the principal means by which these states obtain security is through alliances. Although some alliances are offensive in nature, alliance partners share first and foremost a common negative interest — their fear of another state or bloc of states.[12] Because alliance partners to varying degrees combine their political, military, and economic capabilities to improve their security and enhance their power, they are willing to minimize the cultural and ideological differences among them. Therefore, the foreign policies of their statesmen tend to deemphasize their professed ideological preferences. Rather, statesmen formulate policies to maximize their nation's security and augment its power relative to other nations.[13] Ironically, each state's search for security becomes a cause of insecurity for others:

> In its effort to preserve or enhance its own security, one state can take measures that decrease the security of other states and that cause them in turn to take countermeasures that neutralize the actions of the first state and that may even menace it. The first state may feel impelled to take additional actions that will provoke additional countermeasures . . . and so forth.[14]

This precarious condition is known as the security dilemma. It means that an action-reaction spiral can occur between two states or among several of them so that each is forced to engage in security-seeking measures, such as spending large sums on arms or forging alliances without being more secure than before. Thus, if a nation's security dilemma is unusually acute, a statesman "will deal with almost anyone."[15]

This is precisely the case with Israeli-Iranian relations since 1948. Israel and Iran, by nature of geographical influences on power relationships in international and Middle Eastern relations, have found common ground in opposing threats emanating from the Arab core — and its allies — to the Jewish and Persian identities of their respective states.[16] The acuteness of this security predicament, irrespective of who rules in Tehran or Tel Aviv, is encapsulated by Nicholas Spykman's observation that "although the entire policy of a state does not derive from its geography, it cannot escape that geography. It can deal with [the challenges of its geographic predicament] skillfully or ineptly; it can modify the challenges; but it cannot ignore them. For geography does not argue. It simply is."[17] This geopolitical predicament captures the basic premise of Israeli-Iranian relations. It also explains the durability of the Tehran-Tel Aviv axis: the common interest of Iran and Israel in opposing multiple external threats has impressed upon their various leaders that the stability and security of their regimes can best be protected by joint efforts within the framework of a discreet alliance. In short, the imperatives of both Israel's and Iran's security predicament, which is a function of a patently chaotic and hostile international and regional environment, help explain the inherent logic of the Tehran-Tel Aviv connection.

Demographic Component of Israel's Foreign Policy

The lot of Jewish communities outside Israel, although not a final determinant of Israeli foreign policy, has not remained outside the scope of Israeli decision makers. In many respects, Israel's long-term aspiration is the ingathering of all the "exiles" in the ancient homeland. Israel's current commitment to the ideology of ingathering the exiles, however, is to offer a haven for all Jews in need wherever they are. In other words, Israel is not merely a Jewish state, but a state for all Jews. (Israel's Declaration of Independence reads, "The State of Israel will be open to the immigration of Jews from all countries of their dispersion.") This extremely complex issue, defying the logic of power politics, was forcefully expressed by David Ben Gurion when he addressed a meeting of Israeli ambassadors on July 17, 1950:

> So long as there exists a Jewish Diaspora . . . Israel cannot behave as other states do and take into account only its own geographic and geopolitical situation or limit its concerns to its own citizens and nationals only. Despite the fact that the Jews living abroad are in no legal way part and parcel of Israel, the whole Jewish people, wherever it resides, is the business of the State of Israel, its first and determining business. To this Israel cannot be neutral: such a neutrality would mean renouncing our links with the Jewish people.[18]

Ben Gurion's remarks provide a rationale for such seemingly anomalous incidents as Israel's sale of military equipment to the government of Ayatollah Khomeini. To be sure, the geopolitical consideration of an Iraqi victory over Iran did play a role in Israeli deliberations, but the fate of some 90,000 Iranian-Jews could not have escaped the minds of Israel's decision makers. Interestingly, 40 years ago, when Israel first attempted to cultivate closer ties to Iran, an important motive was to secure safe passage for Iraqi-Jews through Iran.

Containment of Soviet and Sunni Arab Hegemony of the Middle East

Although the demographic component of Israeli foreign policy has played an important role in Israeli-Iranian relations over the last four decades, it has been a prominent theme only when the safety of Jews in Middle Eastern states was in jeopardy. A more persistent factor has been the desire on the part of both Israel and Iran to neutralize Soviet power and Sunni Arab hegemony in the Middle East. With the establishment of the state of Israel in 1948, Iran recognized the potential of using Israel as a fulcrum to counter the Soviet and Arab influence in the Middle East. This constituted the underlying rationale for links with the Jewish state. In many respects, countering the Soviet and Arab threat was also an important motive behind Israel's cultivation of closer ties to Iran, particularly after the Soviets began their courtship of Arab countries in the 1950s. Since then, the imperative of establishing a balance of power against the Sunni Arab core has drawn Iran and Israel together regardless of who rules in Tehran or Tel Aviv.

Trade in Technical Assistance and Oil

Israeli-Iranian relations have also been helped by commercial ties based on the exchange of Israeli expertise in agriculture and military technology for much-needed Iranian oil. By the time the issue of Israel's recognition was brought before the Majlis (Iran's parliament) for ratification in 1951, it was clear to many reform-minded Iranian nationalists that the Jewish state could serve a constructive role as a conduit for information and technology. Israeli expertise could be used to reform agricultural practices and modernize Iran's armed forces. Iranian policy makers believed that Israel's technology was better suited to Iran's small-scale requirements than the highly advanced European or U.S. technologies. This connection became more entangled in 1957 when the Soviet Union stopped its supply of oil to Israel. Henceforth, Iran entered into Israel's energy security calculations. Indeed, under the Shah, the sale of Iranian oil to Israel was one of the most important features of Israeli-Iranian relations.

Iran-Arab and Arab-Israeli Relations

Iran's relations with the Arab world and Arab-Israeli relations have played a prominent role in Israeli-Iranian relations. Although during the period in which Iran and Israel first established contacts Iran's relations with the Arab states were tense, they were not hostile. Nonetheless, tensions between Iran and Iraq and between Iran and Egypt created a favorable environment for Israel to cultivate ties to Muslim Iran, despite the Arab-Israeli conflict. Iran perceived Israel as the meek (mazloom) in its conflict with the Arab states. As a general rule, the history of Israeli-Iranian relations suggests that when Iran-Arab relations were tense and when Israel was viewed as the underdog in its conflict with Arab states, Iran and Israel drew closer together. However, Israeli-Iranian relations were marked by hostility when Iran's cold war with the Arab states thawed and when Israel was perceived to be an aggressor state.

Israel's Special Relationship with Washington

Equally important has been Iran's perceptions of Israel's relationship with the United States and the extent to which this relationship could be exploited for the promotion of Iran's interests in Washington. For example, between 1948 and 1953 Iran sought the support of the United States in countering Soviet designs in the region and in obtaining financial assistance for Iran's development. Iran's de facto recognition of Israel in 1951 was viewed as an important step in winning Washington's approval for Iran's political, military, and economic agenda. The Israelis were keenly aware of this connection. Until 1979, Iran's belief that Tel Aviv could promote and protect Iran's agenda in Washington was an implicit element of Iran's attitude toward Israel and would enter into Iranian policy-making considerations.

Who Rules Iran — Secularists or Traditionalists?

A fundamental lesson of Israel's early encounter with Iran was that Israel's success in fostering its ties to Tehran rested on the Iranian government's ability to control and contain its internal opposition, in particular Shiite fundamentalists. When Shiite clerics have dominated the Iranian political scene, such as from 1948 through 1953 and again from 1979 onward, Israeli-Iranian relations have been at their nadir. In the final analysis, Israeli-Iranian relations have flourished at the expense of Shiite fundamentalist interests. And in all probability, if the Islamic republic of Iran is replaced by a secular government, Israel may once again reestablish diplomatic relations with Tehran.

ORGANIZATION OF THE STUDY

Taken together these factors comprise the major elements of Israeli-Iranian relations since 1948. However, they project themselves with greater or lesser intensity at different times during the last 40 years. This 40-year period can be divided into six periods; each period will be the subject of a chapter.

The first period, "Calculated Ambivalence," begins in 1948 and ends in 1953. It examines the origins of Israeli-Iranian relations, in particular, how the opposition forces in Iran, spearheaded by the religious right, used the issue of Israel's de facto recognition as a political weapon against the central government.

The next period, "Israeli-Iranian Rapprochement," describes how, from 1954 through 1957, Israel's decisive victory over Nasser attracted the Shah and his government's attention. The strategic utility of Israel as a bulwark against Sunni Arab nationalism became obvious for Iranian policy makers during this period.

"The Peripheral Policy" covers the period 1958 through 1967 and examines the growing intimacy between Iran and Israel at a time when their security interests converged. The Shah's positive response to Ben Gurion's invitation for a tacit alliance against Israel and Iran's Sunni Arab enemies led to numerous bilateral projects, including support of Kurdish rebels inside Iraq, efforts to assist Royalist Yemeni forces during that country's civil war, and joint economic projects for the development of Iran's agriculture.

The next period, "The Watershed Years," looks at Israeli-Iranian relations from 1968 to 1974 with particular emphasis on the implications, for both Israel and Iraq, of the 1973 Yom Kippur War and the British withdrawal from the Persian Gulf. Iran's goal of creating a regional environment favorable to a greater degree of security and stability in the Persian Gulf (in spite of Arab opposition to her new role as the "policeman of the Persian Gulf") and Israel's need to secure a reliable source of crude oil contributed to a continuation of Israeli-Iranian relations during this period.

The period from 1974 to the end of the Pahlavi dynasty in 1979 is entitled "Iran's Arab Option." Although during this period the Shah of Iran repeatedly criticized Israeli "intransigence" and praised Sadat's "flexibility" out of fear that the failure of a Middle East peace settlement would lead to the destruction of the Sadat regime and the emergence of an "extremist" regime, Iranian-Israeli cooperation continued at the highest levels. The most important joint venture between the two countries was a plan to develop missiles capable of carrying nuclear warheads.

Chapter 6, entitled "Israel and the Khomeini Regime," examines the evolution of Israel's strategic thought in light of Khomeini's establishment of an Islamic theocracy in Iran dedicated to the "destruction of Zionism." The main question to be answered in this chapter is how does one explain the link between Iran and Israel in light of Khomeini's pledge to "eradicate the Zionist entity."

The last section of this study is devoted to the future of Israeli-Iranian relations. It examines why the Tehran-Tel Aviv axis is likely to be an enduring feature of the Middle Eastern power configuration.

The methodology incorporated into each chapter remains constant throughout and is outlined in Table 1. After an overview of international and regional events for each period, each chapter takes into account the degree to which these seven factors have either contributed to or hindered Israeli-Iranian relations since 1948. This compartmentalization of the issue areas that contribute to an understanding of Israeli-Iranian relations does not mean that they are mutually exclusive; rather, all the factors are interrelated and are mutually reinforcing.

Although each of the seven factors in Table 1 is distinct and contributes to an understanding of certain aspects of the Tehran-Tel Aviv axis, individually they cannot capture the whole story. Thus, although the demographic component of Israel's foreign policy, which triggered Tel Aviv's interest in establishing diplomatic relations with Tehran from 1948 through 1953, is an important factor, it cannot be divorced from the issue of who rules Iran. During those formative years, the influence of Shiite clergy hindered Israeli efforts at cultivating closer ties to Iran. And after 30 years of absence from the Iranian political scene, Shiite fundamentalism reemerged with vengeance in 1979 to derail Israeli-Iranian relations, which had gathered momentum under the secularist rule of Mohammad Reza Shah Pahlavi. This interrelatedness of the factors influencing Israeli-Iranian ties is also a feature of these relations under the Shah. Thus, although Israel's special relationship with Washington was

TABLE 1
Organization of the Study

Issue Area \ Period	Chapter 1 1948–1953	Chapter 2 1954–1957	Chapter 3 1958–1967	Chapter 4 1968–1973	Chapter 5 1974–1978	Chapter 6 1979–1988
Anarchic Nature of the International and Regional Environment						
Demographic Component of Israel's Foreign Policy						
Containment of Soviet and Arab Hegemony of the Middle East						
Trade in Technical Assistance and Oil						
Israel's Special Relationship with Washington						
Who Rules Iran						

an implicit factor in the Shah's decision-making calculus, a far more significant reason why Israeli-Iranian relations flourished was their mutual desire to neutralize Soviet power and Arab radicalism in the Middle East. Throughout this interim period commercial and economic factors such as the exchange of Iranian oil for Israeli expertise played a complementary role and solidified the Israeli-Iranian nexus.

The story of Israeli-Iranian relations has puzzled many students of international politics because of its seeming defiance of conventional wisdom. Yet a closer look at 40 years of friendship and cooperation, disagreement and open hostility suggests that there exists an inherent functional logic to these relations, which can best be described as the Pragmatic Entente. The major objective of this study, to unfold the mystery of the Pragmatic Entente, is expressed by the great Arab historian Ibn Khaldun:

> On the surface, the history of nations is no more than information about political events. On the other hand, the inner meaning of history among nations involves an attempt to get at the truth, the subtle explanation of the causes and origins of existing things, and the deep knowledge of how and why of relations.[19]

NOTES

1. Shahram Chubin, "Israel and the Iran-Iraq War," *International Defense Review* (July 1985): 303–04.

2. Marvin G. Weinbaum, "Iran and Israel: The Discreet Entente," *Orbis* 18 (Winter 1975): 1076.

3. *Israel Export and Trade Journal* (annual edition for 1972): 36.

4. *Kayhan* (Weekly International Edition), August 2, 1975.

5. Benjamin Beit Hallahmi, *The Israel Connection: Who Israel Arms and Why* (New York: Pantheon Books, 1987), p. 12.

6. Avner Yaniv, *Deterrence without the Bomb: The Politics of Israeli Strategy* (Lexington, MA: D.C. Heath, 1987), p. 95.

7. Weinbaum, p. 1070.

8. Aaron S. Klieman, *Israel's Global Reach: Arms Sales as Diplomacy* (New York: Pergamon-Bassey's, 1985), pp. 160–61.

9. Uri Bialer, "The Iranian Connection in Israel's Foreign Policy," *Middle East Journal* 2 (Spring 1985): 314.

10. Kenneth Waltz, *Theory of International Politics* (New York: Random House, 1979), pp. 102–04.

11. Ibid., p. 105.

12. Ibid., p. 166.

13. Hans J. Morgenthau, *Politics among Nations: The Struggle for Power and Peace* (New York: Knopf, 1985 ed.), pp. 6, 8.

14. Robert J. Art and Robert Jervis, *International Politics* (Toronto: Little, Brown, 1985), p. 3.

15. Waltz, p. 166.

16. Although the ethnic problem is an important factor in Iranian society, culture, history, racial consciousness, religion, geography, and language provide a cohesive base for what is referred to in this study as Persian identity. The idea of a Persian identity/statehood (mamlekat) is best exemplified by the foregoing factors, which distinguish Iran from the rest of the Middle East. For a discussion of Iran's ethnic divisions and Iranian nationalism see Farhad Kazemi, "Ethnicity and the Iranian Peasantry," in *Ethnicity, Pluralism, and the State in the Middle East,* ed. Milton J. Esman and Itamar Rabinovich (Ithaca: Cornell University Press, 1988), and Richard Cottom, *Nationalism in Iran,* (Pittsburgh: Pittsburgh University Press, 1964).

17. Nicholas Spykman, *The Geography of Peace* (New York: Harcourt Brace Jovanovich, 1944), p. 25.

18. Cited in Shlomo Avineri, "Ideology and Israel's Foreign Policy," *Jerusalem Quarterly* 37 (1986): 11.

19. Ibn Khaldun, *Ibn Khaldun,* trans. Franz Rosenthal (London: Routledge and Kegan Paul, 1958), p. 6.

THE PRAGMATIC
ENTENTE

1

Calculated Ambivalence: 1948-1953

IRAN, ISRAEL, AND THE SUPERPOWERS

R. K. Ramazani characterizes Iran's attitude toward Israel between 1948 when the state of Israel was born and 1950 when it accorded Israel de facto recognition as "calculated ambivalence" based on the ambiguous nature of Israeli relations with the Soviet Union — Iran's bête noire.[1] From a political and strategic perspective this appears to be a valid argument, for at a time when Mohammad Reza Pahlavi, the Shah of Iran, was drawing U.S. power and influence to Iran to counter Soviet — and British — influence, the official Israeli position vis-à-vis the Soviet Union — and the United States — was one of "ee-hizdahut" or nonidentification. The semiofficial newspaper of the Histradut elaborated the meaning of the Israeli policy of nonidentification by pointing out that "neutrality for Israel must mean dependence on both of the world's large groupings, without favoring either [because Israel depends on the United States for capital and on the USSR for immigration]." It then went on to say, "we cannot therefore hope to terminate this double dependence within the foreseeable future."[2]

Although during its formative years Israel pursued a policy of nonidentification, the weight of available evidence suggests that this policy was not the reason for Iran's calculated ambivalence toward the newly born Jewish state.[3] The establishment of political ties between Israel and Iran was the result of a simultaneous convergence of global and regional

1

factors, on the one hand, and domestic political factors inside Iran, on the other.

On the eve of Israel's independence, the global system was gradually moving toward bipolarity. The United States and the Soviet Union were consolidating their hegemonial status within their respective spheres of influence. The implication of such rigid polarization for most Middle Eastern states was that those who professed friendship toward either superpower "should stand up and be counted."[4] For Iran the choice was clear. Given the history of Soviet — and British — intervention in the internal affairs of Iran, there was a genuine need for alliance with the United States for military and economic assistance. The consolidation of world power into rigid camps did not limit Israel's freedom of choice. Israel continued to cultivate its ties with both superpowers, but not necessarily for reasons that Ramazani offers. Its quest for friendship with both the United States and the Soviet Union was based, in part, on the need for "aliya" or immigration from the large Jewish communities in both countries. Israel depended on immigration to furnish the manpower skills, and, to some extent, capital, without which it could not grow, perhaps not even survive, in the face of entrenched hostility from its Arab neighbors.[5]

ISRAEL'S SEARCH FOR SECURITY

Although the demographic component of Israel's foreign policy would play a crucial role in drawing Israel closer to Iran, it cannot be divorced from, and was indeed accentuated by, the regional predicament the Jewish state faced during its formative years. These regional developments and their implication for Israeli foreign policy were succinctly spelled out by Yaacov Shimoni of the Asia Division of the Israel Ministry of Foreign Affairs in 1950:

> The Arabs regard Israel, and will in all probability continue to do so for some time, as a foreign enclave in their midst; . . . and as making forever unrealizable both the much-desired equation between Middle Eastern regionalism and Arab unity, and the second-choice equation between Middle East regionalism and Islamic unity (embracing Turkey and Iran).[6]

In view of this "sea of Arab hostility" surrounding it, a major goal of Israeli foreign policy has always been to break the wall of isolation that surrounded it. The danger of isolation was clearly spelled out by Moshe Sharett, Israel's foreign minister at the time:

> We are living today in a state of pernicious isolation in the Middle East, we have no traffic with the neighboring countries, we have no recognition of our existence from the neighboring states . . . we cannot ignore the distress that isolation brings to our nation.[7]

The acuteness of Israel's perception of isolation and vulnerability may also be gleaned from the following passage from Yigal Allon's survey of his country's strategic thinking:

> From a demographic point of view, Israel's two and a half million Jews [in the 1950s] had to contend with more than a hundred million Arabs from the Atlantic to the Persian Gulf. Geostrategically speaking, Israel was a narrow strip of land, had its back to the sea, and was surrounded; the lands of the enemy, by contrast, formed a sub-continent. Israel was a country desperately poor in natural resources pitting itself against countries possessing almost inexhaustible natural wealth: oil, big rivers, vast areas of arable land, about half of the world's hydrocarbon reserves. Both in its own region and in the larger world Israel was uniquely isolated. Apart from its bonds with world Jewry, it had no ethnic or religious links with any other nation.[8]

And finally, Israel's geopolitical predicament, a condition accentuated by its anarchic environment, was spelled out by Moshe Dayan:

> The unique vulnerability which geography imposes is aggravated by the fierce antagonism of Israel's neighbors . . . the term frontier security has little meaning in Israel's geographic context. The entire country is a frontier. Not a single state has a firm, unequivocal obligation to help defend Israel against aggression. [Thus] Israel faces formidable dangers and faces them in unusual solitude.[9]

The foregoing remarks by Israeli statesmen capture the heart of Israel's predicament after 1948. Whatever its guiding ideology, whatever its domestic political makeup, and no matter what historical legacy shadowed the minds of its policy makers, Israel's conduct was motivated by the patently anarchic nature of the regional and the wider international environment.[10] The need to pursue a policy of nonidentification, the sense of isolation and vulnerability, and the concern for and attachment to world Jewry were all responses to Israel's predicament. For Israel, a small and isolated country facing a large Arab coalition, this security predicament forced it to explore new opportunities for the cultivation of ties with non-Arab states of the region. The underlying assumption adopted by its policy makers was that the Middle East is not an exclusively Arab area; on the contrary, the majority of its inhabitants are non-Arabs. One such state was Iran, where two of Israel's most important foreign policy thrusts converged: the demographic component, which consisted of links to world Jewry, and the geopolitical component, which aimed at breaking the wall of regional isolation surrounding the new-born Jewish state.

THE GENESIS OF ISRAELI-IRANIAN LINKS

The importance of foreign Jewish communities has had a crucial effect on Israeli foreign policy. Indeed, foreign Jews may be the most important component of the global system for Israel.[11] David Ben Gurion frequently declared that "Israel's only absolutely reliable ally is world Jewry."[12] As regional developments turned against Israel's interests, the demographic component of Israel's relationship with Iran became more pronounced. As early as 1948, Iraqi-Jews, who outnumbered Iranian Jewry two to one, were persecuted, arrested, tried, and sometimes sentenced to death. Zionism was legally declared a serious criminal felony.[13] Late in the summer of 1949 a young Jew was arrested on a charge of clandestine communist activities. He had formerly been a member of the Halutz movement. In an effort to save his life, he informed on members of the Zionist underground, furnishing the names and addresses of four of them. A wave of arrests followed, and many other members of the Halutz and the Haganah organizations were subsequently found and thrown into prison. Of the leadership, however, which numbered 14 instructors and organizers, only one was apprehended. The rest looked to Iran for safety and slipped across the border.[14] Other Iraqi-Jews joined them, encouraged by Iran's tolerance of its Jews. Thus, Iran took on a central importance as an alternate route for Iraqi-Jews fleeing to Israel. In short, the problem of aliyah from Iraq made political relations with Iran into an essential goal of Israeli policy makers.

Beyond the perception of Iran as transit point for Iraqi-Jews, there were a number of factors that encouraged the Israelis to cultivate closer ties to Iran. First, from its establishment in 1948, the Israeli Embassy in Washington, which monitored the Cold War between the United States and the Soviet Union, cautioned Tel Aviv against maintaining a policy of nonalignment. The embassy regarded closer ties to the United States as a prerequisite for receiving continued U.S. aid. From the embassy's point of view, action was imperative because Israel's political isolation in the region decreased its strategic utility to the United States. Therefore, the embassy argued, an intensification of the Cold War would minimize Israel's importance to the United States severely. In early October 1949, after President Truman announced Soviet possession of the atomic bomb, the Israeli Embassy in Washington intensified its warnings, urging Tel Aviv to abandon nonalignment and to break Israel's regional political isolation. While the Israeli foreign ministry found the first recommendation problematic, inasmuch as extreme caution was dictated in matters relating to the abandonment of the nonaligned line, it endorsed the second proposal wholeheartedly.[15] Thus the aim of creating formal political ties with Iran was adopted in October 1949.

A second factor that encouraged the Israelis to move closer to Iran was the special attitude Tehran exhibited toward Israel in her conflict with the Arab states from the outbreak of the 1948 war. Iran tended to stress its solidarity with the Arabs — expressed by Iran's vote against Israel's entry into the United Nations — but at the same time did not disguise its unwillingness to become actively involved in the conflict. The Jewish Agency representative in Tehran, himself a Persian, described the situation in his sarcastic report dated early June 1948:

> Action is being undertaken [by religious elements] to excite and incite the Moslems against the Jews in general and the Jewish population in Israel. Thousands of "Soldiers of Faith" have already enlisted

and the populace and the Parliament are vociferous. But there is no doubt that not even a few tens from among them will cross the borders. There is thus not much to fear from these descendants of Cyrus, the real Aryans of yesterday, who have become blood brothers of the Arabs.[16]

A third factor that moved the Israelis toward Iran was the Israeli perception that Iranian representatives in the United States would overestimate the extent to which Jewish lobbying efforts might promote or hinder the possibility of Iran's receiving vital U.S. aid — a fact that Israel made good use of in a few instances.[17] Iranian officials believed that given Israel's "special links" with the United States ties to the Jewish state could gain Iran considerable mileage in Washington. Indeed, this perception that Israel could serve as Iran's power broker in Washington was an underlying reason for Tehran's cultivation of closer ties to Tel Aviv throughout the Shah's reign.

The fourth factor that facilitated Israel's links to Iran was circumstantial. It was the Israeli perception that local conditions in Iran could be manipulated and that Tehran was mired in chaos, intrigues, and corruption. According to Moshe Tchervinsky, one of the directors of the Mossad in charge of aliyah from the East, "It was possible to achieve almost anything in Iran through bribery."[18]

While links to Iran became an imperative for Israel, Iran's movement toward Israel was less pressing. Israel had won attention and respect in Iran because of its high rate of economic development and military prowess. Iran's chief of staff, General Ali Razmara, praised the Israeli armed forces and the Haganah movement at Tehran's Officers Club for their courage and efficiency during the 1948 War of Independence. They were, he said, a model for the Iranian Army to emulate. The Israeli system of land reform was discussed on the floor of the Majlis (Iran's parliament) as a system that could be emulated by Iran. Despite its natural resources, Iran in the 1950s was an underdeveloped country. It viewed Israel's military and agricultural prowess with great admiration. It also viewed Israel as a potential market for its raw materials. The Israelis were not oblivious to this reality, and the desire to accentuate the profitability of commercial links was expressed in the summary of the brief sent to the Israeli Embassy in Washington on October 30, 1949:

> It must be stressed [to the Iranian] that for obvious reasons Israel is and will for many years continue to be a land of imports and in order for commercial ties to be established, the period during which we do not buy from the neighboring countries should be exploited.[19]

Iran-Arab relations may have played a role as well in drawing Iran toward Israel. Iranian-Egyptian relations were strained after the divorce of the Shah and his first wife Queen Fuzieh. The Egyptian press accused the Shah of mistreating Queen Fuzieh. During the same period, not only did the Egyptian government refuse to lower its flag during the state funeral of Reza Shah (the founder of the Pahlavi dynasty) in Cairo in April 1950, but King Farouq scheduled his engagement party for the same day. Many Iranians were incensed and Iran-Israel relations were encouraged.[20]

Iran's frustration over the long-drawn controversy with Iraq concerning the management of the Shatt-al-Arab may also have caused the Iranian government and the Majlis to lose some of its initial sympathy for the Arabs and consequently move toward Israel. This frustration was borne out by one influential member of the Majlis, Matin-Daftary, who asked, "Although nearly three years have now elapsed since the termination of the World War, why has no action been taken for implementation of the 1937 Frontier Treaty between Iran and Iraq?"[21]

In addition to Iran-Arab relations, intra-Arab rivalries, such as the palace feuds between the Saudi and Hashemite families, led Iran to dissociate itself from the Arab sphere and to follow its own independent policy in the Middle East. This desire was not new but drew upon the Iranians' sense that they are linguistically, ideologically, ethnically, and culturally distinct from Arabs. Equally important was the perception of Israel as the underdog (mazloom in Farsi) and the meek. The regional situation brought out the Iranian national characteristics in a way favoring a pro-Israeli policy.[22]

ISRAEL'S RECOGNITION AND THE
QUESTION OF WHO RULES IRAN

Even though a survey of regional developments suggests that both Israel and Iran had grounds for closer cooperation, perceptions of some policy makers inside Iran would prove to be the major obstacle to establishing links between the two countries.

Throughout the years from 1948 through 1953, the issue of Israel's recognition and the Arab-Israeli conflict was perceived by Iranian decision makers through the kaleidoscope of Iranian cultural values and national characteristics. Pro-Israel observers adhered to the pre-Islamic cultural values and national heritage; those opposed adhered to the Islamic history of Iran and Shia beliefs.

The Shah, members of the military establishment, the technocrats of the foreign ministry, and most of the big landlords and merchants who composed the center of the political spectrum leaned toward Israel.[23] Their attitude was summed up by the Shah in his book, *Mission for My Country*, which reflects his emphasis on Iranian cultural values of tolerance, universalism, nationalism, and expediency. His sympathetic attitude toward the Jews — and indirectly Israel — is reflected in the following passage:

> We never believed in discrimination based on race, color, or creed, and have often provided a haven for oppressed people of backgrounds different from our own. . . . For example, it was characteristic of Cyrus the Great that, when he conquered Babylon, he allowed the Jews, who had been exiled there by King Nebuchadnezzar after the conquest of Jerusalem in 597 B.C., to return to Palestine with their sacred vessels and rebuild their destroyed temples.[24]

If the Shah tended toward the recognition of Israel, the question is, what prevented him from following this tendency in 1948? Ramazani contends that once the state of Israel was born, Iran began to perceive its relationship with Israel primarily within the large context of the emerging antagonism between the Soviet Union and the United States. And since the attitude of Israel toward the superpower antagonism had seemed ambiguous, Tehran pursued a policy of calculated ambivalence in its relations with that emerging state. However, the weight of available evidence suggests that the Shah's calculated ambivalence toward Israel stemmed from internal politics. It was a concession to opposition groups made up of the Ulama, mullahs, supporters of an Islamic community, spearheaded by Ayatollah Abol-Qassem Husseini Kashani, an openly political mullah who had been exiled by the British to Palestine in 1941 because of his pro-Nazi activities.[25] In a May 1948 issue of *Etelaat Haftegi* (a Farsi weekly), Kashani's role and his anti-Israel activities were praised and his view of the Palestine issue and Arab-Israeli conflict were elaborated:

> The Arab people in Palestine are fighting for their independence and integrity against wealth and power supported by international Jewry. The Palestine problem is basically an East-West issue which has taken new face at the time when the Arab and Muslim countries represent one side and the Western countries the other. Neither side is ready to receive the unwanted Jews who, before arriving, claim the ownership of the place.[26]

Kashani was not a mere extremist outside the political process. He was made speaker of parliament and in this position wielded considerable power. This is best reflected in the special act that he had passed in 1951 quashing the death sentence for Khalil Tahmasebi, Prime Minister Ali Razmara's assassin, and declaring Tahmasebi to be a "soldier of Islam."

It should, therefore, not come as a surprise when the Shah, during his first state visit to the United States in November 1949 answered a question regarding the recognition of Israel by hedging, "We are a true Moslem country, but casting back through the history of Iran, to the very old and ancient days of the great kings we have always been tolerent of all religious minorities. . . . We have not yet recognized Israel and as a Moslem country we will naturally have to discuss it with other Moslem countries before we do."[27]

Having escaped an assassination attempt in February of that same year by the Fedayeen Islam, it is clear that an immediate determinant of the Shah's ambivalent policy toward Israel was his fear of his domestic opposition and that any concern over Israel's policy toward the conflict between the superpowers was secondary.

The motives of Israeli and Iranian policy makers that were outlined determined the course of events between the two countries from 1948 to 1954. This can be seen especially in Israel's decision to obtain Iranian recognition in order to provide an escape channel through Iran for Iraqi-Jews, who from the later months of 1949 through the first months of 1950 crossed into Iran at a rate of 1,000 a month. Through a U.S. intermediary code-named "Adam," Mossad agents in January 1950 arranged for the payment of $240,000 to the Iranian government in exchange for de facto recognition. The money was to be used to generate favorable publicity in the Iranian press regarding de facto recognition. On February 14, the Associated Press published reports of Prime Minister Mohammad Saed's proclamation opening the gates of Iran to any and all refugees and transient persons. Five days later, the Mossad representative in Tehran met with the prime minister. As a result of the meeting Saed instructed the director of the Passports Department of the Iranian Foreign Office, the head of the state police, and the chief of border police to recognize the Mossad agent as representing the State of Israel in regard to refugees and the emigration of local Jews from Iran to Israel. On March 6, 1950, the Iranian cabinet decided on de facto recognition of Israel, and Iran's United Nations representative was asked to make the formal announcement: "Iran is planning its own independent foreign policy and has decided to recognize Israel."[28] And Prime Minister Saed, in defense of the recognition of Israel, addressed the 18th session of the Senate:

> The government and people of Iran in their long history have never had anti-racial or anti-religious policies ... the establishment of relations with the government of Israel ... was a normal action and in line with our peaceful policies that the Iranian people have believed in and will always believe in. Of course Arab countries have been our foundation of faith, belief, and Islamic truth and no policy has ever been formed in this country against their interests. But the international situation made it necessary that we respect the United Nations decision. As the honorable gentlemen are aware, we owe this to the United Nations which has aided us on many occasions. The de facto recognition of Israel was therefore in accordance with our national interests and reputation. In fact, it was in deference to the Arab countries that we had delayed this decision for two years.[29]

Although Saed mentioned the Iranian government's allegiance to Islam, it was his — and the Shah's — respect for, and fear of, Islamic interest groups and the religious culture of Iran that was responsible for the two-year delay in recognizing Israel. Prime Minister Saed's efforts collapsed, however, when the new Iranian prime minister, Ali Mansur, failed to convince the Majlis of the wisdom of his predecessor's efforts and was vigorously attacked. At the same time, international pressure from Arab states mounted, prompting one member of Majlis to say, "We have always supported the Arabs, the Islamic cause and Islamic issues and we should continue."[30] Indeed, the issue of Israel's recognition degenerated into a three-way political struggle between the National Front of Mohammad Mossadeq, the religious ulama led by Kashani, and the centerists led by the Shah and his advisors. Mansur's next move was to invite Kashani to return to Iran (he had been in exile since February 1949) in an attempt to win the support of the ulama, the mullahs, and other influential religious leaders who were being courted by the Mossadeqists. The move, it was hoped, would prevent unification of the Kashani forces with Mossadeq supporters.

An alliance between Kashani and Mossadeq, however, faced significant barriers. Opposition to Iran's recognition of Israel by the clergy was based on Islamic pride whereas the Mossadeqists opposed the government on the basis of its domestic policy, the legality and constitutionality of the decision to recognize Israel, and the government's method of foreign policy decision making in general.[31] However, the opposition was united in its criticism that the government was weak, corrupt, unpatriotic, and did not represent the wishes and interests of the Iranian people. Senator Tadayon, a critic of the government, used this issue to emphasize the government's weakness, arguing that "our government, in relation to foreign influence has nothing to show but weakness. You say we are an independent nation. On the same grounds we should not have accepted Israel just as the Moslem world doesn't accept her."[32]

In June 1950, while under pressure from the religious right and the National Front, Prime Minister Mansur died, and General Ali Razmara — well known for his pro-Western ideology — became prime minister. As a military man,

General Razmara was open to an idea of a de jure recognition of Israel and suggested that commercial ties be emphasized to overcome domestic opposition. As early as 1947, Sayyed Zia Tabatabai, an influential politician who had been exiled to Palestine by Reza Shah (father of Mohammad Reza Shah Pahlavi and founder of the Pahlavi dynasty), had approached General Razmara and lobbied for closer ties to the yet-to-be-born Jewish state. Tabatabai's interest in promoting closer ties with the Jews was that he had acquired large land holdings from the indigenous Palestinian population.[33] However, on March 7, 1951, General Razmara was assassinated by Khalil Tahmasebi, a member of the extremist Fedayeen Islam, and any Israeli hopes of de jure recognition faded.

With the assassination of Prime Minister Razmara, the road was opened for Dr. Mohammad Mossadeq to become the next prime minister. Mossadeq was an aristocrat with strong nationalist sentiments and a firm determination to make parliamentary democracy work in Iran.[34] Initially, Mossadeq and Kashani became reluctant allies. Mossadeq needed the mullahs to counterbalance the power of the Left, and the mullahs considered Mossadeq indispensible for reducing the power of the Court and thus making sure that no Reza Shah could emerge in the future.

The issue of recognition, however — as well as numerous other issues — soon created a rift between the two. In early June 1951, *Etelaat* (one of Tehran's major newspapers) published a telegram sent by Kashani to the Egyptian newspaper *al-Misir* claiming that "Iran would soon withdraw its recognition of Israel which did not have any legal basis."[35] And indeed, in 1952, the Iranian Consulate in Israel was closed. According to the government, the decision was prompted primarily by budgetary pressures: "Mr. Safinia will be asked to return to Iran. But this has nothing to do with Iran's de-facto recognition of Israel. The decision is based on financial difficulties of the Treasury Department."[36] Ramazani tends to agree with this assessment, pointing out that the reduction of the principal Iranian source of revenues, as a consequence of the oil nationalization dispute with Britain, lay at the heart of that decision.[37] But the government did not close any of its foreign posts. Opposition from the clergy certainly played a role as did the desire to obtain Arab support for Mossadeq's oil nationalization policies at the United Nations. Although the Mossadeq government had distinguished the withdrawal of the mission and the withdrawal of de facto recognition, the Arabs were led to believe that the move was a withdrawal of de facto recognition. In fact the Egyptian ambassador in Tehran was asked on behalf of President Nasser to "thank the Iranian government and promise that all Arab countries will fully support Iran in her conflict with the British."[38]

But in 1952, the circumstances governing Iran's relationship with Israel changed. Kashani broke ranks with Mossadeq and was cooperating with the young Shah in a united front against the threat of the pro-Moscow Tudeh Party. In June 1953, Mossadeq was overthrown, and the Shah — who had briefly fled the country — was restored to the throne by a coup d'état led by General Fazllolah Zahedi. Kashani played a prominent role in the enterprise, which enjoyed financial and logistical support from both the CIA and MI-6.[39] The return of the invigorated monarch marked the beginning of his move to consolidate power inside Iran and would allow him to cultivate Iran's ties to Israel with minimal internal opposition.

The period 1948 through 1953 served to establish the basic structure of Israeli-Iranian relations. Although the immediate reason for cultivating closer ties to Iran was Tel Aviv's concern for the safety and well-being of Iraqi-Jews, closing the Iranian mission in Israel brought to a clear and disappointing end Israeli hopes for diplomatic relations between the two countries.[40] Israel also realized the limitations of securing bilateral relations with a country, which despite its non-Arab culture, was divided along secular and religious lines, thus making for a weak central government. This meant that Israeli policy makers would have to wait until the secularist forces consolidated their power within Iran, something the Shah and his supporters would concentrate on beginning in 1954. For Iran, the connection with Israel proved to be a liability for the central government, which was under attack by religious interest groups and the Arab world. Nevertheless, the Shah and his advisors were not oblivious to the potential advantages of ties to the Jewish state.

However, although the ascendency of the Shah and his government, supported as they were by Kashani, would provide fertile ground for closer relations between Iran and Israel, not all the clergy supported the Shah-Kashani alliance. A cleric by the name of Hojatolislam Ruhollah Khomeini was breaking ranks with both Kashani and Ayatollah Borujerdi (Iran's Grand Ayatollah), calling the young monarch a "Zoroastrian fire-worshipper." By the mid-1950s Khomeini had his own circle of "talabehs" (students of theology) and was already recognized as a leading "modares" (teacher of theology) at the Fazieh School in Qom.[41]

NOTES

1. See R. K. Ramazani, "Iran and the Arab-Israeli Conflict," *Middle East Journal* 32 (Autumn 1978): 413–28.

2. Cited in Michael Brecher, *The Foreign Policy System of Israel* (New Haven: Yale University Press, 1972), p. 40.

3. For a detailed discussion of the formative years of Israeli-Iranian relations see Uri Bialer, "The Iranian Connection in Israel's Foreign Policy," *Middle East Journal* 39 (Spring 1985): 292–315, and E. E. Shaoul, "Cultural Values and Foreign Policy Decision Making in Iran: The Case of Iran's Recognition of Israel" (Ph.D. dissertation, George Washington University, 1971).

4. Brecher, *The Foreign Policy System of Israel,* p. 41.

5. Ibid., p. 38.

6. Yaacov Shimoni, "Israel in the Pattern of Middle East Politics," *Middle East Journal* 4 (July 1950): 286.

7. Cited in Uri Bialer, "The Iranian Connection in Israel's Foreign Policy," *Middle East Journal* 39 (Spring 1985): 293.

8. Cited in Avner Yaniv, *Deterrence without the Bomb: The Politics of Israel Strategy* (Lexington, MA: D. C. Heath, 1987), p. 13.

9. Cited in Brecher, *The Foreign Policy System of Israel,* p. 66.

10. Avner Yaniv, *Dilemmas of Security: Politics, Strategy, and the Israeli Experience in Lebanon* (New York: Oxford University Press, 1987), p. 11.

11. Brecher, *The Foreign Policy System of Israel,* p. 39.

12. Cited in ibid.

13. Bialer, p. 299.

14. Nissim Rejwan, *The Jews of Iraq* (London: Westview Press, 1985), p. 244.

15. Bialer, p. 295.

16. Ibid., p. 297.

17. Ibid., p. 299.

18. Ibid.

19. Ibid., p. 301.

20. Shaoul, p. 152.

21. Ibid., p. 153.
22. Ibid., p. 155.
23. Ibid., p. 157.
24. Mohammad Reza Shah Pahlavi, *Mission for My Country* (London: Hutchinson Press, 1961), p. 30.
25. Amir Taheri, *The Spirit of Allah* (Bethesda, MD: Adler & Adler, 1986), p. 107.
26. Cited in Shaoul, p. 188.
27. New York *Times*, November 18, 1949, p. 5.
28. Shaoul, p. 170.
29. Ibid., p. 133.
30. Ibid., p. 173.
31. Ibid., p. 203.
32. Ibid., p. 209.
33. Interview with former Iranian official, Washington, D.C., 1987.
34. Taheri, p. 110.
35. Cited in Shaoul, p. 194.
36. Ibid., p. 196.
37. Ramazani, p. 415.
38. Shaoul, p. 199.
39. Taheri, p. 111.
40. Bialer, p. 314.
41. Taheri, p. 112.

2

Israeli-Iranian Rapprochement: 1954-1957

NASSER AND THE SHAH'S POLICY OF POSITIVE NATIONALISM

According to Murad Ghalab, who served as ambassador to Moscow under Gamal Abdel Nasser and who guided Egypt's relations with the Soviet Union during the Nasser era, when the Egyptian revolution of 1952 occurred, "it immediately directed its efforts toward the liberation of the country and its people from imperialist domination and British bases." He noted that "from its inception, the revolution realized that to face imperialism we must turn to the Soviet Union. This direction crystallized early."[1]

One of the fundamental reasons for the Israeli-Iranian rapprochement after 1954 was what Ghalab referred to as the "crystallization of Egyptian-Soviet relations." Indeed, from 1954 through 1957, the main villain of the Middle East from both Tehran and Tel Aviv's perspective was the militant, anti-Western, pro-Soviet, pan-Arab regime in Cairo. The basic rationale behind Israeli-Iranian relations during this period was to neutralize and curtail the Moscow-Cairo axis.

By 1955, President Nasser of Egypt had emerged as the leader of pan-Arabism. He led the junta that toppled the discredited Faruq regime in 1952 and established himself as a Third World leader after his exposure to various Asian nationalist and Communist leaders at the 1955 Bandung Conference. He stayed aloof from the West, while Iraq, a potential rival joined the pro-Western Baghdad Pact.

Furthermore, he went ahead and purchased $200 million in weapons from Communist countries after the West had refused to sell arms that might be used against Israel.[2] Most important, Nasser effectively articulated the unique relationship between Palestine, imperialism, and Arab unity to the Arab masses. Within a few years of the Egyptian revolution, Nasserism was a powerful force in the Arab world. As an ideology, it represented a platform against foreign domination of the Arab world or, as Nasser saw it, the Middle East. Within this context, the Arab-Israeli conflict was seen to be closely associated with the intrusion of Western powers into the Middle East, and Nasser placed Egypt into the Arab vanguard by leading the "struggle" for Arab independence and unity against powerful external forces allied by regional "reactionary" regimes.[3]

One of Nasser's prime targets was the government of Iran and its young monarch, Mohammad Reza Shah Pahlavi, who was pursuing a pro-Western course called "positive nationalism." This phrase was coined in reply to two concepts that the Shah's government was trying to combat: the "negative nationalism" of the Mossadeq era, which brought Iran to the verge of ruin, and Nasser's "positive neutralism" which, the Iranians thought, tended to facilitate Soviet infiltration into the area.[4] The Shah defined this policy as follows:

> Positive nationalism implies a policy of maximum political and economic independence consistent with the interests of one's country. On the other hand, it does not mean non-alignment or sitting on the fence. It means that we make any agreement which is in our own interest, regardless of the wishes or policies of others. We are not intimidated by anybody who tries to tell us whom we should have for our friends, and we make no alliances merely for the sake of alliances or of vague principles, but only in support of our enlightened self-interest. We cultivate the friendship of all, and are prepared to take advantage of every country's technical skills if to do so does not prejudice our interests or our independence. This gives us great freedom of action — much more than that enjoyed by any dogma-ridden state. . . . We energetically seek to strengthen our defense establishment with these particular aims in view: to help ourselves and our friends by honoring our collective security agreements; to safeguard my country's sovereignty and territorial integrity; and to maintain internal security for the protection of our citizens.[5]

The foregoing statement captures the essence of the Shah's plans for his country in the post-Mossadeq era. On the one hand, it consisted of a tactical, temporary alignment with the United States, in order to maximize Iranian security against the Soviet Union. On the other hand, it was an attempt to lay the foundations for Iran's economic development through agricultural projects with the assistance of, as he put it, "countries [such as Israel] whose technical know-how could be shared by Iran." The Shah's basic philosophy was that a stable and secure Iran, at peace with herself and her neighbors, was a prerequisite to his country's economic development and prosperity. In the context of regional politics, positive nationalism meant facing "dogma-ridden" states like Egypt both unilaterally and with the help of other states that shared the same security dilemma. Israel fitted perfectly into the Shah's policy of positive nationalism because an alliance with Tel Aviv could have fulfilled two of the most important goals of Iran's monarch: to provide Iran with technical expertise for economic development and to serve as a balance against the menace of a Moscow-Cairo axis in the region.

While the Shah would privately pursue his Israel option, the third principle of his policy of positive nationalism, which was to join collective security arrangements of a pro-Western orientation, gained a public dimension. In the spring of 1955, when Hussein Ala replaced General Zahedi as Iran's prime minister, his first decision was whether to join the Baghdad Pact, recently concluded by Turkey, Iraq, Pakistan, and Britain and designed to serve as a defensive regional alliance. The pact clearly fitted the Shah's policy of positive nationalism, but the decision was not easy to make because the Soviet Union, in the course of the year, had twice warned Iran not to contemplate such a step. Soviet objections were based on the Irano-Soviet Treaty of February 26, 1921, which stipulated, in Article 3, that neither party could participate in alliances or political agreements that might be directed against the security of either signatory. In addition to the Soviet warnings, the move to join a Western alliance system was not very popular among some circles in view of Mossadeq's legacy of suspicion and dislike of the West. However, the Shah and his prime minister realized the importance of being formally included in the Western defense system and benefiting from the military guarantees and economic aid that this participation was likely to provide. More specifically, adherence to this pact meant an opportunity to modernize and strengthen Iran's army largely at Western expense. On October 11, 1955, Prime Minister Ala announced his government's resolve to sign the Baghdad Pact, and within a week this decision was ratified by both houses of Parliament.[6]

Joining the Baghdad Pact (later named Central Treaty Organization after the 1958 revolution in Iraq) also served to counter the pressure Nasser placed on Iran. The Shah raised this issue in the following exchange with E. A. Bayne:

E.A.B.: Was it your thought that CENTO might be a defensive instrument against Nasser? He was already active at the time [1955].

H.I.M.: Maybe this was really the reason why we joined. It was at a time when Nasser was discussing the problem of the British [withdrawal of the garrison stationed in the Suez Canal Zone]. Nasser had agreed that if the Russians attacked Turkey, he would permit a reactivation of the Suez Canal base, but he refused to do this in the event of a Russian attack on Persia. That was the real motive for our joining CENTO.[7]

Although Iran joined the Baghdad Pact for the reasons cited above, she complained from the beginning about U.S. nonparticipation in the organization. Washington did not believe it would be prudent to join the alliance because such a course might have aggravated the Cairo-Baghdad cold war and antagonized Israel since Iraq was a member of the alliance. Iran, however, feared that U.S. nonparticipation might mean that the alliance would prove an ineffective defense against the Soviet Union.[8] The desire to assume closer ties with the United States was motivated by several major considerations. First of all, the Shah recognized in the United States the "third power" that could countervail against both residual British interests and Russian expansionism. Second, the young monarch attached the highest priority to strengthening the Iranian armed forces. Finally, the Shah concluded that neutralism was no longer feasible. Although abidingly suspicious of British and Western imperialist impulses, the danger he faced was from the Soviet Union. The Shah explained that "in our experience it is the new imperialism — the new totalitarian imperialism — that the world's less developed countries have most to fear. It concentrates on negative, destructive nationalism and thrives on the chaos that follows."[9]

THE SHAH CONSOLIDATES HIS POWER

Having charted the course of Iran's foreign policy by joining the Baghdad Pact and choosing closer military ties with the United States, the Shah turned his attention to consolidating his rule inside Iran. In December 1956, with the approval of the Majlis, the Sazeman Etellat Va Amniyat-e Keshvar or Savak was established, and General Teymour Bakhtiar was named its director. The Shah explained the reason for Savak's creation as follows:

> First of all, you foreigners all had such a service — the British, the United States, almost all the countries. It is unfortunate, maybe, but in every kind of society you need one. We are really not much safer than you are, nor any more immune to subversive activity and it becomes almost an obligation, a duty, to have one.[10]

The raison d'être of Savak was the tumultuous events of the 1950s. The Communist Tudeh Party espoused the overthrow of the central government while religious extremist groups such as the Fadayean Islam continued their campaign of selective terrorism. Iran also faced threats from abroad. Soviet involvement in the Azerbiajan crisis and its connections with the Tudeh had left a legacy of mistrust and fear. The need for a security apparatus to guard against Iran's internal and external enemies became necessary. During its formative years, particularly under the directorship of General Bakhtiar, Savak developed into an inquisitional agency with abuses of power by its rank and file. With the removal of Bakhtiar and under the directorship of General Hasan Pakravan, Savak's activities centered on counterespionage and foreign intelligence gathering; however, it never relinquished its role as a political watchdog inside the country. It should be noted that the British had initiated a drive to organize Iran's intelligence gathering capabilities several months before Savak was officially established in order to maintain a close eye on internal developments inside the country. British efforts were coordinated by one of their agents, Donal Makenson, who was supposedly the British Embassy's Press Attache. The Central Intelligence Agency became aware of the British plans and immediately countered by offering its own "good services" — yet another example of British and U.S. competition for influence in Iran.[11]

From 1954 through 1957 one of Savak's major tasks was to crush the Communist Tudeh Party. This policy was necessary in view of the Tudeh Party's close association with Moscow and its infiltration of Iran's military and security establishment. Furthermore, forcing the Tudeh Party to go underground matched the Shah's belief that Iran's economic and social development required he consolidate his power. Savak's surveillance of potential sources of dissidence also included the clergy. However, during the 1950s, clergy-state relations were, on the whole, more accommodative than conflictual. Kashani, who had close ties with the terrorist Fadayean Islam group, was shunned and sank quickly into oblivion. Moderate clerics like Ayatollah Borujerdi and Ayatollah Behbahani (Tehran's leading ayatollah), both of whom shared the Shah's concern with the Tudeh Party and the Soviet Union, forged a "tactical alliance" with the Shah.[12] The net effect of Savak's simultaneous campaign against the Tudeh Party and appeasement of the Shia hierarchy through a number of monetary inducements provided the Shah an opportunity to establish his control over Iran.

And, indeed, the period between 1954 through 1957 saw the consolidation of power by the Shah. It enabled him to stabilize his personalist regime, increase and modernize Iran's armed forces, crush the Tudeh Party, forge a "tactical alliance" with the clerics, and settle the oil nationalization problem by creating an international consortium in which the United States and the United Kingdom each had 40 percent right to produce and market oil. He assured himself of sufficient U.S. economic and military aid so that he could gradually free his country from what he saw as undue U.S. influence on Iranian affairs. He thus began to cut the ground from under his opponents.[13] The young monarch was fully aware of his changing role as the vanguard of the Iranian nation, for as early as 1955 he made the following observation: "You know, there is no more lonely and unhappy life for a man than when he decides to rule instead of reign. I am going to rule!"[14]

The policies that led to the consolidation of his power gave Mohammad Reza Shah Pahlavi the confidence and the power base he needed to respond to the challenges of Iran's internal and external predicament. It allowed him to forge new friendships and alliances with countries that shared Iran's interest in stemming the tide of Soviet influence and Arab nationalism that was sweeping the region in the 1950s. Of all the nations in the region, none fitted better into the Shah's strategic thinking than Israel. Not only could an Iran-Israel connection serve as a balance against the Cairo-Moscow axis, it could also play an important role in the plans for Iran's modernization. In the meantime, however, the Iranian monarch had to wait for Israel to consolidate its position in the region.

ISRAEL TURNS TO THE WEST

If 1948 to 1953 can be described as the phase of Israel's nonidentification, the period 1954 through 1957 witnessed the emergence of its pro-Western orientation. By the mid-1950s Israel's relations with the Soviet Union had deteriorated as the Soviets persisted in wooing the Arabs through such means as the "Czechoslovakian Deal." The Czechoslovakian Deal referred to the 1955 arms deal between Egypt and Czechoslovakia in which Egypt was to get a wide range of weapons including 80 MiG 15s, 45 Ilyushin 28 bombers and 115 heavy tanks equal to the best in the Soviet army and superior to anything Israel had.[15] In addition, Israel's relations with Britain remained cool. Under the circumstances Israel was compelled more than ever before to look to the United States for economic aid and political friendship. Ben Gurion expressed this clearly:

> The "Czechoslovakian Deal" is only a new and pointed expression of a process which began with the Bolshevist Revolution and sharpened after Lenin's death ... [indicating] the Soviet Union's constant opposition on principle to Zionism, which is the lifeblood of the State of Israel; the United States, to whom we owe our thanks for much political and financial assistance from the day the State

was founded.... Hence we insist on our demand for arms — first of all from the United States, which does not desire war in the Middle East and wishes well both to Israel and the Arab peoples.[16]

In the meantime, the U.S. government had had a second look at the Arab-Israeli problem, and its response to Israel had lost some of its earlier cordiality. Earlier, the United States had extended economic aid and allowed the issuance of a $500 million State of Israel Bonds obligation. By 1955 it had become apparent that the United States did not want a public image in the Middle East as Israel's ally or protector. It declined to supply arms or enter into a formal security agreement with Israel. This negative response to Israel's overtures for a security guarantee drew Israel toward the French and culminated in the de facto alliance of September 1956.[17]

The French motives for an alliance with Israel were various. There was a feeling of obligation to the Jews as a people who had suffered too much, as well as a sense of admiration for what the Jews had achieved in Israel. Men like Guy Mollet and Ben Gurion shared a sense of socialist solidarity. These affinities were played upon by skillful Israeli statesmen who found their task much facilitated when Nasser helped the Algerian rebels in 1954. His actions led many Frenchmen to conclude that a blow at Nasser was the right way to solve their troubles in Algeria — or at any rate a necessary precondition. In addition, some Frenchmen shared Anthony Eden's view that Nasser was a menace like Hitler and must be stopped before it was too late. Therefore, French policy, traditionally pro-Arab, was pulled in a new direction.[18] On June 23 1956, in an address to French military officers outside Paris, Israeli Chief of Staff Moshe Dayan conveyed with typical directness Israel's view of the evolving Middle Eastern power configuration and the dangers it posed to the Jewish state:

There are two dangers threatening the Middle East — the annihilation of European influence and Soviet penetration. Egypt is gradually turning into a Soviet base, and the West is losing its influence in this part of the world. To Israel and France there is a common enemy in the region — Gamal Abd-el Nasser. For the purpose of the struggle against him Israel is prepared to cooperate with the French.[19]

While Israel searched for and found allies in the West, escalating border violence from the Arab zone made the Israeli government increasingly uneasy. The Soviet-Arab arms agreement in September 1955 transformed the military balance in the region. Egypt enlarged its blockade of the Tiran Straits to include air traffic. Israeli casualties from Arab hit-and-run raids mounted. With the formation of a unified command over the armies of Egypt, Jordan, and Syria (October 23, 1956), Israel felt its back against the wall and invaded Sinai on October 29.[20] By the time Israel's military campaign was completed on November 5, her armed forces had occupied the Gaza Strip and virtually all of Sinai, the Tiran Straits were opened, the Fedayeen bases had been destroyed, and Egypt's military power had been crushed.[21]

Although from a military standpoint the Sinai War was an Israeli success, it did not alleviate the fundamental nature of Israel's security predicament. This was clearly spelled out by Abba Eban at a speech to the United Nations General Assembly on November 1, 1956:

> Surrounded by hostile armies on all its land frontiers, subjected to savage and relentless hostility, exposed to penetration, raids and assaults by day and by night, suffering constant toll of life amongst its citizenry, bombarded by threats of neighbouring governments to accomplish its extinction by armed force, overshadowed by a new menace of irresponsible rearmament, embattled, blockaded, besieged, Israel alone amongst the nations faces a battle for its security anew with every approaching nightfall and every rising dawn. In a country of small area and intricate configuration, the proximity of enemy guns is a constant and haunting theme.[22]

Although Israel did not achieve absolute security, its military success dealt a crushing blow to Nasser. Chief of Staff Moshe Dayan explained why:

> The military victory in Sinai brought Israel not only direct gains — freedom of navigation, cessation of terrorism — but, more important, a heightened prestige among friends and enemies alike. Israel emerged as a state that would be welcomed as a valued friend and ally, and her army was regarded as the strongest in the Middle East.[23]

Another important result of the 1956 war for Israel was the opening of its southern port of Eilat to Red Sea shipping. This allowed access to Persian Gulf oil, specifically that of Iran, which came to be a major supplier of Israel (as well as user of its new pipelines to the Mediterranean Sea) after 1957.[24]

ARAB NATIONALISM AND THE
ISRAELI-IRANIAN CONNECTION

These two major consequences of the 1956 war changed the Iranian attitude toward Israel. Initially, Iran's reaction to Israel's military victory was ambivalent. On the one hand, echoing the exceedingly harsh reaction of Washington and reflecting some deference to Arab indignation, Iran issued a sternly worded note of censure condemning Israel. On the other hand, Iran, fearful of growing Soviet influence in the reigon, was duly impressed with Israel's performance. Iran was also worried that Nasser would succeed in turning his military defeat into a political asset.[25]

As Iran's young monarch was pondering the means to counter the tide of Arab nationalism that was originating in Egypt, he could not but appreciate the strategic utility of Israel as a bulwark against Nasser. Equally important, from the Shah's point of view, the Suez War had opened Israel's southern port of Eilat to Red Sea shipping. This meant that Nasser could no longer use the Suez Canal, through which 73 percent of Iran's imports and 76 percent of her exports (mostly oil) passed, as a trump card against Iran.

Meanwhile, Israel's perception of Iran as an asset in the region had encouraged it to keep a presence in Iran. The task of keeping the "fire burning" was assigned to Dr. Zvi Doriel, who came to Iran in 1953 and served as Israel's unofficial representative until Meir Ezri, an Iranian Jew from Esfahan, became the official representative in 1960. The following confidential cable from the U.S. Embassy in Tehran offers a candid explanation of Dr. Doriel's mission to Iran:

> Dr. Zvi Doriel, the Israeli Representative here, leads an ambiguous existence. He circulates widely in the Diplomatic Corps, but he is not of it. An attempt about a year ago to represent himself as "Ambassador" was decisively rebuffed by the Iranian government. (He was forced to withdraw a circular letter in which he signed himself as Ambassador of Israel.) Yet he has widespread and no doubt productive contacts with Iranian officials. Doriel has been in

Iran for eight years and carries on a number of activities. . . . One difficulty we have in dealing with him is that it is quite clear that among his manifold activities, which include the blowing-up of alarmist reports about Nasser, is his encouragement of the line that "Nasser is being propped up by American aid."[26]

One of Dr. Doriel's activities was to ensure that Israel's perception in Iran as a country surrounded by hostile Arab neighbors and a friend and potential ally of Iran be maintained. Toward this end, he established contacts with the Iranian press, particularly after the 1956 war. The following cable from the U.S. Embassy dated November 19, 1956, is insightful:

> Dr. Doriel, Israel's unofficial representative in Tehran has been very active in placing pro-Israel material in the local press. His contacts are through Abas Shahandeh, Editor of Farman, and Abdullah Vala, Editor-owner of Tehran Mosavar. He is rumored to have paid out 100,000 rials (approximately $1500) to newsmen during the first week of November.[27]

Dr. Doriel also maintained a working relationship with the directorate of Savak's counterintelligence bureau, General Kia, but contacts between the two men did not lead to a formal intelligence agreement. Rather, the decision to approach Israel's intelligence services at an official level was made by the Shah.

Early in 1957, the Shah asked General Bakhtiar to contact the Israelis in order to determine whether they would be interested in cooperating with Iran in intelligence. There were a number of reasons for this decision. First, the Shah and his advisors realized that in order to keep Israeli-Iranian relations discreet, the intelligence services of both countries must be brought in to manage the relationship. He had decided that overt diplomatic relations between the two countries would not be in Iran's best interest and that the best way of ensuring secrecy was to delegate the task of carrying out the Israeli connection to Savak. Second, the Shah and Savak officers were of the opinion that the CIA's view of intelligence matters centered on its competition with the KGB and was framed in the context of the Cold War. What Savak trainees needed, and the Shah agreed, was a regional perspective to intelligence gathering and counterespionage, particularly in light of Nasser's threats against Iran. The Mossad, given its vast experience in the Middle East, would be a perfect partner for Savak. Third, many of Savak's section chiefs complained about the training they and their trainees were receiving from the CIA. Finally, Savak officials believed that in their work against Iran's internal and external enemies, the technical expertise that Mossad could provide would be more valuable than that of any other intelligence organization willing to assist Iran.

Upon orders from the Shah, Bakhtiar flew to Israel aboard a Dakota DC-3 military aircraft avoiding the air-space of Arab countries. In Israel he had a formal meeting with Isser Harel, the director of Mossad, at which time he was introduced to one of Harel's associates, Yaakov Karoz. Karoz, Mossad's station chief in Paris, later coordinated all contacts with Iran. Karoz met with General Bakhtiar several times, and Karoz was subsequently invited to Tehran. The result was that in 1958, an Israeli "trade mission" was opened in Tehran, and this remained the official cover for the Israeli operation for years.[28]

The working relationship between Mossad and Savak developed to the point that the number of Israeli espionage and counterespionage experts who were conducting courses for Savak exceeded the number of U.S. trainers. At the same time, a large number of Savak trainees flew to Israel, where they were trained at Mossad's headquarters in Tel Aviv, in communications, espionage, counterespionage, and break-ins. The newly arriving Iranian officials were impressed by the many uses of wireless interceptors. For example, on one occasion, Mossad was able to pick up, through its interceptors, a message from Jordan that some weapons that had recently been purchased from England were lost in the port of Aqaba. The Israelis later directed the Jordanians to the lost crates, much to the amazement of both their Iranian guests and Jordanian "enemies." Equally impressive for Savak was the massive work carried out by approximately 200 Mossad officers who translated every single Arabic newspaper published in the region. This source accounted for a large percentage of Mossad's information on its Arab neighbors.

An important feature of Mossad-Savak relations was the Trident meetings held every six months (or if deemed necessary more often) in either Tehran, Tel Aviv, or Ankara, and attended by the heads of Mossad, Savak, and the Turkish intelligence organization. The major purpose of Trident was to exchange intelligence information gathered by the three services, and, when necessary, recommend appropriate policy responses. A typical conference agenda would usually include information on Arab countries, Palestinian organizations, Armenians, Kurds, and Soviet activities in the Middle East. Disagreements at Trident meetings were rare and, when they occurred, were usually related to regional issues. For example, the Turks considered Kurds "mountain Turks" and so were not pleased with the assistance provided by both Iran and Israel to the Kurds. The Iranians, in view of their close relations with the Armenians, protested the Turkish persecution of Armenians who lived near the Turkish-Iranian border. In general, although the Turks were a member of Trident, they played a peripheral role in the organization. In part this was because they did not share the same security problems that both Iran and Israel faced.

Trident was composed of two working committees and a council. The security committee dealt with internal security matters through espionage and counterespionage. In this committee the Israelis shared with Iran and Turkey any new techniques on intelligence gathering. The intelligence committee provided what is called in the vernacular of the intelligence community "positive intelligence." This was information gathered by the three services from Arab countries and hard-line African countries. The council was the policy-making body that was composed of the three chiefs of intelligence.

The working relationship that developed between Mossad and Savak stemmed from a deep-seated understanding of the dangers both Israel and Iran faced within the region and the equally important need for cooperation to respond to these challenges. For Mossad and Savak, ignorance of what was transpiring in the region would have been disastrous. It was imperative, therefore, that the two intelligence agencies keep in constant contact to ensure the security and stability of their respective countries.

By the end of 1957 the rapprochement between Iran and Israel had ushered in a new era in Middle East politics, one in which Nasser's Arab radicalism and Soviet penetration into the region would be balanced and challenged by a "discreet entente" between Shiite Persian Iran and the Jewish state of Israel. Both countries considered the other as a strategic ally in their war against radical forces in the Middle East. The positive feedback of the 1954 through 1957 period for both Iran and Israel meant that there were enormous gains to be made by including themselves in one another's deterrence calculus.

While the discreet entente between Iran and Israel was taking shape, in a not so discreet fashion, Ruhollah Khomeini was also shaping his future by surrounding himself with such future prominent leaders of the 1979 uprising as Shaikh Sadeq Khalkhali, Hussein Ali Montazeri, Mohammad-Javad Bahonar, and Mohammad Hussein Beheshti. As the 1950s drew to a close, Khomeini was already established as an ayatollah. He belonged to a group that could be described as the second division, consisting of three Grand Ayatollahs with Borujerdi presiding over all.[29] However, as the Shah consolidated his power, Khomeini realized that his reputation as a radical was a liability and limited his chances of succeeding Borujerdi and becoming the "mantle of the Prophet." He therefore limited his attacks on the Shah, although still addressing him as a "Zoroastrian fire-worshipper." This would soon change, for as the 1960s approached, the "vicar of Shiism" found a new ally in Gamal-Abdul Nasser, the leader of Sunni Arab radicalism and the most vociferous opponent of Israeli-Iranian relations.

NOTES

1. Tareq Y. Ismael, *International Relations of the Contemporary Middle East* (Syracuse: Syracuse University Press, 1986), p. 173.

2. Arthur Goldschmidt, *A Concise History of the Middle East* (Boulder: Westview Press, 1983), p. 257.

3. Ismael, p. 53.

4. George Lenczowski, *The Middle East in World Affairs* (Ithaca: Cornell University Press, 1962), p. 220.

5. Mohammad Reza Shah Pahlavi, *Mission for My Country* (London: Hutchinson Press, 1961), pp. 125, 297.

6. Lenczowski, pp. 218–19.

7. E. A. Bayne, *Persian Kingship in Transition* (New York: American Universities Field Staff, 1968), p. 211.

8. R. K. Ramazani, *The United States and Iran: Patterns of Influence* (New York: Praeger, 1982), p. 38.

9. Cited in Lenczowski, p. 397.

10. Bayne, p. 181.

11. Interview with former Iranian official, Washington, D.C., 1988.

12. Ramazani, p. 74.

13. Lenczowski, p. 375.

14. Bayne, p. 66.

15. Peter Calvocoressi, *International Politics since 1945* (New York: Praeger, 1968), p. 181.

16. Cited in Michael Brecher, *Decisions in Israel's Foreign Policy* (New Haven: Yale University Press, 1975), p. 239.

17. Brecher, p. 227.

18. Calvocoressi, pp. 180–81.

19. Cited in Brecher, p. 246.

20. When Nasser turned down a joint ultimatum by France and Britain for a ceasefire, a coordinated Anglo-French force bombarded Egypt's airfields, landed paratroopers at Port Said, and occupied the northern half of the Suez Canal. For a discusison of the events leading to the Suez War, see Brecher, p. 229.

21. Ibid., pp. 281–82.

22. Cited in Brecher, pp. 280–81.

23. Ibid., p. 312.

24. Edward R. Rosen, "The Effect of the Relinquished Sinai Resources on Israel's Energy Situation and Politics," *Middle East Review* (Spring/Summer 1982): 5. It should be noted that Israel's oil connection to Iran intensified after the Soviet Union stopped its supply of oil to Israel in 1957.

25. Avner Yaniv, *Deterrence without the Bomb: The Politics of Israeli Strategy* (Lexington, MA: D. C. Heath, 1987), p. 93.

26. Documents of the United States Embassy in Tehran, Volume 13, 1979, p. 5.

27. Ibid., p. 8.

28. Benjamin Beit-Hallahmi, *The Israeli Connection: Who Israel Arms and Why* (New York: Pantheon Books, 1987), p. 9.

29. Amir Taheri, *The Spirit of Allah* (Bethesda, MD: Adler & Adler, 1986), pp. 113–15.

3

The Peripheral Policy: 1958-1967

The following secret Central Intelligence Agency (CIA) report on Israel's foreign policy orientation from the late 1950s onward captures the essence of what came to be known as the Periphery Doctrine:

> The Israelis have over the years made efforts to break the Arab ring encircling Israel by involvement with non-Arab Moslem nations in the Near East. A formal trilateral liaison called Trident organization was established by Mossad with Turkey's National Security Service (TNSS) and Iran's National Organization for Intelligence and Security (SAVAK) in late 1958. . . . The main purpose of the Israeli relationship with Iran was the development of a pro-Israel and anti-Arab policy on the part of Iranian officials. Mossad has engaged in joint operations with Savak over the years since the late 1950s. Mossad aided Savak activities and supported the Kurds in Iraq. The Israelis also regularly transmitted to the Iranians intelligence reports on Egypt's activities in the Arab countries, trends and developments in Iraq, and Communist activities affecting Iran.[1]

Indeed, looking at the political map of the world and the Middle East in 1958, Israeli policy makers could not but notice the isolation they faced. Therefore, it should come as no surprise that when the architect of the Periphery Doctrine, David Ben Gurion, was about to attend a political session of Mapai's Foreign Affairs Committee on March 4, 1958, he said:

> Something happened to me that had happened several times before, but not for a long time: all of a sudden I saw before me a picture of the

world, and I sensed our position in it very clearly; and when it came to my turn to speak, I didn't use one word of what I had prepared but instead described what I had suddenly seen, and I knew that this picture was right even if it was "cruel." And it seemed that those who heard also felt that this was an accurate picture of how we were seen by the Arab world, Russia, China, India, the small nations of Asia and Africa — and the countries of America and Europe — and the political line we must take.[2]

That "political line" Ben Gurion had in mind was a "peripheral pact": the establishment of a bloc of states situated on the periphery of the Middle East, and connected to Israel in a triangle, with Turkey and Iran in the north, and Ethiopia in the south. The Periphery Doctrine was designed to create the image in the region and in the world at large, that the Middle East is not exclusively Arab or even Islamic but rather a multireligious, ethnic, cultural, and national area. Its initiator was Reuven Shiloah, a Foreign Office specialist, but it was Ben Gurion who gave it policy significance:

> The Middle East is not an exclusively Arab area; on the contrary, the majority of its inhabitants are not Arabs. The Turks, the Persians and the Jews — without taking into account the Kurds and the other non-Arab minorities in the Arab states — are more numerous than the Arabs in the Middle East, and it is possible that through contacts with the peoples of the outer zone of the area we shall achieve friendship with the peoples of the inner zone, who are our immediate neighbours.[3]

The underlying rationale for the periphery policy was Israel's understanding that it could not achieve security through a military victory by eliminating millions of Arabs in the Middle East. Israel's response, therefore, to its pressing security concern was to formulate a policy that would drive a wedge among its enemies by forging alliances with non-Arab nations. The common denominator of these states was expressed mainly in their political position: sharp opposition to Nasserist expansionism and subversiveness and the hope of halting Soviet influence. The unwritten pact had a clear implication for the West. The United States was most concerned in view of the Soviet penetration of the Middle East: the Eisenhower Doctrine had not succeeded in stemming the tide.[4] For the first time, Israel sensed that it had something to offer the Americans and realized that it was terribly important to win U.S. political and financial support for the clandestine organization.[5]

Although Ben Gurion's peripheral pact policy received lukewarm treatment from President Eisenhower, Israel's Ambassador to the United States, Abba Eban, was able to persuade the U.S. Secretary of State, John Foster Dulles, to encourage Iran to cooperate with Israel. Dulles replied: "I see no reason why I shouldn't notify Iran of our satisfaction with the development of ties between you."[6]

IRAN'S QUEST FOR SECURITY

It appears that Dulles was indeed successful in obtaining an Iranian agreement for cooperation with Israel, for in response to Ben Gurion's letter of 1958 to the Shah, in which he mentioned Cyrus's policy toward Jews, the Shah replied: "the memory of Cyrus's policy regarding your people is precious to me, and I strive to continue in the path set by this ancient tradition."[7]

Although it is reasonable to argue that the Shah accepted the U.S. suggestion of establishing closer ties with the Jewish state in order to take advantage of the "Jewish lobby" in the United States, his perception of the developing power configuration in the Middle East and the assistance that Israel could offer in neutralizing and reversing this trend was far more important.[8] This perception was based on Iran's sense of isolation in the wake of an increasingly hostile Soviet Union to the north and the rise of Arab radicalism in many Middle Eastern countries. From the Shah's vantage point, the emergence of these regional threats to Iran's security exposed the limitations of his U.S. connection in dealing with Iran's enemies and, therefore, solidified his positive perception of Israel. In short, the Shah recognized that Iran's security, in the face of a hostile international and regional environment, could best be maintained within the framework of the Periphery Doctrine.

The most immediate threat to Iran's security came about with the collapse of Iraq's monarchy in 1958. On July 14, 1958, units of the 20th Brigade under the command of Brigadier-General Abdul Karim Qassim seized control of Baghdad. King

Faisal II was shot while pleading for his life, and the heir to the throne, Abdullah, was also put to death. Federal and Iraqi cabinet ministers were placed under arrest, except for Nuri es-Said, the premier, who went into hiding but was discovered a few days later disguised as a woman and killed. General Qassim then went on to deliver his first public statement in which he proclaimed the deliverance of "our beloved country from the corrupt clique of imperialism," announced "the formation of a popular republic adhering to complete Iraqi unity," and called for "brotherly ties with the Arab and Moslem states."[9] While most Arabs rejoiced at the fall of the monarchy, Iran and her Western allies were horrified. Iraq was perceived to be the central link in the Northern Tier, which the West had set up against the Soviet Union. Now the new regime seemed to be the embodiment of both Arab nationalism and Communism, a triumph for Nasser, a harbinger of the fate awaiting Jordan and Lebanon, and a stalking horse for Soviet imperialism in the Middle East.[10]

Iran's fears seemed to be realized almost immediately. Within a few days after the coup, Deputy Premier Colonel Abdul Sallam Aref traveled to Damascus, where on July 19, after a meeting with Nasser, he signed an agreement pledging close cooperation between the two countries in military, political, economic, and cultural spheres. The rapprochement with Nasser was accompanied by the establishment of diplomatic relations with the Soviet Union and other countries of the Soviet bloc, none of which had been represented in Baghdad during the former government. Before long various political exiles began returning to Baghdad. Foremost among them was Mullah Mustafa Barzani, a Kurdish rebel chieftain who had lived in the Soviet Union since the downfall of the Kurdish Republic of Mahabad (inside Iran) in 1946.[11]

After cultivating ties to Egypt, Syria, and the Soviet Union, Abdul Karim Qassim turned his attention to Iran. He declared that the 1937 Treaty between Iraq and Iran concerning the Shatt-al-Arab waterway was unacceptable to his government and laid claim to the entire river separating the two countries. In 1959, he ordered his troops to prevent National Iranian oil Company (NIOC) tankers from moving down the Shatt-al-Arab and blocked their passage to the Iranian port of Khosrow

Abad. In an interesting turn of events, Qassim invited Barazani to Iraq and provided him and his troops with arms. From northern Iraq, Barazani forces made a number of attacks into Iran and created disturbances in the border towns of Baneh and Marivan. Although the Barazani alliance with Iraq was short-lived, the perception inside Iran that Iraq was a sworn enemy lived on and would enter into the Shah's strategic calculus.

Iran's sense of isolation within the region and the danger of Arab radicalism increased as Nasser continued his attempts at destabilizing Iran. In September 1962 a group of Yemeni army officers seized control of Sana and proclaimed a republic. Elated, the Egyptian government hailed the new regime and assumed that Imam al-Badr, Yemen's young monarch, had been killed. Actually, he and his followers had taken to the hills, where monarchist tribesmen were ready to fight for their imam. They were backed by the Saudis, who did not want a Nasserite republic on their southern border. Nasser backed the republican leader Brigadier Sallal without realizing that he would thereby entangle himself in Yemen for several years and to the tune of 50,000 to 60,000 troops. What seemed to be a contest between followers of the young imam (mainly Shiites in the hills) and republican officers (mainly Shafii-rite Sunnis living near the coast) became a struggle by proxy between conservative Saudi Arabia and revolutionary Egypt. This struggle lasted until 1967.[12] Nevertheless, after 1962, Nasser's attempts at establishing a foothold in Yemen was perceived as a threat to Iran's petroleum export route, which traveled through the Bab-al-Mandab and then to the Suez Canal or to the Israeli port of Eliat. This prompted the Shah to cooperate with Saudi Arabia over Yemen under the guise of a new Islamic Alliance.

In May 1963 Nasser sent an agent named Colonel Abdul Hamid Saraj to Qom in order to deliver $150,000 to Khomeini for antigovernment riots.[13] Until this date Khomeini primarily focused on the Shah, whom he referred to as the "Zoroastrian fire-worshipper." After his alliance with Nasser, he introduced his new theme: Israel was plotting against Islam. "Israel does not want the Quran to be in this kingdom. Israel does not want the ulama of Islam to be in this kingdom. Israel does not want the rule of Islam to be in this country."[14]

From this point on, Khomeini would refer to the Shah as "an agent of Zionism."

And finally, Nasser's assumption of an ideological mantle for the establishment of a radical pan-Arab state stretching into the Persian Gulf, which he referred to as the Arabian Gulf, was viewed by the Shah as a direct threat not only to Iran's national security interests but also to its Persian identity. As early as 1959, the Shah, threatened by Nasser's propaganda, sent an envoy to Cairo to explore the possibility of toning down Egyptian attacks on Iran. The meeting began with Nasser insulting and accusing the Shah of "selling out to the Zionists." Although, after regaining his composure, Nasser assured the special envoy that "Iran has to remain a monarchy," it was nevertheless reported in Tehran that Nasser was "too caught up in his image as the vanguard of the Arab world and will continue to pose a danger to His Majesty's plan for the development of Iran."[15]

Iran's sense of regional isolation took a turn for the worse when in October 1965 the Syrian cabinet officially claimed the province of Khuzestan in southern Iran as part of the "Arab homeland," henceforth to be called "Arabistan." The oil-rich province of Khuzestan was — and is — of strategic importance to Iran. Any suggestion by radical Arab states of the "Arabization" of Khuzestan was a direct threat to Iran's national security interests. Not surprisingly, the Shah immediately recalled Iran's ambassador and broke off diplomatic relations with Syria. Iran's cold war with the Arab states was now well under way.

Although relations with the Soviet Union stabilized after September 1962 with Moscow's accepting Tehran's assurances regarding the U.S. military presence and its denial that there was a missile base on Iranian soil, Soviet intrigues inside Iran continued to alarm the Shah and his advisors. They had some justification. Note, for example the following secret memo to the United States Information Service (USIS) in Tehran dated June 6, 1963, concerning the Soviet Ambassador to Iran:

> Gregor Zeitsev entered the Soviet Ministry of Foreign Affairs in 1944 and served in Iran from 1945 to 1949, the period when the Tudeh Party became well organized and very active in Iran. . . . In 1953 he visited Egypt, Syria, and Lebanon and participated in all talks between the Soviet Union and the Arab states. . . . Zeitsev is an

outstanding expert in organizing political parties and perpetrating disturbances. Following the coup which brought Qassim to power in Iraq in 1958, Zeitsev was named Soviet Ambassador to the new regime of Iraq. He was assigned to organize a powerful Communist party, an assignment which he successfully carried out. We should look for troubles and many headaches after his arrival in Iran, as he has been a prominent member of KOMSOMOL (Communist Youth Organization) and knows very well how to organize the dissatisfied people into a very destructive force against Iran.[16]

Soviet intrigue inside Iran continued despite high-level exchanges between the two countries, culminating in the 1966 purchase by Iran of a steel mill and some unsophisticated military transports. Indeed, in April 1966, Soviet agents were engaged in subversive acts against Iran, as evidenced by the following secret U.S. Intelligence Information Cable:

> Senior officials of the National Intelligence and Security Organization (Savak) are concerned by Soviet officials' recent spreading of unfounded rumors and propaganda among various levels of Tehran society. They feel it is a concerned campaign by the Soviets to sow suspicion and discord in the minds of Iranian people in an effort to worsen Iranian-Western relations ... two of the most active Soviets in this campaign are Fedor Saulchenkov and Viktor Osipov ... Saulchenkov is known to be a Soviet intelligence officer and Osipov is suspected of being a KGB officer.[17]

In addition, U.S.-Iran relations were not always harmonious in this period. At the beginning of the decade, the Kennedy administration sought to engage in social engineering, tying military assistance and budgetary support to the creation of democratic institutions, which it believed ought to be a major new U.S. export. Furthermore, Washington used its considerable economic leverage to dictate the size of Iran's armed forces.[18] At the same time, at least in the Shah's view, the United States did not appreciate Iran's geo-strategic position, particularly in light of the "nonaligned" position of such states as Egypt and India. This prompted him to say to an Israeli official, "I don't know who is smarter, Nasser, Nehru, or me."[19] His suspicions of U.S. intentions were heightened when President Kennedy met with a confidant of the former director of Savak, General Bakhtiar, who was in exile in Iraq and had plans of overthrowing the

Iranian government. Despite Professor James Bill's assertion in his well-researched book *The Eagle and the Lion: The Tragedy of American-Iranian Relations* to the contrary, as early as 1958, General Valiullah Qarani, the chief of military intelligence, was planning a coup with U.S. support. The government of Iran became aware of the plot, which was to include a number of National Front sympathizers, when U.S. Ambassador to Tehran Selden Chapin offered to pay a high-ranking Iranian official for all confidential information on Qarani in Savak's files.[20] By the late 1950s and early 1960s, the Shah's reservoir of trust for the United States was beginning to diminish.

In view of the global and regional power configurations confronting Iran between 1958 and the late 1960s, the Shah's policy of positive nationalism evolved into what he, in 1964, called a "national independent policy" (Seyasat-e Mostaghel-e Melli). It basically signaled Iran's intention of assuring its own interests by seeking to distance itself from the United States and from the Soviet Union. Although this policy did not portend warm ties with Moscow, the Shah's declaration reflected Iran's intention to judge other states by their contributions to its interests. In other words, relations with other states would be based on the extent to which they could help Iran respond to the twin challenges of Arab radicalism and Soviet influence in the Middle East. From 1958 through 1967, the strategic utility of Israel for Iran in meeting these twin challenges would set the stage for the cultivation of closer ties with the Jewish state.

On July 23, 1960, the eighth anniversary of the Egyptian revolution, the Shah, at one of his monthly press conferences, was asked by a reporter named Faramarzi to elaborate on Iran's stance on Israel. He replied, "Iran's de facto recognition of Israel since its existence is not something new. However due to circumstances that prevailed during those days [1951–1953] and budgetary reasons we had to recall our envoy."[21] Although the Iranian monarch responded to the question without finding anything extraordinary about its content, Nasser attacked the Shah the very next day and ordered the expulsion of Iran's Ambassador to Cairo: "the Shah has shown a hostile attitude toward Egypt, the Arab nations, and Arab nationalism since 1952. Now that the Shah has loudly proclaimed that he recognized Israel, America is pleased and so are Britain, Zionism, and Israel."[22] In response, Iranian Foreign Minister Abbas Aram ordered the expulsion of Egypt's Ambassador to Tehran and described Nasser as "this light-headed pharoah who is ruling by bloodshed." He then went on to announce the severance of diplomatic relations with Cairo.[23]

A few days later, Sheikh Mahmoud Shaltout of Cairo's Al-Azhar Mosque (Center of Islamic Teaching) said in a telegram to the Iranian monarch, "Your recognition of the gang in Israel has shocked Muslims everywhere . . . recognition of Israel by Iran is tantamount to siding with an enemy — an act forbidden by the Quran."[24]

In a carefully drafted letter, the Shah responded to Shaltout's accusations, in light of his own interest in keeping Iran's relations with Israel at a de facto level — something the Israelis were pressuring the monarch to upgrade to de jure recognition:

> I received your telegram concerning the need for unity among Muslim nations and am happy that the misunderstanding has allowed me an opportunity to address this matter. Of course, as you are aware Iran granted Israel de facto recognition in 1950 and in 1951 during Dr. Mossadeq's tenure, our envoy was recalled. However, we have not extended de jure recognition and this has been viewed positively by Muslim nations and we are not about to change our policy. Therefore, I see no reason for your worrying about this issue. However, in order to assure your Holiness and other respected members of Al-Azhar of our position, I would like to emphasize that our methodology in dealing with issues concerning the Muslim nations has been clear and rests on our support for the rights of Muslims around the world.[25]

ISRAEL'S PURSUIT OF FORMAL PUBLIC RECOGNITION

During the early 1960s, and whenever an opportunity presented itself, Israel attempted to take advantage of the Shah's precarious situation — which was to keep a balance between Iran's obligations as a Muslim nation and her need to neutralize and reverse the tide of Arab radicalism — in order to obtain de jure recognition by publicizing Iranian-Israeli contacts in the media. For example, according to former high-ranking Savak officials, Faramarzi, the reporter who asked the question concerning Iran's de facto recognition of Israel at the July 23, 1960, news conference had a file at Mossad headquarters. In addition to his photograph, the file contained a copy of the question he asked the Iranian monarch at his news conference.[26]

In December 1961 when David Ben Gurion arrived at Tehran's Mehrabad Airport from his trip to Burma, he expected an official welcoming ceremony. However, the Iranian government resisted. Prime Minister Ali Amini stepped into the Israeli prime minister's plane and explained, "Iran's relations with Israel cannot be made public. Let us keep it a secret between ourselves . . . our relationship is like the true love that exists between two people outside of wedlock. It is better this way."[27] When Prime Minister Amini resigned and moved to Switzerland, Israeli officials made another attempt to publicize Iranian-Israeli relations by inviting Dr. Amini to Israel for an official visit. He politely declined. Even during his tenure as Iran's Ambassador to Washington, Dr. Amini would ask Israel's Ambassador Abba Eban to park his care several hundred feet away from the Iranian Embassy and walk to the compound in order not to be seen in his official car.

A more serious incident occurred when, in late 1962, at the request of the Israeli government, Prime Minister Amini agreed to meet Foreign Minister Golda Meir at Tehran's Mehrabad Airport for one hour during a stop on her way to West Africa. Prime Minister Amini gave strict orders that the meeting be classified as "top-secret" and not be publicized in the foreign press. Israeli officials, however, intended to broadcast Mrs. Meir's visit on Israeli radio as soon as her plane landed in Tehran. Unfortunately for Israel, the El-Al plane carrying Mrs. Meir, which was scheduled to land at half past midnight, was delayed for four hours in Cyprus because of mechanical problems. Meanwhile, General Pakravan, director of Savak, and officials of the Iranian Foreign Ministry awaited her arrival at the airport. At approximately 11:00 p.m. Tel Aviv time, which was 1:30 a.m. Tehran time, Radio Israel announced the news of "the meeting" between Mrs. Meir and Prime Minister Amini. The announcement was picked up by BBC's Arabic News Program and broadcast an hour later.

Savak's communications center immediately relayed the news to Prime Minister Amini. He was shocked and angered and ordered the welcoming party to leave the airport with only one low-level official left to greet the Israeli Foreign Minister.[28]

Not all Israelis were so intent on receiving formal recognition. Israel's representative in Iran during the incident, Meir Ezri, came to appreciate Iran's reasons for not wanting to publicize its relations with Israel. This explains why he disagreed with Israel's Agriculture Minister, Gvati, who in 1963 insisted that Israel present Iran with a fait accompli by unilaterally mounting a plaque at the entrance to Israel's mission in Tehran reading: "Embassy of Israel."[29]

Ezri was not alone. The following confidential memorandum of conversation between David Tourgeman, Second Secretary of the Israeli Mission in Tehran, and Thomas Greene, political office of the U.S. Embassy, dated April 2, 1965, summarizes the nature of Iranian-Israeli relations in light of the foregoing incidents:

> Mr. Tourgeman commented that the Israeli operations here in Iran are almost clandestine. He said that while his government was eager to expand relations with Iran, it realized the delicate position of the Iranian Government in recognizing both Israeli and many Arab countries, and therefore did not push contacts too much.[30]

In short, Israel's eagerness to elicit formal, public recognition from the government of Iran, which was a major objective of Ben Gurion's peripheral policy, had to be tempered. In view of Iran's precarious position within the Muslim world, the modus vivendi of Israeli-Iranian relations would have to be cloaked in secrecy.

THE DISCREET ENTENTE

Although Iran persisted in her refusal to publicize relations with Israel and to upgrade them to the exchange of embassies, she also refused to yield to Nasser's heavy-handed pressures and cooperated with Israel to make certain that his expansionist schemes failed. One example of cooperation occurred during the Yemen civil war.[31]

By November 1962, the Soviet Union began supporting Nasser's policies in Yemen and provided him with military equipment to support his adventure there. The Soviets sent 450 technicians to Sanaa, and by July 1963 it was reported that about 500 Soviet technicians were constructing a modern jet airport for Yemen. Although Nasser's decision to intervene in Yemen was more a product of ill-conceived hopes of reestablishing Egypt as the leader of the Arab world, Soviet strategy in Yemen appeared to be aimed at establishing a sphere of influence in the Arabian peninsula.[32]

Despite the fact that North Yemen is politically, economically, geographically, and militarily important to the Kingdom of Saudi Arabia, the coup d'état was initially perceived by the kingdom as a "domestic affair" that should be solved by the Yemeni people themselves, without any outside interference either from Arab or non-Arab powers. However, Saudi Arabia was pushed to interfere and extend its political, financial, and moral support to the ex-imam and his followers as a result of three major factors: the Egyptian air raids on Saudi border towns, the hostile attitude of the new republican regime in Sanaa toward the Kingdom, and the constant aid requests by the Yemeni royal family. Thus, in a speech in 1963, King Faisal recalled that "Egypt's rulers declared that they had sent their expeditions to fight in Yemen to destroy our country and capture it." He then went on to say, "We were, therefore, driven into a position where we had no alternative but to defend ourselves. Every state and every country in the world is entitled to self-defense."[33] Despite Saudi support for the royalists and attempts at getting Egypt to agree to a ceasefire, by early 1966, Nasser introduced his so-called "Long Breath Strategy," which resulted in increasing Egyptian involvement in Yemen.

By this time, the Shah and his advisors had resolved to stop Nasser's drive into the Arabian peninsula. In Trident meetings, Mossad and Savak officials discussed the means of thwarting Nasser's efforts and supporting Imam al-Badr's royalist forces.[34] The logic of an Israeli-Iranian intervention in this inter-Arab conflict was quite clear: to prevent Arab unity under the banner of Nasserism and to channel Arab energies into internal rivalries. The goal was to ensure that an Arab coalition against Iran and Israel did not develop. At the same time, both countries were committed to the stability and survival of conservative Saudi Arabia — as long as it opposed Arab radicalism. Equally important from a strategic standpoint was the need to keep the Bab-al-Mandab straits open to Israeli and Iranian shipping.

Accordingly, a high-ranking Savak official was dispatched to Saudi Arabia in order to coordinate the anti-Nasser campaign. Soon after his arrival he had established a working relationship with Kamal Adham, director of Saudi intelligence services. At the same time, one of General Nematollah Nassiri's deputies (General Nassiri had been appointed director of Savak after the 1963 uprising by Khomeini and his followers) was sent to northern Yemen in order to assure Imam al-Badr of military support and training for his guerrilla units. Initially, Iranian C130 military aircraft delivered ammunition and other equipment twice a week, flying from Tehran to Taif (western Saudi Arabia). From Taif the materiel was transported by trucks to the rugged terrain of Yemen. Later, when the royalists needed more weapons, the Israelis flew Soviet-made munitions captured in their wars with the Arabs to Tehran where they would be repaired and renumbered and flown to Taif. On two occasions, the Israelis flew directly over Saudi airspace using IIAF (Imperial Iranian Air Force) stickers on their aircraft and parachuted ammunition to the Yemeni rebels. Aside from Savak officials who knew the true identity of the Israeli aircraft flying over Saudi airspace, the only other person aware of this Israeli-Iranian joint venture was Kamal Adham, who was put in touch with Zvi Zamir, director of Mossad, for the first time, in Tehran at Savak's officers' club in 1969. The General Nassiri acted as host. This meeting was arranged at the request of General Zamir, who would use the good offices of Savak as intermediary between Mossad and the director of Saudi Arabia's Intelligence Services.

In 1974, President Anwar Sadat showed a secret Egyptian military balance sheet of his country's Yemenese adventure to the high-ranking Savak official sent by the Shah to Yemen (who was then stationed in Cairo). According to this account 25,000 of Egypt's best soldiers and officers lost their lives. And while in the final analysis Saudi Arabia's campaign against Nasser was of greater importance, Iranian-Israeli intervention on behalf of royalist forces in Yemen did indeed cost Nasser militarily and politically. It undoubtedly damaged the Egyptian army and contributed to the weakening of its morale and cost Nasser prestige in the Arab world.

Although the Yemen intervention was a far cry from Ben Gurion's grand design, in which emphasis was on the public commitment of the partners to come to each other's aid in the event of an attack by a third party, the degree of coordination with which Iran and Israel conducted their anti-Nasser campaign was a clear indication that the peripheral pact could exert political, economic, and military pressure on Israel and Iran's common enemies. Another such enemy was the revolutionary regime in Iraq.

As has already been noted, Iran and Israel saw the Iraqi revolution of 1958 not only as a victory for Arab radicalism but also as a magnification of the threat from the Soviet Union. By extending their influence to Baghdad, the Soviets had found a springboard for infiltrating the Persian Gulf region as well as a proxy with which to disrupt the then prevailing pro-Western status quo. Iran and Israel's apprehensions had been sharpened by arms shipments to Nasser's Egypt. Both Iran and Israel perceived the revolt in Iraq as an extension of Soviet power through the very center of the Middle East.[35]

A major Israeli-Iranian tactic was to arm the Kurds. The rationale behind this move was clear: to keep Iraqi forces engaged in the north and thus to prevent them from exerting pressure on Iran at the southern border and on Israel on its eastern flank. Toward this end, Savak officials arranged a meeting between Mullah Mustafa Barazani, Israeli Chief of Staff, Lieutenant General Tsvi Tsur, and two other high ranking officials from Israel's Defense Ministry. The Israeli delegation was flown from Tehran to Rezaieh and driven to the border town of Piranshahr. There, they changed into local clothes and walked over the border into Iraq. After walking two kilometers they were met by Barazani and approximately 200 of his men. Barazani needed weapons and training for his men and advocated a policy of direct attacks against Iraqi units. The Israeli and Iranian officials agreed that conducting a guerrilla campaign against the Iraqi military would not be very productive and agreed to train the Kurdish rebels and provide them with sufficient arms to conduct a full-scale offensive.

The meeting ended after a day and a half of talks concerning logistical matters. Barazani escorted the Israeli delegation back to the Iran-Iraq border.[36] Thereafter, large-scale aid, in the form of arms, ammunition, and Israeli military advisors began in 1963 and was channeled through Iran with assistance from Savak. In August 1965, the first training course for Kurdish officers run by Israeli instructors was held in the Kurdistan mountains. When Iran's budget for its Kurdish operations diminished, the Israelis filled the vacuum, and after the 1967 war the Kurds we supplied with Soviet equipment captured from the armies of Egypt and Syria. Israel also provided the Kurds with $500,000 a month. Barazani visited Israel in September 1967 and again in September 1973.[37] The following, prepared by the National Foreign Assessment Center (U.S. government agency), is a summary of Iran's and Israel's involvement in Kurdistan against the Iraqi regime:

> Between 1961 and 1970, the [Iraqi] government initiated a number of offensives against Kurds, but none were successful in suppressing the Barazani-led forces, in large part because of Iran's [and Israel's] willingness to aid the Kurds and to allow its — Iran's — territory to be used for their supply and support. Despite Iran's experience with its own Kurdish minority, the Shah [and the Israelis] perceived support for the Kurds in Iraq as a means of containing a pro-Soviet socialist neighbor. Both the Kurds and the Iraqi military, which at times had as much as 80 percent of its forces deployed against the rebels, suffered heavy losses.[38]

Clearly then, for Israel and Iran, the periphery policy was paying handsome dividends, for despite its informal nature, both countries seemed to be moving toward an alliance that would add important increments of security to Israel and Iran by increasing the burden on the Arabs and thereby forcing them to be more preoccupied with their security.[39]

One move that did add significantly to Israel's and Iran's security was the establishment of offices in the southern Iranian port city of Khoramshahr to conduct their "interborder activity." Savak and Mossad followed this unique technique of intelligence gathering through the use of the local population in order to protect the national origins of the operation. For example, in this particular case, Iranian Arabs were recruited by Savak and Mossad agents (who were themselves fluent in Arabic) from the large Iranian-Arab community of Iran's Khuzestan province. These ethnic Iranians, who spoke Arabic, would in turn cross the border with fake passports and establish links with their relatives and friends on the Iraqi side of the border and, over time, infiltrate the military and political establishments in Basra and Baghdad. The advantage of this type of intelligence gathering was that maximum use was made of local contacts, thus minimizing the direct involvement of Mossad and Savak agents.

Through the use of the Khoramshahr office, Iran and Israel were able to obtain valuable information on Soviet arms transfers to Iraq, such as the number of Soviet advisors assisting the Iraqi military and the exact types of weapons delivered. This information was used by the Iranian and the Israeli military establishment and was relayed to members of the NATO and CENTO alliances. In addition, this joint venture between Iran and Israel succeeded in obtaining information on the Soviet MiG aircraft delivered to Iraq. Savak immediately told the CIA about the Soviet MiG, and when Mossad officials attempted to sell the same information to the CIA they were informed that Savak had already supplied the information free of charge.

One of the most important accomplishments of Israeli-Iranian interborder activity was the discovery of an Iraqi plot to establish a republic in the Iranian province of Khuzestan (which Iraq and Syria called Arabistan). After the coup led by Abdul Sallam Aref in 1963, Iraq's anti-Iranian activities increased. Aref decided to use the indigenous Arab population of Khuzistan to foment an uprising and establish an independent state hostile to Iran. For this purpose he organized his agents in Khuzestan, established the Hizb-al-Tahrir al-Arabi (Party of the Arab Liberation) of Southern Arabia with Mohiedin Nasser, a high-ranking official of the National Iranian Oil Company, as its leader, and invited Nasser to Iraq. After his meeting with Abdul Sallam Aref, Mohiedin Nasser was given 300,000 British pounds and some light arms. Upon his return to Iran, Nasser created his government, consisting of 11 so-called cabinet members, and established chapters of Hizb-al-Tahrir al-Arabi in Khoramshahr, Ahwaz, Abadan, and Dezful. He was even successful at recruiting members from the local military and police units. This plot, however, was soon uncovered by members of the Iranian-Israeli interborder activity team, and with Israeli assistance, 82 of Mohiedin Nasser's men were identified and apprehended. Nasser and two coconspirators were found guilty by a military court and executed. Eighteen members were given life sentences, and the remaining members got long prison terms. Once the plot was uncovered, the Shah insisted that its members be arrested, but an Israeli agent named Erel advised against it, arguing that by waiting a little longer, more incriminating evidence could be discovered for prosecuting the conspirators in the military tribunal. The Shah followed Erel's advice.

While the joint Israeli-Iranian interborder activities were producing results close to the Iraqi border, Mossad and Savak agents were busy laying the foundations for counterespionage activities within Iran, particularly in Tehran. In 1962, a meeting took place between Meir Amit, head of Israel's military intelligence, and a high-ranking Savak official. The purpose of the meeting was for the Savak official to get to know Amit better and to discuss his request to meet privately with the Shah. It appears that during his meeting with the Iranian monarch, General Amit was able to obtain the Shah's agreement to train Savak agents in the art of counterespionage and to conduct joint intelligence gathering operations by breaking into embassies of hostile countries in Tehran. Indeed, after this meeting, according to high-ranking Savak officials, Mossad's Arabic-speaking agents were able to take full advantage of the weakness Arab diplomats in Tehran displayed toward money and women and were able to break into a number of their embassies and open diplomatic pouches and photograph their contents.

Israeli-Iranian relations during the period 1958 through 1967 were not confined solely to the task of stemming the tide of Arab radicalism and neutralizing Soviet influence in the region but gradually expanded into the development of Iran's armed forces. In addition to becoming a reliable "second source" for her arms supplies, Iran recognized the important role Israel could play in the modernization of the Imperial Iranian Armed Forces. Henceforth, this factor would play an increasingly important role in Israeli-Iranian relations.

After the overthrow of the Mossadeq regime, when the Iranian military rallied to their commander-in-chief, the Shah focused on strengthening Iran's ground forces. Deeply concerned about Iran's internal security problems and her vulnerability to pressures from the Soviet Union, with which Iran shared a 1,300-mile border, the Shah was determined to improve his country's military security. The ground forces were steadily upgraded until, in the mid-1960s, two basic developments combined to force a reexamination of Iran's strategic interests.[40]

One event was the Indian-Pakistani War of 1965. The Shah and his military advisors could not but notice how the United States abandoned Pakistan in favor of an even-handed policy. In effect, this policy was hardly even-handed. The United States had frozen its arms shipments to both belligerents, but only the Pakistani army depended on U.S. equipment and spare parts. The Shah became determined to pursue a policy of self-help and decided in favor of an independent Iranian military establishment, because as he put it, "these Pacts will not save us."[41] The Shah's critics, who like to link his military programs to the "oil windfall," overlook the fact that the pivotal point in his plans to develop Iran's armed forces came in the wake of this Indo-Pakistani conflict of 1965, long before the impact of the oil price hikes, which were later factored into the modernization of Iran's armed forces.

A second development, alluded to earlier, was the growing influence of radical Arab movements along the periphery of the Arabian peninsula and the need to upgrade Iran's arsenal in view of their procurement policy. Thus, in January 1964 the Israeli chief of staff, Lieutenant General Tsvi Tsur, and the director-general of the Ministry of Defense, Asher Ben Nathan, stopped in Tehran for two days of talks with the Iranian chief of staff, General Abdulhossein Hejazi, and senior members of his staff. This meeting led to the sale to Iran of Uzi submachine guns, which were on display by the parading Iranian soldiers during King Faisal's 1965 visit to Tehran.[42]

Later, in 1966, in order to cultivate its second source further, Iran signed a $6 million arms package with Israel which included overhauling 35 Iranian F-86 combat planes, the sale of 106 mm. antitank recoiless guns, 120 mm. heavy mortars (made by Tampella), and 160 mm. heavy mortars

(5.8-mile range). Iran's procurement officers were able to recall the type of weapons in the Iraqi arsenal from Iraq's days in the Baghdad pact and chose their weapons accordingly. In the mid-1960s, Israel sold prefabricated desert kitchens to Iran's military, along with radio equipment for armored vehicles and targeting devices for mortars in order to enhance their accuracy.

These purchases from Israel occurred at a time when the Democratic administrations of Kennedy and Johnson were generally opposed to the sale of military hardware to Iran. Iran, in turn, looked to Israel as "little America," one whose Third World experience matched Iran's regional military concerns. For example, in the late 1960s, when Iran decided to purchase 460 British-made Chieftain tanks, General Hasan Toufanian, director of military procurement, sought the advice of the Israelis. The Israelis recommended that the tank's horsepower be upgraded from 650 to 750 in order to operate better on Iranian terrain. For General Toufanian and the Shah, it was quite clear that Israel could contribute in a variety of ways to the modernization of Iran's armed forces, and more important, could be trusted to deliver on its promises during periods when other suppliers were less than willing to sell arms to Iran.

It also became clear to the Shah and his advisors that, aside from Israel's direct aid to Iran in terms of arms procurement, it could further Iran's efforts in the United States to procure more advanced weapons during periods when the U.S. administration or Congress was not forthcoming. One such Israeli lobbying effort on behalf of Iran occurred during the tenure of Armin Meyer as U.S. Ambassador to Iran.[43] In 1966, Washington was strongly opposed to providing any arms to Iran. Faced with what it considered an extreme policy, the U.S. Embassy recommended that a military mission be brought to Iran to assess the Shah's real military needs. As a result, a survey was made by a mission headed by Air Force General Peterson. To the surprise of the embassy, the Peterson mission, among its recommendations, suggested that the United States supply Iran with F-4 Phantom fighters, aircraft considerably more advanced than the F-5's then in the Iranian inventory. The Shah was delighted and promptly supported F-4 procurement.

Because Washington was basically opposed, Ambassador Meyer went to Washington to seek some reasonable solution. In a talk with President Johnson, he explained that in light of the fact that the Soviets had provided $2.3 billion in arms to Iraq, including MiG-21 aircraft, it was not a good policy to leave the Shah without the means to defend Iran. Meyer stressed that it was important to maintain the close military relationship which the United States had had with Iran since World War II. President Johnson, aware of Washington opposition, replied, "Mr. Ambassador you make a good case. I hope you can get our government to go along with you." The ambassador then took his case to Defense Secretary McNamara, who was opposed to selling the Shah even a "nickle's worth" of arms. The conversation concluded with McNamara asking his Defense Department colleagues to study Iran's economic ability to afford the arms. Mindful of the Peterson recommendations, Ambassador Meyer suggested to McNamara rehabbed F-4's. McNamara said if aircraft were to be supplied, they should be new ones. Others in Washington who opposed any arms sales to Iran included Senate Foreign Relations Committee Chairman William Fulbright, who told a Congressional hearing: "I believe we are doing Iran a great disservice by selling these arms."[44]

Upon his return to Tehran, Ambassador Meyer was contacted by Zvi Doriel, the Israeli representative, who had apparently read, in the Tehran press, stories that the United States was strongly resisting arms supplies to Iran. The Israeli asked Ambassador Meyer, "What are you [the United States] trying to do? Throw the Shah into the arms of the Russians?"

Noting that the Israeli President was on an official visit to Washington, Ambassador Meyer told the Israeli representative: "If you have such strong convictions you might wish to suggest that your Prime Minister raise the subject with President Johnson." It appears that this suggestion was followed, for in one of his Tuesday meetings of his four key security advisors in November 1967, President Johnson informed them that the Israelis were greatly concerned that Iran would stray away from ties with Washington and gravitate toward Soviet military purchasing. The upshot was that the decision was made to proceed with a four-year program in which Iran would be allowed to purchase $50 million worth of military equipment each year. Thus, by the end of 1967, McNamara authorized the sale to Iran of two squadrons of Phantom jets, each aircraft costing $2 million.

GENESIS OF THE ISRAELI-IRANIAN OIL CONNECTION

During the period 1958 through 1967, while Israel helped develop Iran's armed forces, Iran accelerated its sale of crude oil to Israel. Indeed, one of the most significant components of Israeli-Iranian relations, and one that aroused Arab hatred toward Iran the most, was the sale of Iranian petroleum to Israel from 1957 through 1977.[45] The Shah's rationale for selling oil to Israel was, initially, based purely on Iran's budgetary problems. The need to raise foreign exchange in order to begin the process of economic development meant that any country willing to purchase Iranian crude would not be discriminated against. Equally important was an understanding by the Shah and his advisors of the special relationship between the United States and Israel. By selling oil to Israel, Iran hoped its agenda for economic and military development would receive the blessing of the U.S. administration and Congress.

The logistics of transporting Iranian oil to Israel is captured in the following secret United Stated *Intelligence Information Cable* dated May 27, 1967:

> Tankers engaged in Iran to Eilat run:
> A. Nora-Hariz Tanker Corp., Monrovia, Liberia.
> B. Leon-Trans World Tanker Corp., Monrovia, Liberia.
> C. Samson-Supertanker Corp., Monrovia, Liberia.
> D. Siris-Astro Armada Nav. S. A., Panama.
> E. Patria-Zas Tanker Co. Ltd., Monrovia, Liberia.
> The oil comes from stocks owned by two members of IRICON group: Signal-Iran of Los Angeles and SOHIO of Cleveland. The Siris and Patria travel regularly between Kharg Island and Eilat with oil for Israel, a round trip of about 20 days. Other ships are also known to carry oil from Iranian ports to Israel, but a number of them are falsely manifested on leaving port so that Eilat is not listed as their destination.[46]

There were instances, however, when the supply of Iranian oil to Israel did not always correspond to Israel's demand. In the fall of 1965, with the prospect of increasing domestic consumption and stable or reduced production, Golda Meir came to Tehran in order to persuade Iran to increase the sale of Iranian oil to Israel. The Shah, however, turned her down, because her request came after the second and third Arab summits, in which Iran was criticized for its relations with the "Zionist entity." After the 1967 Arab-Israeli War, however, the Shah's oil strategy would change.

ISRAEL AND IRAN'S AGRICULTURAL DEVELOPMENT

By the 1960s, the major factors that prompted Iran to cultivate closer ties to Israel came into sharper focus: the need to neutralize and curtail Soviet power and Arab radicalism in the Middle East, Israel's contribution to the modernization of the Imperial Iranian Armed Forces and its reliability as a source of arms in exchange for Iranian oil, and the lobbying efforts of Israel on Iran's behalf in Washington. One other major factor that contributed to Israeli-Iranian relations peculiar to this period is captured in the following exchange between Mohammad Reza Shah Pahlavi and E. A. Bayne concerning the Iranian monarch's philosophy about development:

E.A.B.: A national administration of water resources could work, given an ideal administration.

H.I.M.: Of course, everything boils down to that. They have this in Israel. They have to.

E.A.B.: But in Israel you have a democratically developed society that grew out of another tradition. Here the tradition was hierarchical and even absolutist. There is a different approach to administration.

H.I.M.: The goals are the same. Every country that wants to come abreast of the advanced nations has the same goal, although the forms may be different . . . while we have devised many things out of our own brainpower, we have taken what seems best from here and there. Some things might look communistic to you, or socialistic to people in European countries — or liberalistic. Our ideology is an amalgam of whatever we thought would best suit our interests and needs. So, you cannot put a trademark on us.

E.A.B.: Well, perhaps there is a name for it: pragmatism.[47]

The Iranian monarch was clearly impressed by the rapid pace of development in Israel and believed that Israel's technical expertise could be used to Iran's advantage. At the same time, Israel's export of its technical knowledge more or less paralleled the development of Israel's foreign policy, and it did not escape the minds of Israeli policy makers that closer ties to Iran in the form of economic assistance could extend into other areas of cooperation.

Following the visit to Iran of Moshe Dayan, who was highly respected by the Shah and his advisors as the chief architect of the Israeli victory in the 1956 Israel-Egypt War, and who, since 1959, had been the minister of agriculture in Ben Gurion's government, Israel launched a major reconstruction project in Iran's earthquake-damaged region of Ghazvin.[48]

In 1962, an earthquake shook the Ghazvin Plain, about 65 miles west of Tehran, destroying 300 villages, 123,000 acres of land, and leaving 22,000 farming families (125,000 people) homeless. Iran's Ministry of Agriculture, after taking a hard look at the devastation, decided to undertake a comprehensive development scheme for the area with the assistance of an Israeli government corporation — Tahal (Water Planning) Ltd. of Tel Aviv. When the by-laws of the project were presented to the Iranian Senate for approval, no mention was made of Israel's cooperation, although Dr. Sadjadi, president of the Senate, was aware of Israeli assistance. Once the $20 million World Bank loan for the project was secured (after an Israeli lobbying effort in Washington[49]), an Israeli team headed by Lova Eliav (who was a prime mover in developing the Lachish area in Israel between Tel Aviv and the Negev) developed — and implemented — a four-part plan for the development of the Ghazvin Plain.[50]

The Ghazvin project was unique in terms of providing Israeli specialists an opportunity to work directly with Iranian villagers. The following account of the Ghazvin project by Susan Levine, the associate editor of the *Near East Report*, provides a lucid description of Iranian-Israeli cooperation from a human angle:

> The Israelis had learned that they could not successfully propagandize the villagers. The village of Gomieq, without water since the earthquake knocked out its qanats, would not hear of a

well. So Tahal escorted Gomieq leaders to Dowlatabad [where the Israelis had built a well] and left the citizens of Dowlatabad to convince the citizens of Gomieq that the well made good sense. The skeptics however, will never be secure that this new well which comes from the Shah is given in good faith, prompting one of them to say to an Israeli technician: "I understand everything but this. Why should the Shah want to build a well for me?"

By fall 1965, over 50 wells had been drilled; 28 were equipped. By spring 1966, 85 more will be drilled and equipped. When everything is finished, there will be 250 wells. A long-experienced Israeli engineer, whose home-sick wife and children want to go back to Tel Aviv, is resisting because of the challenge which all this digging promises. "Israel is the holy country you know? Full of holes. Will I get the chance to dig 200 new wells if I go back to Israel now?"

Zalman Abramov was responsible for sinking the Farouk, one of the few victories of Israel's miniscule navy in the war of 1948. He is a national hero and presumably not afraid of much. But when he tried to invite some Ghazvin villagers to come to have their sheep dipped in harmless disinfectant, he ran like crazy, so hard and fast flew the stones of rejection. However, Tahal went ahead and built a dipping pond on its experimental land and sent the herds of some cooperative villagers through. In ten days, the ticks which made Ghazvin's 180,000 sheep worth next to nothing wool-wise, were gone. Representatives from three villages sneaked in to verify the phenomenon. Then came six more. Then 12 more. By fall of 1965, 14 dipping ponds had been constructed and 117,000 sheep belonging to 76 villages had been pushed through them. Abramov no longer feels rejected.[51]

For the Iranian peasant it did not matter that a "Yahudi" (Jew) was teaching him how to make the best use of the possible resources available to him, nor did it matter for his government that citizens of a non-Muslim state were engaged in the development of their Muslim country. As Iranians, they welcomed the Israeli assistance and cooperated because it was the most pragmatic entente for Iran, given the difficult circumstances of the mid-1960s and the requirements of development.

The success of the Ghazvin project was in no small part also due to the Iranian authorities, who trained and prepared a suitable national group to take responsibility gradually for the project. From more than 50 Israeli experts in 1969, the number had declined to about 15 at the beginning of 1972; by the end of the year almost all of them had terminated their assignments. It should be noted that from among the original number of

Israelis, 12 were agents who entered Iran under the guise of working for the Ghazvin project. They actually worked at Ahwaz Radio, rebutting Arab propaganda directed at Iran's ethnic minorities in the Khuzestan province.

The economics of the project demonstrated several impressive results as well. Between 1966 and 1971, at the end of the first stage of development, many changes had occurred. The irrigated area had increased from 2,600 hectares to 23,000 hectares; the number of wells, from 95 to 272; field crops, from 5,500 hectares to 20,600; and deciduous irrigated fruit trees, from 910 hectares to 1,630. The yield in tons per hectare increased in wheat cultivation from 0.75 to 3.00, and in record yields up to 4.40; sugarbeets, from 12.00 to 33.00, and in record yields 52.00; and tomatoes, from 9.00 to 32.20, and in record yields 45.00. The average income per family increased from $180 per year to $370. By 1975 it had met the target of $620 for a family of six.[52]

In view of the close cooperation between Iran and Israel in the military, security, and economic fields and the cementing of these ties from 1958 through 1967, it is not surprising that despite her public pronouncements, Iran welcomed Israel's victory in the 1967 War. Throughout this period, Iran perceived the Israeli strategic utility primarily in terms of the balance of power between Israel and the Arab states and the extent to which her alliance with Israel would add to Iran's national interests. As such, the unprecedented rise of the Israeli preponderance of power after the 1967 War was more than welcomed by the Shah and his administration, for it in effect neutralized the tide of Arab radicalism that could have swept the Middle East had the Arab states won. Equally important, the withdrawal of Egyptian forces from Yemen removed the perceived Egyptian threat to the Arabian peninsula.[53]

One man who continued, however, to attack the Shah and his endorsement of Israel's peripheral policy was Ayatollah Khomeini. Although the rise of Islamic fundamentalism was kept in check during this period and allowed Israeli-Iranian relations to flourish, Khomeini's rhetoric was a constant reminder of the danger he and his vision of an Islamic Republic in Iran would have for the "unholy alliance" between Iran and Israel:

> We tell you that Israel has formed your land reform laws. You are always stretching out your hands like beggers to the Israelis for new programs. You are bringing Israeli military experts to this country. You are sending your students to Israel. I wish you would send them to England. We oppose these policies. We don't want our Sunni brothers to think we are Yahudi worshippers. People of the world beware! Our people are against Israel. These are not our people who support these relations. Our religion does not allow us to support the enemies of Islam.[54]

Khomeini's rhetoric soon gave way to open hostility and in 1963, with some financial assistance from Egypt's Nasser, he called on his followers to overthrow the central government. The uprising was unsuccessful. Through the intervention of General Pakravan, director of Savak, Khomeini was not executed but was sent into exile in Turkey. General Pakravan was a deeply cultured man, believing that he could win over any opponent by being sincere and logical. Yet his efforts on behalf of Khomeini cost him dearly, for soon after Khomeini's return to Iran in 1979, Khomeini ordered his execution without trial. His corpse, or what remained of it, was left at the Tehran morgue for weeks as Khomeini's henchmen refused to issue burial permission.[55]

By the end of 1967, Khomeini was living a life of isolation in Najaf (occasionally a representative from the British Embassy would pay him a visit), while his arch rival, Mohammad Reza Shah Pahlavi, was busy explaining his plans for Iran to visiting guests. One such visitor was Richard Nixon. During the course of their meeting, the Iranian monarch made a very important point that caught Nixon's attention and which would later become the cornerstone of the Nixon Doctrine: "Let me take care of my regional problems. Why should the United States or the Soviet Union intervene in an Iran-Iraq war? The lesson of Vietnam is clear: stay out of irregular wars, because yours are regular troops."[56]

A RETROSPECT

The lessons of Iranian-Israeli cooperation from 1958 through 1967 did not escape the Shah either, for the success of his plans of taking care of all the regional problems rested, to a large extent, on the continuation of Iran's pragmatic entente with Israel. By the end of 1967, this entente rested on several premises.

Anarchic Nature of the International and Regional Environment

From a global perspective, despite their pro-Western stance, U.S. guarantees of assistance were perceived by both Iran and Israel as fragile. Concomitantly, the rise of Arab nationalism with its aim of establishing hegemony in the region accentuated Tehran's and Tel Aviv's sense of isolation. Thus, with no international arbiter powerful enough to allay the Israeli-Iranian security imperatives, Iran and Israel, in their search for self-help, entered into a pragmatic entente.

Contain Soviet and Sunni Arab Hegemony of the Middle East

The intersection of David Ben Gurion's peripheral doctrine with Mohammad Reza Shah Pahlavi's national independent policy during this period was premised on the mutual need to contain the Soviet-Arab alliance in the region. In other words, the purpose of an Israel-Iran axis was to serve as a balance of power against the rising tide of Arab radicalism, which was aided by the Soviet Union.

Trade in Technical Assistance and Oil

Israel's expertise in military technology and agricultural development fitted perfectly into Iran's plans to modernize its armed forces and to increase agricultural productivity. The period between 1958 through 1967 was a good example of adapting Israeli technology to fit Iran's development requirements. In view of the Shah's basic philosophy of safeguarding his country's domestic development in an environment of peace and stability, Israel's technical assistance played a twin role: its expertise in agriculture would contribute to economic development in such areas as Ghazvin while its military assistance contributed to the ability of the Imperial Iranian Armed Forces to defend the country's territorial integrity. This trade relationship was not one-dimensional.

While Israel provided valuable technical assistance, Iran helped Israel's energy security by selling much-needed crude oil to that country.

Iran-Arab and Arab-Israeli Relations

The Iran-Arab cold war that began in 1952 continued unabated into the 1960s, pitting conservative Iran against revolutionary states like Iraq, Egypt, and Syria. The threat of interference by these Arab states in the internal affairs of Iran in order to destabilize the Iranian government was genuine. Indeed, within the ideology of Arab nationalism, Iran was seen to be closely associated with the intrusion of Western powers into the Middle East and, as the Arabistan issue illustrates, was itself viewed as a colonizer of Arab territory. Nevertheless, the centrality of Arab irredentist policy, manifested in terms of claims to Iran's Khuzestan province and attempts at redefining the Persian Gulf as the Arabian Gulf, was perceived as a threat not only to Iran's security interests but also to her identity as a non-Arab Persian state. Therefore, information on Arab activities and means of thwarting their plots against Iran required a closer relationship with the only country in the Middle East capable of providing such intelligence, namely, Israel and its superb intelligence organization, Mossad. Not surprisingly, when the 1967 Arab-Israeli War erupted, Iran's overt sympathies for the "Muslim brothers" were outweighed by her covert satisfaction at the success of the "Jewish cousins." In short, the Arab challenge — a function of the geopolitics of the region — was a major factor in Iran's decision to ally herself with Israel.

Israel's Special Relationship with Washington

One major lesson for Iran during this period was that relations with Israel carried an important by-product: getting approval for Iran's agenda in Washington at times when the United States appeared reluctant to help. To Israel's friends in the United States, it was clear that relations between the Jewish state and Iran contributed to the former's security. To the extent that Israel's security would be enhanced by its continued discreet entente with Tehran, the "special relationship" factor would be invoked on behalf of Iran.

Who Rules Iran: Secularists or Traditionalists?

With the exception of 1963, when Khomeini's attempt at overthrowing the central government failed, clergy-state relations during this period were not polarized to the extent of derailing relations with Israel. Although one reason for such a state of affairs might have been the continued financial support the Shiite clerics received during this period, an equally important factor may have been the persistently hostile nature of attacks by the Sunni Arab states against the Shah personally and Iran in general. For example, attempts at "Arabizing" the Khuzestan province or expelling Shiites from Iraq were viewed as an insult to Iranian clerics and an affront to Shiism. To the extent therefore that the Iran-Arab cold war was encapsulated into a Sunni-Shiite rivalry, traditionalists sided with the secularists in defending Iran's national integrity, even if that defense included an alliance with Israel.

NOTES

1. Documents from the United States Embassy in Tehran, Volume 11, 1979, p. 24.
2. Michael Bar Zohar, "Ben Gurion and the Policy of the Periphery," in *Israel in the Middle East*, ed. Itamar Rabinovich and Jehuda Reinharz (Oxford: Oxford University Press, 1984), p. 171.
3. Cited in Michael Brecher, *Foreign Policy System of Israel* (New Haven: Yale University Press, 1972), p. 278.
4. The Eisenhower Doctrine was a joint resolution of the Congress designed to protect the territorial integrity and independence of Middle East states requesting aid when threatened by "international communism." In 1957 Iran announced its enthusiasm for the Eisenhower Doctrine, and on March 5, 1959, following the 1958 revolution in Iraq, the United States and Iran signed a bilateral defense agreement.
5. The Periphery Doctrine was enunciated at a time when the international system was entering a new phase: balance of terror. Although superpower competition as a global phenomenon persisted, a balance of terror served as an effective deterrent to nuclear war. The constraint on the use of force was clearly evident in the Cuban missile crisis of 1962 and the 1967 Arab-Israeli conflict. However, the patron relationship that the United States and the Soviet Union had developed with regional actors continued unabated. Within the Middle East, the Soviet Union continued its patron

relationship with Egypt and Syria while it attempted to lure new entrants like revolutionary Iraq and Northern Yemen into its camp. The United States, meanwhile, had "recruited" Israel, Iran, and Turkey, and with British assistance, in 1958 had established a regional alliance called the Central Treaty Organization (CENTO) consisting of Iran, Turkey, Pakistan, and the United Kingdom. The major thrust of CENTO was to serve as a cordon sanitaire along the Soviet Union's southern borders. Thus, the superpowers had managed to turn the Middle East into another area in which they could, by supporting their respective regional allies, hope to gain the upper hand in their Cold War.

For a detailed account of the genesis of the Periphery Doctrine see Michael Bar Zohar, "Ben Gurion and the Policy of the Periphery," in *Israel in the Middle East*, ed. Itmar Rabinovich and Jehuda Reinharz (Oxford University Press, 1984), pp. 164–71.

6. Ibid., p. 170.

7. Ibid., p. 166. It should be noted the Cyrus, King of the Persian Empire in the sixth century B.C., was the first non-Jew to recognize the longing of the Jews for Zion and prompted the reestablishment of a Jewish community in Judea, thus ending the First Babylonian Exile.

8. Some U.S. officials, like Ambassador Meyer, contend that the idea of using the Jewish lobby in Washington played a secondary role in the Shah's cultivation of ties to Israel.

9. George Lenczowski, *The Middle East in World Affairs* (Ithaca; Cornell University Press, 1962), p. 298.

10. Arthur Goldschmidt, *A Concise History of the Middle East* (Boulder: Westview Press, 1983), p. 271.

11. Lenczowski, p. 299.

12. Goldschmidt, p. 272.

13. Shojaedin Shafa, *Jenayat va Mokafat* Volume 3 (Paris: 1986), p. 1777.

14. Amir Taheri, *Spirit of Allah* (Bethesda, MD: Adler & Adler, 1986), p. 139.

15. Interview with former Iranian official, France, 1987.

16. Documents of the United States Embassy in Tehran, Volume 47, 1979, p. 17.

17. Ibid., p. 29.

18. Shahram Chubin, "Iran's Foreign Policy 1960–1976: An Overview," in *Twentieth Century Iran*, ed. Hossein Amirsadeghi (London: William Heinemann, 1977), p. 198.

19. Interview with Shmuel Segev, Israel, 1988.

20. Interview with former Iranian official, Washington, D.C., 1988; General Qarani became the first Joint Chief of Staff of the Iranian Armed Forces under the Khomeini regime and was assassinated on April 23, 1979.

21. Shafa, p. 1688.

22. New York *Times*, July 28, 1960.

23. New York *Times*, July 29, 1960.

24. Cited in Shafa, *Jenayat va Mokafat*, p. 1689.

25. Ibid., p. 1690.

26.   Interview with former Iranian official, Washington, D.C., 1988.

27.   Interview with former Iranian Prime Minister, Dr. Ali Amini, France, 1987.

28.   Interview with former Iranian official, Washington, D.C., 1988.

29.   Interview with Shmuel Segev, Israel, 1988.

30.   Documents of the United States Embassy in Tehran, Volume 11, 1979, p. 48.

31.   For a comprehensive analysis of the Yemen Civil War see Saeed M. Badeeb, *The Saudi-Egyptian Conflict over North Yemen, 1960–1970* (Boulder: Westview Press, 1986).

32.   Badeeb, p. 67.

33.   Ibid., p. 50.

34.   The first Trident meeting was held in Tehran in 1961. Isser Harel represented Mossad; Savak was represented by General Pakravan. Trident's second meeting was held in Tel Aviv and after the conference, Harel invited the Iranian officials to his home for an informal gathering. What struck the Iranian officials most was Harel's simple lifestyle and his small quarters.

35.   Alvin Cotrell, "Iran's Armed Forces," in *Iran Under the Pahlavis*, ed. George Lenczowski (Stanford: Hoover Institution Press, 1978), p. 416.

36.   *Oral History of Iran*, Foundation for Iranian Studies, Bethesda, Maryland.

37.   Benjamin Beit-Hallahmi, *The Israeli Connection: Who Israel Arms and Why* (New York: Pantheon Books, 1987), p. 19.

38.   Documents of the United States Embassy in Tehran, Volume 31, 1979, p. 15.

39.   Avner Yaniv, *Deterrence without the Bomb: The Politics of Israeli Strategy* (Lexington, MA: D. C. Heath, 1987), p. 95.

40.   Cotrell, p. 419.

41.   Interview with former Iranian official, Washington, D.C., 1987.

42.   Yaniv, p. 95.

43.   Interview with former U.S. Ambassador to Iran Armin Meyer, Washington, D.C., 1987.

44.   U.S. Congress, Senate, Committee on Foreign Relations, *Arms Sales to Near East and South Asian Countries*, 90th Congress, 1st Session, Hearing, March–June, 1967, p. 17.

45.   For a detailed study of Israel's energy security see Edward Rosen, "The Effect of Relinquished Sinai Resources on Israel's Energy Situation and Policies," *Middle East Review* (Spring/Summer 1982): 5–11; and Benjamin Shwadram, *The Middle East, Oil, and Great Powers* (New York: John Wiley & Sons, 1973), pp. 449–59.

46.   Documents of the United States Embassy in Tehran, Volume 36, 1979, p. 18.

47.   E. A. Bayne, *Persian Kingship in Transition* (New York: American Universities Field Staff, 1968), pp. 100–01.

48.   Yaniv, p. 95.

49.   According to interviews with former Iranian officials who negotiated the World Bank loan, there were some initial reservations on the part of the bank to extend the $20 million. However, Israelis who

accompanied the Iranian delegation to Washington, D. C., assured them that the loan would be approved and that there was nothing to worry about because, as they put it, "we have already arranged the loan's approval through our friends in Washington."

50. The four-part plan included:

> Water development: the replacement of Ghazvin's ancient underground water carrier system (qanats) by deep wells and a regulated flow of irrigation water. Villagers living on the periphery of the Ghazvin Plain with no access to water were each given 500 Israeli chickens.
>
> Agricultural planning: in addition to the adoption of new techniques for higher crop yields, improved animal husbandry such as artificial insemination and crossbreeding of Israeli sheep with Iranian sheep was implemented.
>
> Farming community development: the adoption of kibbutz-style farming communities where possible.
>
> Marketing: the reorganization of transport, communications, and farm credits.

51. Susan Levine, "A Study of Development: Iran," *Near East Report* 10 (January 1966): 24–25.

52. Shimeon Amir, *Israel's Development Cooperation with Africa, Asia, and Latin America* (New York: Praeger, 1974), p. 31.

53. R. K. Ramazani, "Iran and the Arab-Israeli Conflict," *Middle East Journal* 32 (Autumn 1978): 417.

54. Cited in E. A. Shaoul, "Cultural Values and Foreign Policy Decision Making in Iran: The Case of Iran's Recognition of Israel" (Ph.D. dissertation, George Washington University, 1971), p. 167.

55. Taheri, p. 145.

56. Interview with former U.S. Ambassador to Iran Armin Meyer, Washington, D.C., 1987.

4

The Watershed Years: 1968-1973

On June 3, 1969, in an article entitled, "Growing Importance of a Very Discreet Friendship," *The Financial Times* offered the following assessment of Israeli-Iranian relations:

> One of the most fascinating and significant relationships on today's international scene is the strange friendship which has developed over the past few years between Iran and Israel. It could, indeed, be called an alliance, even an axis, though it is only rarely acknowledged or discussed. The reason is simple: abroad, few people appreciate the extent of the links between the two countries, while at home officials are reluctant to admit to something so delicate and controversial at a time of acute Middle East tension. Yet the evidence of Irano-Israeli friendship and cooperation has recently become so overwhelming that the alliance will soon be as undeniable as the El Al airliners which regularly pass on scheduled service between Tehran and Tel Aviv and so, almost symbolically, offer travellers one of the few methods of access to Israel from the Muslim Middle East.[1]

As the 1960s came to an end, the growing significance of the Tehran-Tel Aviv axis was, indeed, becoming an integral element of Middle East politics. Israeli trade with Iran amounted to $250 million annually; they trained and instructed the Iranian secret service; they cooperated with Savak in smuggling remaining Iraqi-Jews out of Iraq; they bought Iranian oil and piped it through a special pipeline from Eilat on the Gulf of Aqaba to Ashkelon on the Mediterranean; and they employed Iranian territory as a forward base for substantial assistance to the Kurdish rebels of Barazani in the northern part of Iraq.[2]

The underlying basis for the increasingly strong ties between Tehran and Tel Aviv was a convergence of geopolitical and economic interests that continued to arise from their common security interests. In the period 1968 to 1973, both states found themselves confronted with an international and regional environment whose major characteristic was unruliness. Thus, although close ties to the United States provided a semblance of security, neither Iran nor Israel was able to obtain a formal treaty with the United States as a guarantee against third-party aggression. And in light of continued Arab hostility, Iran and Israel found themselves embracing one another, albeit under the cover of secrecy. In short, Israeli-Iranian relations flourished during this period as a result of mutual security imperatives that continued to plague both states.

Certain conditions, however, were changing. While the discreet entente between Iran and Israel was making very few headlines, the relaxation of tensions between the Soviet Union and the United States was grabbing the international spotlight under a new buzz-word: detente. One catalyst appears to have been the 1967 Arab-Israeli War, for it demonstrated the limits of intervention by Moscow and Washington in a local war and the desire to avoid direct confrontation at all costs. Detente would, henceforth, provide the underpinning of stability to superpower relations.

CHALLENGES OF THE MIDDLE EAST SYSTEM

While superpower relations tended toward stability, the Middle East remained unsettled, and new faces that posed threats to Iran and Israel emerged during the period 1968 through 1973. In Iraq, Abd al-Rahman Aref, who had replaced his brother Abd al-Salam Aref (who died in a plane crash in 1966), was overthrown by a Baathist coup led by Hasan al-Bakr and his deputy Saddam Hussein in 1968. The new Iraqi regime did not get along well with Syria because of their dispute over the use of Euphrates River waters and differences concerning the ideology of the Baath Party. Iraq's incompatibility with Syria did not mean that Iraq would seek reconciliation with

Iran. Relations with Iran took a turn for the worse as both countries renewed their claim to the Shatt al-Arab. Iraq continued to seek to destabilize the Iranian government. In addition, Iraq criticized Egypt and Jordan for having accepted United Nations Resolution 242, tacitly recognizing Israel. In northern Iraq, the Kurds (with Israeli-Iranian assistance) went on fighting for their independence, while the Baath regime tried to distract popular opinion at home by publicly hanging 14 convicted Israeli spies (nine of whom happened to be Jewish) in Baghdad.[3]

In 1969, a military coup in Libya brought to power an impetuous army colonel named Muammar Qaddafi, who soon emerged as a promoter of militant Arab nationalism. He ejected the Americans from Wheelus Air Base, forced all tourists to carry travel documents written in Arabic, and offered his troops to Nasser to fight for the Suez Canal and volunteered his forces to reinforce the Fedayeen in Jordan and Lebanon.[4] Despite these gestures, he never achieved Nasser's stature in the Arab world.

By September 1970, the Palestinian problem surfaced again. After the disastrous 1967 Arab defeat, Syria had become the major Arab supporter of PLO activity. It encouraged raids from Jordan — much to the displeasure of King Hussein — to minimize Israeli reprisals into Syria. Furthermore, Syria increased its support for the PLO by forming al-Saiqa, a guerrilla unit under the aegis of the PLO but strictly following the political orientation of the Syrian Baath Party and manned largely by Palestinian volunteers from the Syrian army. As the PLO and its various factions, including al-Saiqa and the Popular Front for the Liberation of Palestine (PFLP), grew in strength, they tried to establish a territorial base for themselves in Jordan. Indeed, by September 1970 PLO organizations in Jordan had grown extremely powerful, and their secular, leftist ideology included the goal of deposing King Hussein, who felt increasingly threatened by the PLO presence. Meanwhile, the leader of the PFLP, George Habash, believed that by striking against Western governments and civilians he could dramatize the Palestinian cause and extract concessions from these governments. Four Western planes carrying summer travelers heading for home were hijacked and forced to land in a desert airstrip near Amman. The harsh treatment of the passengers (especially those who happened to be Jewish) embarrassed the Jordanian government and served as catalyst to King Hussein's decision to crush PLO influence inside Jordan. His army began fighting against the Palestinians, civilians as well as Fedayeen, destroying many sections of Amman and other cities. By mid-September Jordan was torn by a full-scale civil war. On September 18, Syria sent an armored column into Jordan to help the Palestinians, but withdrew after a few days when Israel (with U.S. encouragement) and Iran threatened to intervene in the fighting. Nasser tried to act as mediator between the PLO leader Yassir Arafat and King Hussein, but he had made little progress when he died of a heart attack.[5] And while clashes between PLO guerrillas and the Jordanian army continued throughout 1971, the remaining guerrillas left Jordan for other Arab states like Syria, Libya, and Lebanon.

The 1970 Jordan crisis expanded into Syria, where an ongoing leadership struggle was being waged between President Salah Jedid, who ordered the Syrian intervention on behalf of the PLO, and the minister of defense, General Hafez al-Assad, who refused to send air support for the ground units in Jordan. Two months later, in November 1970, Assad ascended to power in a bloodless coup. One element of Assad's defense and foreign policy was — and is — to achieve strategic balance with Israel. His reasons were twofold. First, he wanted to pressure Israel into withdrawing its forces from the Golan Heights and other "occupied" territories. Second, he hoped to become the Arab leader to be reckoned with in the Arab-Israeli conflict.

In Egypt, Anwar-al-Sadat, Nasser's vice-president and one of the last of the original "free officers" group, was chosen to succeed him. By May 1971, Sadat had eliminated all major contenders for power and was well poised to make the far-reaching changes he termed, the "corrective revolution." Nasser's elaborate security apparatus was dismantled. Sadat tried to encourage native and foreign capitalists to invest in Egyptian enterprises, even though this meant a move away from socialism. The official name of the country, which had remained the United Arab Republic even after the Syrian breakaway, was changed to the Arab Republic of Egypt. And although Egypt's ties with the Soviet Union were seemingly strengthened by a 15-year treaty of alliance signed in May 1971, they were in fact becoming strained because of Soviet reluctance to supply Sadat with offensive weapons for use against Israel. A year later, Sadat ordered all Soviet advisors and technicians to leave Egypt.[6]

By September 1973 the Middle East seemed deceivingly calm, and an Arab-Israeli war seemingly improbable. Although the period from June 1967 to September 1973 was one of continued tension in the Middle East, the Arab states were weakened by factionalism, internal strife, differences over their goals and methods of achieving them, and a general mood of self-doubt caused by their humiliating defeat in the 1967 War. Israel seemed to be the most powerful state in the area. And when as early as September 24, 1973, the CIA and the National Security Agency (NSA) were convinced that a major Arab attack was coming and warned Israel, the Israeli Command rejected the warning. They were too confident in their knowledge of the Arabs and underestimated their potential enemies' ability to keep secrets.[7]

With financial backing from King Feisal of Saudi Arabia, Egypt launched a massive air and artillery assault on Israel's Bar-Lev line east of the Suez Canal. This attack was coordinated with a large-scale Syrian tank invasion into the Golan Heights on the Jewish Day of Atonement, Yom Kippur, October 6, 1973. The underlying rationale for Sadat was clear: a war with Israel would be costly to Egypt, but if his army and air force, equipped with an impressive arsenal of Soviet tanks, planes, and missiles, could regain some of the lands Nasser had lost in 1967, Egypt would be in a better bargaining position to make peace with Israel. Although the Israeli armed forces were taken by surprise and the Egyptians were able to cross over onto the East Bank of the Suez Canal, Israel contained the Egyptian advances in the Sinai and encircled one-third of Egypt's armed forces. By the third week of the war the United States persuaded all parties to accept a cease-fire, much to Israel's resentment. But U.S. Secretary of State, Henry Kissinger, reasoned that Egypt would be more apt to make peace if it were allowed to leave the war with some of its initial gains, thus ending another chapter in the long and bloody Arab-Israeli conflict.

ISRAEL'S RESPONSE TO THE INTERNATIONAL
AND REGIONAL CHALLENGE

The anarchic nature of the Middle East environment between 1968 through 1973 with its coup d'états, civil wars, revolutions, and interstate conflicts could not have escaped the minds of Israeli policy makers and had major implications for Israel's foreign policy toward its friends and enemies during this period.

The period from 1955 to 1966 saw an Israeli foreign policy built upon the twin pillars of a tacit alliance with France and a multidimensional friendship with the United States. Israel's foreign policy options narrowed, however, after 1968 because of her decision makers' perceptions that only the United States could counteract the menacing Soviet presence in Egypt and Syria. This perception was reinforced by the fact that U.S. deterrence of direct Soviet military intervention in the Middle East had several important consequences for Israel. It intensified Israel's dependence on Washington (and Egypt's on Moscow) and deepened the hostility between Israel and the Soviet Union; in substance, it influenced the images of Israeli leaders in the direction of the need for greater security with U.S. assistance, and at times when such aid was not forthcoming, to provide for its own security; and in technique, it strengthened Israel's policy predisposition to "bargain from strength."[8] As the degree of Israel's dependence on the "American factor" intensified, so did her search for regional allies; hence, the conspicuous change in the nature of Israel's relationship with Jordan.

The tacit friendship between Israel and Jordan (which had developed as early as 1936 and later in 1948) from 1968 onward, derived, in part, from a shared interest in opposing the fedayeen movement and King Hussein's awareness that Israel would not stand idle if his regime were in danger of collapse. The following account by Yitzhak Rabin, Israel's ambassador to the United States during the 1970 Jordan crisis, is insightful in this regard and seems to support this hypothesis:

> The Palestinian terrorist organizations based [in Jordan] were at the peak of their strength and conducted themselves like a state within a state. As control progressively slipped out of his hands, King

Hussein realized that the hour of decision was drawing near. . . . By that time Golda Meir had completed her visit to Washington and on her last evening in the United States was scheduled to address a large United Jewish Appeal dinner at the New York Hilton. It was there that I was asked to call Henry Kissinger. . . . He spoke with a ring of urgency in his voice: "King Hussein has approached us, describing the situation of his forces, and asked us to transmit his request that your airforce attack the Syrians in northern Jordan. I need an immediate reply." When I met Kissinger at nine the next morning the American reports on the military situation were still sketchy. . . . Although the Syrians had penetrated northern Jordan, Hussein's armoured units were holding on to the two routes leading south and had inflicted losses on the invasion force. In response, the Syrians were massing further armoured units near the border, but they had refrained from using their air power. . . . Israeli-U.S. cooperation in planning the IDF intervention, together with the Israeli troop concentrations near the Syrian border convinced the Russians and the Syrians that they should halt the advance into Jordan. . . . Soon afterward the Syrians withdrew from Jordan and the risk of a broader war was averted.[9]

IRAN'S RESPONSE TO THE INTERNATIONAL AND REGIONAL CHALLENGE

While Israel's willingness to cooperate closely with the United States in protecting U.S. interests in the region altered her image in the eyes of many officials in Washington, another U.S. ally, Iran, was also winning friends in the United States. In explaining the major thrust of the Nixon Doctrine to a group of reporters, in the aftermath of the British withdrawal from the Persian Gulf, Henry Kissinger said:

There was no possibility of assigning any American forces to the Indian Ocean in the midst of the Vietnam War and its attendant trauma. Congress would have tolerated no such commitment; the public would not have supported it. Fortunately, Iran was willing to play this role.[10]

Indeed, the single most important regional development that deepened U.S. reliance on Iran and hence increased Iranian influence in Washington was the departure of the British forces from the Persian Gulf region, U.S. reluctance to act as the British legatee, and the eagerness of the Iranian monarch to play a leading role in the region.[11] Historically

Iran was concerned with the southern shore of the Persian Gulf. By the early 1970s many Iranians lived in the Persian Gulf sheikhdoms, notably in Bahrain, to which Iran had an old claim. Moreover, the Persian Gulf, and notably the narrow exit from it through the Strait of Hormuz into the Arabian Sea and the Indian Ocean, had become much more important for Iran because through it was a conduit for Iranian oil. Iran, therefore, considered it essential that the Arab side of the Persian Gulf, and particularly the shores of the Strait of Hormuz, Iran's "jugular vein," not fall under the hostile control of such countries as Iraq.

To attain this objective, Iran acknowledged Bahrain's independence in 1971, but took over three small yet strategically located islands in the Persian Gulf, Abu Musa and the Great and Little Tunbs. Although little military force was used, Iran's moves were a blow to Arab pride, and Libya used the occasion to sever diplomatic relations with Iran. Iraq also denounced the Iranian moves. Two years later, Iran dispatched an expeditionary force of several thousand ground troops and helicopters to the Sultanate of Oman to help Sultan Qabus suppress the Dhofar rebellion in the Western part of the Sultanate bordering on the People's Democratic Republic of the Yemen (Aden). The rebellion was led by the People's Front for the Liberation of the Occupied Arab Gulf (PFLOAG) and supported by the pro-Soviet PDRY regime, as well as the government of Iraq. Iran's primary motives for complying with Oman's request (after all Arab states had refused similar requests) were two: to prevent Oman, and therefore its enclave of territory on the south side of the Strait of Hormuz from falling into pro-Soviet hands and to counteract PFLOAG attempts to subvert the Persian Gulf sheikhdoms.[12]

Another major development that entered into Iran's foreign policy calculus was the gradual trend away from radicalism and Soviet influence in the Arab world. As has already been noted, the radicalism and pro-Soviet policies of Nasser and the Syrian and Iraqi Baath regimes were seen in the late 1950s and 1960s as a major threat to her security and, in particular, as an opportunity for the Soviets to encircle Iran from the west and south as well as from the north. However, Nasser's defeat by Israel in 1967 and his consequent abandonment of his operations in the Yemen marked a decline in the danger posed by Arab radicalism. Nasser's death and President Sadat's friendship with the Iranian monarch intensified this trend. Sadat's rapprochement with the conservative, oil-rich Arab states as well as the United States and his rebuff of the Soviet Union represented a "bouleversement des alliances" in Arab politics. The Shah welcomed this trend and was quick to take advantage of this development. He wished to improve his relations with the Arab states in order to diminish Soviet influence among them and to gain their support for his oil diplomacy and his leadership in the Persian Gulf. He consequently moved rapidly to improve Iran's relations with Egypt and Saudi Arabia.[13]

The Shah's closer ties with the Persian Gulf states and Egypt were tempered during the period between 1968 and 1973 by Iran's tense relations with Iraq and the Soviet Union. One of the first acts of the Baathist regime in Baghdad was to begin subversive activities against Iran, something Abd al-Rahman Aref had discontinued in exchange for $10 million (the sum was transferred to his Swiss bank account).[14] Saddam Hussein invited to Baghdad former director of Savak General Teymour Bakhtiar, who was in exile in Switzerland, in order to make arrangements to overthrow the monarchy in Iran. He was soon joined by almost the entire Tudeh Party leadership, headed by Reza Radmanesh and Danesh Panahian. The three men decided to join forces with Khomeini who was living in Najaf.[15] At the same time, the Iraqi regime embarked on a massive campaign of harassment and persecution of Iranians living in Iraq. Thousands were relocated and sent to the border town of Qasr-e-Shirin; their properties were confiscated. Iran's suspicions of Iraq's hostile intentions were confirmed by the historic April 9, 1972, Treaty of Friendship between the Soviet Union and Iraq that involved a 15-year Soviet military and economic commitment to Iraq.

The alliance between her northern and western neighbors clearly aggravated Iran's security dilemma, and the Shah was now forced to rethink his country's distrustful coexistence with the Soviet Union. Although Iran's regional importance constrained Soviet attacks, Iran remained skeptical of Soviet intentions. For example contacts between the Iranian Foreign Ministry and the Soviet Embassy were kept at a minimum, as evidenced in the following confidential memorandum of conversation dated April 9, 1973:

> In answer to a question, Vlassov (first secretary of Soviet Embassy in Tehran) remarked that Iraq's actions in recent months have had a deleterious effect on Iran/Soviet relations. He wondered if the Government of Iran really believes that Russia is attempting to encircle it using Iraq and India as proxies. The reporting officer replied that Iranians might very well feel this way.... Renewing an old complaint, Vlassov said that personal relations between Soviet Embassy officers and Iranian officials remain stiff.[16]

The Shah embarked on a strategy of diminishing Soviet belligerency toward Iran by entangling them in commercial relations involving Iran's natural gas and other bilateral projects. He hoped that these gestures might restrain Soviet attitudes toward Iran and give substance to the Soviet slogan, "frontiers of peace and good neighbourliness."[17] However, by the early 1970s, Iran began to perceive the Soviet naval buildup in the Indian Ocean as a danger to her interests in the Persian Gulf. Given the hostility of India toward Iran, the weakness of Pakistan as a buffer, and the looming U.S. defeat in Indochina, the Soviet Union appeared more menacing than ever from Tehran's vantage point.

Thus Iran, like Israel, was engaged in a war of attrition from 1968 through 1973. Traditional enemies such as Iraq, the Soviet Union, and the PLO continued to threaten her national security. Although Tehran did seek her own version of detente with some Arab states when the opportunity presented itself, like Israel, Iran accelerated her arms purchases and deepened her relationship with the West hoping to stay one step ahead of the enemy. Indeed, both Iran and Israel realized that despite assurances from the United States, the emergence of rough strategic equivalence between the superpowers raised serious questions about superpower propensities for risk taking, particularly in marginal areas like the Middle East. The Israelis no doubt shared the Shah's view that a geographically limited detente could constitute a "hunting license" for enemies of Israel and Iran. The basic premise, therefore, for the continuation of cooperation between Iran and Israel was the absence of any third party powerful and willing to counter the menace of an Arab-Soviet attempt to dominate the Middle East.

DIPLOMATIC RELATIONS

Although Israeli-Iranian relations increased in intensity and scope form 1968 through 1973, Iran persisted in its flat refusal to sign a treaty of alliance and continued to prefer — much to the annoyance of the Israelis — a low public profile for her Israeli connection. By the early 1970s, however, Israel had come to accept this modus vivendi. In fact, the head of Israel's burgeoning mission in Tehran (#5 Takht-e-Jamshid Street) carried ambassadorial rank and had easier access to the Shah than did most of the latter's own advisors.[18] The choice of Meir Ezri as Israel's representative to Iran was suggested and strongly supported by the Shah, who had developed a good working relationship with Ezri. The following confidential memorandum of conversation dated October 14, 1972, is insightful in this regard:

Mr. Ben Yohanan stated that the Israeli Mission in Tehran is in a very substantive respect treated by the Government of Iran like any other Embassy. Ambassador Meir Ezri has ready access to the Shah and other high officials of the Iranian government. When the Ambassador is away, Mr. Ben Yohanan is also able to see those Iranian officials, including the Shah, that he needs to see to carry on business between Israel and Iran. It is only on the ceremonial side that the Israeli Mission is treated differently from other regular Embassies in Tehran. No Israeli flag is flown at the Mission and no sign on the front of the building identifies it as the Israeli Mission. Ambassador Ezri does not attend ceremonies which protocol requires other Ambassadors to attend. However, Ben Yohanan saw an advantage in not having to play a ceremonial role which often took up too much of the time of other Ambassadors. Embassies of the Arab countries in Tehran were fully aware, Ben Yohanan said, that the Israeli Embassy was actually like all other Embassies here except for the ceremonial aspects. They fully accepted this unusual state of affairs and made no remonstrations about it with the Iranian Government. Thus, the Israeli Minister continued, the situation was that the Israelis were willing to forego the ceremonial trappings of diplomacy as long as the real substance was present while the Arabs could tolerate the substance of close Iran-Israel relations as long as this was not apparent from surface indications. Ben Yohanan realized that the strongly Islamic orientation of many Iranians, inclining them to sympathize with their fellow Muslims in the Arab-Israel dispute, made it useful for Iran to mask its true policies by publicly pretending not to recognize Israel.[19]

In line with the Shah's desire to keep Israeli-Iranian relations shrouded in secrecy, Iran's embassy in Tel Aviv continued to be regarded as a section of the Swiss Embassy. Officials of the Iranian Embassy in Tel Aviv who were actually assigned to that country were listed in the Iranian Foreign Ministry Directory as serving in Bern, Switzerland. Their work was limited to such routine matters as gathering information on political developments inside Israel and providing assistance to Iranian-Jews and Bahais who visited Israel. The following U.S. Department of State document dated January 6, 1971, offers some interesting observations on the Iranian Embassy in Tel Aviv:

> Teymuri [head of the Iranian Mission to Israel] indicated that the Iranian Government believes Israel should display more flexibility in its negotiations with the Arabs. He argued that it was not to Israel's long-term advantage to insist on the retention of Arab lands since this would only aggravate and prolong the Arab-Israel conflict. Teymuri inquired whether the U.S. would put pressure on Israel to withdraw in accordance with something like the Rogers Plan. . . . Teymuri seems to be friendly to the United States and its Near East policies. . . . I assume that Teymuri's status is the same as that of his predecessor, Ferydoon Farrokh, i.e., that he is technically a part of the Iranian diplomatic staff at Bern, Switzerland, but who is actually in charge of the semi-covert Iranian Mission in Israel. . . . The Iranian Mission in Israel seems to have about three officers, including Teymuri. The others I have met were H. Ghazi-Zadeh who dealt mainly with Iranian-Jewish students in Israel, and Mahmoud Izadi, a political officer. . . . The Mission is located in a villa at 28 Jabotinski Street, Ramat Gan. Teymuri lives in the villa. . . . Switzerland protects Iranian interests in Israel and applicants for Iranian visas are directed to the Swiss Embassy in Tel Aviv. However, an Iranian Mission employee handles the visa issuances.[20]

It is not surprising, therefore, that during an interview with the *Financial Times* in which he indicated his approval of Iran's ties with Israel and her right to exist, the Shah, in response to a question concerning the possibility of a more official relationship with Israel, said, "Diplomatic relations are not really necessary. This is not the time, especially when the UN Resolution of November 1967 has not been carried out."[21]

In many respects, the Iranian monarch was right. From the Iranian point of view, diplomatic relations were not really necessary in order for Iranian-Israeli relations to be viable. The Shah continued to meet privately with Israel's prime ministers and discussed with them areas of mutual interest. For example, in May 1972 he met with Golda Meir and agreed with the Israeli prime minister that detente would be beneficial to both Israel and Iran. And as in all his meetings with Israeli leaders, the Shah touched upon some of the major points of Iran's relations with Israel. From the Shah's perspective, the basic ingredients of the Tehran-Tel Aviv axis, which included clandestine operations against radical elements in the Arab world, procurement of Israeli arms, and the sale of petroleum to Israel, had to remain a secret to avoid aggravating Arab hostility toward Iran.

THE ISRAELI-IRANIAN PETROLEUM CONNECTION

Although the Shah insisted that Iran's relationship with Israel be played down, by 1969 one element of the Tehran-Tel Aviv connection had already deepened Arab hostility toward Iran. Arab objections were clearly expressed by the distinguished Arab oil expert, Sheikh Tariki, in a letter to the Shah:

> You are aware of what Israel is doing to your Muslim brothers, you know how it is desecrating the al-Aqsa mosque and its soldiers setting foot in the mosque and minaret. Yet you insist on forging close relations with it, and supplying it with crude oil, which plays a basic role in propelling its armed forces against your Muslim brothers. After all this, do you imagine it is possible to have neighborly relations with the Arabs?[22]

While the Shah's rationale for selling oil to Israel was, initially, based on Iran's budgetary problems, his reasons for continuing the sale of Iranian crude to Israel evolved. They were, in his own words, "to circumvent the Consortium [i.e., the multinational oil companies operating in Iran] and to show the world who's the boss."[23] This latter attitude is captured in the following letter from the Department of State to Armin H. Meyer, United States ambassador to Iran, dated February 13, 1969:

> In our sessions with the oil companies and the British, when we were comparing notes on the Shah's January 31 meeting with Consortium representatives, we learned of a definite statement by the Shah about the Israeli pipeline [Eilat-Ashkelon Pipeline]. He said that Iran had a financial interest in the line and planned to continue using it regardless of any Arab complaints. He added that he was confident that the Arabs would not be able to defeat Israel and Israel looked to Iran as a friend.[24]

Aside from the Shah only a handful of National Iranian Oil Company (NIOC) executives were privy to the intricacies of Israel's Iranian oil connection during this period. In NIOC board meetings Israel was never mentioned by name. Only the names of dummy companies created to purchase the oil were mentioned. And decisions regarding the price at which Iran sold its crude to Israel and the quantity were made by the director of NIOC's international operations. Although Iran and Israel were usually in agreement over issues concerning pricing and quantity, on one occasion a disagreement developed between Uri Lubrani, Israel's representative in Tehran, and the director of NIOC's international operations. The oil company official demanded that Israel pay a 14-cent/barrel premium on that portion of Iranian oil traveling through the Eilat-Ashkelon Pipeline that was for Israel's domestic consumption.

Despite occasional differences over pricing, Iranian oil continued to reach Israel. Table 2 offers a close approximation of Iranian exports of crude to Israel based on Israeli production and domestic consumption figures (consumption minus production equals imports) from 1959 through 1971. As Table 2 indicates, Israel's oil imports gradually increased from 30,000 barrels per day in 1959 to 106,284 barrels per day by 1971. It is highly possible that between 80 percent to 90 percent of these imports originated in Iran, which translates into 24,000–27,000 barrels per day of Iranian crude imports in 1959 to approximately 85,000–95,000 barrels per day by 1971.

A major event that affected Iran's sale of crude to Israel was the 1967 Arab-Israeli War. After the Six-Day War, Israel controlled the Sinai Peninsula, which contained several significant oil fields along its Gulf of Suez coast (Ras Sudr, Asl, Abu-Rodeis, and Sidri). By 1972, however, output from the Sinai had dropped from its peak of 120,000 bpd to some 90,000 bpd, or about 80 percent of Israel's consumption; by 1974, production averaged 86,000 bpd and was, according to the government "dropping steadily." Iran's goal of exporting oil to Eastern Europe was frustrated by the war. Israel had captured the east bank of the Suez Canal and was in favor of opening it on the assumption that it would reduce Egypt's inclination to initiate fighting in the canal area. Egypt refused to accept a ceasefire when it appeared that the reopening of the Suez was postponed indefinitely. Iranian and Israeli officials consulted their mutual needs and entered into a joint venture by constructing the Eilat-Ashkelon Pipeline, running from the Gulf of Aqaba to Israel's Mediterranean coast. It was agreed that the NIOC and Israel would each have a 50 percent equity interest in the Eilat-Ashkelon Pipeline Company (Iran's interest was held by APC Holdings of Montreal, a subsidiary of NIOC). Profitability would be maintained from the rent the company would demand for oil traveling through its pipeline from Eilat to Ashkelon, i.e., Cost/Insurance/Freight (CIF) Ashkelon. The following secret cable from the U.S. Department of State dated May 27, 1968, sheds some light on the rationale for building the pipeline:

The following observations regarding the Israeli pipeline were gleaned from a long conversation with Israeli officials on May 14:

1. *Economic Justification*

   A. Cheaper than around Africa. While oil companies claim the pipeline is not economic, they know better. As Israelis see it, 29 ships of 200,000 ton (one ton = 7.33 barrels) capacity can move 50 million tons of oil through the pipeline in the course of a year. To move the same amount in the same time span with the same size ships around Africa would require 50 ships. Each ship costs $20 million, and since this would mean 21 more ships, the extra cost is over $400 million, which is two or three times the cost of the pipeline.

   B. Lower Maintenance Costs. The Israelis claimed that maintenance costs are much higher for ships than for pipeline, with ratio of maintenance to capital costs being 2:1 for ships versus 1:2 for the pipeline.

   C. Superior Port Handling Facilities. The Port of Eilat is so deep it can handle ships of any size. At the other end, the port will be able to shuttle smaller ships to European ports in the Eastern Mediterranean which in any case can handle only smaller ships

TABLE 2
ISRAEL'S OIL PRODUCTION, CONSUMPTION, AND IMPORTS, 1959–1978

Year	Production barrels per year	Consumption barrels per year	Imports barrels per year	Imports barrels per day
1959	927,000	11,949,300	11,022,300	30,198
1960	936,000	12,503,100	11,567,100	31,690
1961	978,000	14,043,800	13,065,800	35,796
1962	967,000	15,371,500	14,404,500	39,464
1963	1,082,000	17,040,000	15,958,000	43,720
1964	1,439,425	18,303,800	16,864,375	46,203
1965	1,469,079	19,170,000	17,700,921	48,495
1966	1,352,954	21,300,000	19,947,046	54,649
1967	974,000	23,087,070	22,113,070	60,583
1968	823,191	28,224,630	27,401,439	75,072

Year				
1969	725,000	30,601,000	29,876,000	81,852
1970	555,000	35,939,490	35,384,490	96,943
1971	540,000	39,340,000	38,794,000	106,283
1972	-	41,062,500	-	50,000*
1973	-	51,708,090	-	56,660*
1974	-	-	-	81,000*
1975	-	-	-	80,328*
1976	225,500	-	-	135,000*
1977	-	-	-	80,000*
1978 (1st half)	-	-	-	80,000*

*Indicates direct imports from Iran.
Source: Compiled from industry statistics.

and would be unable to receive supertankers coming from around Africa; i.e., double handling would be necessary in any case.

Thus, the Israelis are convinced that a pipeline is fully justified economically, even if Suez were to be reopened.

2. *Financing*

In response to a query about the reason for Baron Rothschild's withdrawal, the Israelis said he was never in.

3. *Availability*

They said this would be a transit facility open to anyone. They noted that all the oil for the present 16″ pipeline is currently coming from Iran.

4. *Supply of Crude*

They added that they are not worrying in the slightest about availability of sources of crude for deliveries through the pipeline; the only problem was finding customers at the other end of the line.[25]

On February 5, 1970, Israel announced that the pipeline had been completed at a cost of $136 million. Concomitantly, Petroleum Press Service reported that Iran was the major source of crude arriving at Eilat for transport through the pipeline. This report seems to be accurate and is substantiated by the following U.S. Department of State cable dated March 17, 1970:

Our estimates based on available information is that about three-quarters of the oil going through the Israeli pipeline comes from Iran. The rest, amounting to some 75,000 to 100,000 barrels per day, comes from the Bela'im offshore and onshore fields in Sinai, occupied by Israel since June 1967. Of the oil going through the Israeli pipeline from Iran, we believe most of it is owned by the National Iranian Oil Company (NIOC). In January, Iranian offshore concessions produced 340,000 bpd, of which NIOC's share would be about 170,000 bpd. However, not all of this is available to go through the Israeli pipeline since NIOC has some customers East of Suez. As much as another 100,000 bpd of NIOC oil could be going through the Israeli pipeline under barter oil agreements between NIOC and the Consortium, by which up to a certain amount of oil can be purchased by NIOC from the Consortium at a "quarter-way" price for sale only to specified countries in Eastern Europe. Much of the oil is believed to be going to Romania. It is possible that some Iranian oil from Iricon members or other small companies without interests in Arab countries are using the Israeli pipeline. However, we have no evidence that any of the major oil companies or companies producing in any Arab country are using the line. And we doubt that they would do so.[26]

NIOC viewed the Eilat-Ashkelon Pipeline primarily as a first step toward the vertical integration of Iran's oil industry into the global oil system. Indeed, Iran was one of the first nations to expand its role into international marketing. In the late 1960s, when there was an abundance of crude in the world oil market, Iran began to integrate vertically into the refinery markets overseas. The NIOC's first participation in a refinery outside its own territory was the Madras refinery (Indian government, 84 percent; Amoco India, 13 percent; NIOC, 13 percent). As a large producer, Iran's motives for establishing joint ventures abroad was clear: to guarantee a market for its crude in a way that would minimize crude price fluctuations. However, when the Israelis pressured NIOC to agree to another joint venture for the purpose of building a refinery at Ashdod, the director of international operations refused, claiming that Israel was not a large enough market for refined crude products.

If Iran's refusal to cooperate with Israel on building an export refining facility was based on purely economic grounds, the U.S. decision not to be associated in any way with Israeli-Iranian relations as they pertained to oil is addressed in the following United States Embassy document dated August 22, 1970:

> At this critical time, we believe any U.S. association with the Eilat-Ashkelon pipeline scheme might involve dangerous risks vis-à-vis our relations with friendly Arab oil-producing states and would provide badly-needed ammunition in Arab extremists fight against current peace effort launched by U.S. Popular Front for Liberation of Palestine in July 11 issue of Beirut weekly *Al-Hadaf* has already accused us and Iran of plotting against Arab interests by arranging to have additional Iranian oil pumped through the Israeli line. In short, we feel this is essentially a matter between Iranians and Israelis.[27]

The Arab-Israeli War of October 1973 saw considerable disruption of both Israel's and Egypt's oil operations along the

Gulf of Suez. Although the news of Iran's sale of crude to Israel at that critical juncture in its history is well publicized, what is not known is that Egypt made an urgent request for Iranian oil as well. During the early days of the war, President Sadat called the Shah, urging him to supply Egypt with crude oil. Within 24 hours after the request, one million tons of crude oil and refined products were delivered to Egypt. This act of generosity and friendship made a lasting impression on Sadat and explains why he referred to Mohammad Reza Shah Pahlavi as "my brother."

COOPERATION IN AN ANARCHIC REGIONAL SYSTEM

Apart from oil, another factor that drew Iran and Israel together during the period between 1968 through 1973, was the deteriorating political climate in the Middle East. By 1970, the political storm that was developing in Jordan was viewed by both Tehran and Tel Aviv as another attempt by radical elements to wrest control of the military and political agenda of the Arab world. Mossad and Savak followed the developments in Jordan closely, and the crisis was discussed at Trident meetings. Both intelligence services and their respective governments agreed that King Hussein was in serious danger of being overthrown by the PLO and its allies, Syria and Iraq. A high-ranking Savak official was sent to Jordan in hopes of persuading Yasser Arafat to come to terms with King Hussein in exchange for $200,000. Later, the same official met with King Hussein and promised the delivery of F-5 aircraft, but the Jordanian monarch, although appreciative of the Iranian offer, seemed to have lost all hope. In fact, King Hussein told Iran's ambassador to Jordan that he had already made arrangements for a government in exile in Saudi Arabia should he fail to crush the PLO and asked that the Iranian envoy convey his plans to "my brother Mohammad Reza Shah Pahlavi." In an interesting turn of events, the Shah called the besieged king and told him to "use your airforce (at that time Jordan had only twelve British made Hawker aircraft) against Syria's armored units and do not worry about a thing." Within days, Jordan was able to repulse Syria's armored units (295 Syrian tanks were either destroyed or captured) after Hafiz Assad refused to send air support, and the PLO commandos were soundly defeated. Throughout this military operation, the Israeli air force flew over Jordan at about 20,000 feet to guard against any possible aerial intervention by Syria while the U.S. air force flew its aircraft from aircraft carriers in the Mediterranean at about 40,000 feet to deter any Soviet action. Although this joint operation prevented the PLO from establishing a state within a state, thus saving Jordan's Hashemite dynasty, it leaves the question of Assad's rise to assume Syria's presidency open to interpretation. In view of the Shah's encouraging words to King Hussein regarding the use of Jordanian Hawkers against Syria, is it possible that the Iranian monarch knew of a deal between the United States and Assad, in which the latter, in exchange for refusing to engage Syrian MiGs in combat, was promised support in his bid to the presidency, which he assumed in a bloodless coup two months after the Jordan crisis. Although beyond the scope of this study, in view of the kaleidoscopic nature of Middle East politics, the question is a valid, though nonfalsifiable, proposition worthy of further research and analysis.

During the period 1968 through 1973, Iran and Israel continued their campaign against Iraq by providing military and economic support to the Kurds. Although by 1970 its military support for the Kurdish rebels had somewhat weakened because of a shortage of weapons, Iran continued its financial assistance of the Kurds. Israel, for its part, provided the Kurds with weapons and communications equipment. After the 1970 Jordan crisis, King Hussein joined the Israeli-Iranian campaign of support for the Kurdish rebels by sending weapons and ammunitions captured from PLO stockpiles to Iran on C-130 Hercules aircraft for delivery to the Kurds. Jordan, Iran, and Israel shared a common feeling of enmity toward the Iraqi regime, although each had its own particular reason for taking part in the Kurdish campaign. King Hussein wanted to divert at least part of the 26,000 Iraqi troops on the Jordanian border to the northern Kurdish provinces. (Iraq's three armored divisions stationed on Jordan's borders were supposedly for combat against Israel, but were used by the Iraqi regime as a means of destabilizing the Hashemite kingdom.) Iran wanted to pressure the Iraqis to accept the thalweg line on the Shatt-al Arab (Arvandrood in Farsi) waterway as the international boundary between the two countries. And Israel wanted to keep the Iraqi forces bogged down in northern Iraq to divert their attention and resources away from Israel's northern borders.

Another dimension of Israeli-Iranian cooperation inside Iraq involved the smuggling of the remaining Iraqi-Jews from that country. The importance of this demographic component of Israel's foreign policy, which played an important role in drawing Israel closer to Iran in the early 1950s, is evident from the following U.S. government memorandum dated November 12, 1970:

> Ben-Yohanan of the Israeli Mission in Tehran said there were approximately 3,000 Jews left in Iraq. He doubted there was much hope of their early departure from that country. Things were increasingly unstable in Iraq, and there were rumors of new executions, but he had no definite information.[28]

With assistance from Savak, a large number of Iraqi-Jews were smuggled out of Iraq through Kurdistan, arriving at Rezaieh, the capital of Iran's province of West Azerbiajan. Once in Iran, Jewish organizations such as the Joint Distribution Committee took over the responsibility of resettling the freed Iraqi-Jews. In short, the policy of assisting Kurdish rebels is a clear example of how the demographic component of Israel's foreign policy was enhanced, albeit indirectly, by its strategic component.

Israeli-Iranian cooperation was not always confined to campaigns against common enemies outside their borders. By the early 1970s, as opposition to the Shah's modernization plans intensified, Mossad provided valuable information to Savak on the activities of urban guerrilla groups such as the Mohahedeen Khalgh and Fedayeen Khalgh which had PLO ties and offered to cooperate with Savak in neutralizing them. Such cooperation, however, remained a well-guarded secret in order not to provoke the opposition, which insisted that Iran abandon Israel in favor of a pro-Arab policy.

Iranian officials, on occasion, had to go to tremendous lengths to keep their working relationship with Israel out of the headlines. One such incident occurred during the tenure of Meir Ezri, when the government of Switzerland lodged a protest against the Imperial Iranian Air Force for attempting to sell some old World War II weapons through Geneva to an African state the Swiss had blacklisted. The Shah's principal advisor for military procurement, Deputy Defense Minister General Hassan Toufanian, conducted his own investigation, fully aware that all military hardware bought and sold by any branch of the Imperial Iranian Armed Forces had to be on his letterhead and his signature. Upon reviewing the end-user certificate that was presented to the Swiss government on behalf of the Imperial Iranian Air Force, he realized that it was on the Chief of the Imperial Iranian Air Force's letterhead, the late General Khatam, and therefore a forgery. It was later discovered that an employee of the Israeli Mission in Tehran had smuggled a blank letterhead from General Khatam's office and forged the end-user certificate. General Toufanian informed Ezri, with whom he had a good working relationship, of his finding. It was decided that the employee responsible for smuggling General Khatam's letterhead be asked to leave Iran but that the Iranian Foreign Ministry not be advised of the incident because the general felt that "the Foreign Office will blow the incident out of proportion in view of their pro-Arab tendencies." The employee responsible for this act was Israel's military attache to Iran, Yaacov Nimrodi.[29] Yaacov Nimrodi was not the only official to leave Iran. By 1973, Meir Ezri's 12-year tenure as Israel's representative to Iran ended; he was replaced by Uri Lubrani, a seasoned Israeli diplomat.

ISRAEL, IRAN, AND THE YOM KIPPUR WAR

By the time Uri Lubrani assumed his post as Israel's representative to Iran, the Yom Kippur War of October 1973 was under way. General Dayan suggests in his biography that before the Egyptian attack the Israelis and the Americans could not find any hard evidence of a major coordinated Egyptian offensive across the Suez Canal and a Syrian offensive into the Golan Heights area. He writes, "At the beginning of October 1973, the Israeli intelligence branch reported that the Egyptians were engaged in military exercises but not preparing to launch a war. This was not only the view of the Israeli Intelligence, but also of American Intelligence Services." He then goes on to cite a CIA bulletin dated the day before the attack stating that "the exercise and alert activities may be on a somewhat larger scale and more realistic than previous exercises, but they do not appear to be preparing for a military offensive against Israel." Dr. Ray Cline, former director of the State Department's Intelligence section and once a senior CIA officer, takes a different view. He blames the intelligence breakdown partly on Secretary of State Henry Kissinger's "unwillingness to accept the conclusions reached by the intelligence community."[30]

Cline's point seems plausible. Early in 1973, Kamal Adham, director of Saudi Arabia's intelligence services, came to Tehran and met with the Shah and General Nassiri. During the course of their meeting, Adham provided them with the approximate date of Egypt's offensive into the Sinai and the military plans that were to be carried out by the Egyptian armed forces. Under normal circumstances General Nassiri would have relayed the information to his Israeli counterpart, General Zvi Zamir. Two possible reasons might explain Iran's silence in this regard.

First, in view of the close ties between the Shah and the Nixon administration, particularly Henry Kissinger, it is unlikely that the Iranian monarch would have kept Adham's information from Kissinger. Because both men wanted to break the deadlocked Middle East peace process, it is conceivable that the Shah did indeed relay the information to Kissinger but that the U.S. secretary of state decided the only way to break the deadlock in the Middle East was to allow Sadat to execute his offensive and therefore asked the Shah not to inform the Israelis.

A second reason for Iran's silence may be gleaned from the Shah's meeting with Golda Meir in 1972, in which he tried to impress upon the Israeli prime minister that Anwar Sadat "is a good man who is willing to make peace with Israel if the opportunity presented itself."[31] From the Shah's vantage point, "the opportunity presented itself" when Sadat decided that a war with Israel, although costly to Egypt, might help regain some of the lands Nasser had lost in 1967, thus putting him in a better position (and a better frame of mind) to make peace with Israel. Therefore, in order not to jeopardize Sadat's opportunity for peace, it is possible that the Shah withheld

Adham's information from both the Israelis and the Americans. This also helps explain why Iran's sympathies with Egypt and the other Arab states found more concrete expression during the 1973 October War, for she not only extended medical supplies to them but also sent pilots and planes to Saudi Arabia to help with logistical problems, permitted the overflight of Soviet civilian planes carrying military equipment to Arab states, and did not allow the transfer of Jewish volunteers from Australia to Israel via Iran.[32]

Of course, the Arabs were not the only recipients of Iranian assistance during the October War. When the hostilities broke out, Israel not only received vital supplies of Iranian crude but asked for and got delivery of a number of 160 mm. heavy mortars from the Iranian armed forces. Indeed, by the end of 1973, the Israeli Mission in Tehran was conducting its business as usual while some of its newly appointed personnel were offering their impressions of Iran's development and its policy toward the Arab-Israeli War of 1973:

> At the suggestion of Ambassador Lubrani, Areyeh Levin, Counselor of the Israeli Mission in Tehran, called on me December 5, 1973. Returning to Tehran after a long period, Levin said he was astonished at the changes that had occurred. These included not only all the usual evidences of change in a city like Tehran, with better facilities, bigger buildings, higher standards of living, etc., but more important, he felt, there was evidence of more fundamental changes which suggested that the Shah was indeed successful in moving the country into the 20th century and changing some of its outlook. In short, Levin says he is impressed by what he had seen. . . . Levin said he has experienced no difficulties or hostility since he has been here. He moves around freely and no one has refused to see him. In this connection he mentioned a recent conversation with an editor with whom he was discussing anti-Israel sentiment in Tehran during the recent war. The editor told him that pro-Arab support that developed during this period should be interpreted not only as an indication of popular support for the Arabs but also as an expression of opposition to the Shah. There were few ways in Iran that one could demonstrate against the present regime and being pro-Arab is a safe way to express one's self without getting into trouble. Many feel that the Shah does not favor a pro-Arab policy.[33]

The underlying rationale for the Shah's favorable attitude toward Israel rested on a number of factors. Aside from the exogenous factor of shared security imperatives, the momentum that thrust Israeli-Iranian relations into the anarchic Middle East environment rested upon deep-seated geopolitical factors such as the containment of Sunni Arab power in the Middle East, which during this period was allied with Moscow. Furthermore, economic interests also entered into the decision-making calculus of Iranian and Israeli leaders and was encapsulated in the sale of Iranian crude oil to Israel. Finally, throughout this period, despite protests from the leftists and the religious right, the Shah and the secularists around him were in firm control of Iran and, thus, in a formidable position to direct Iran's foreign policy in a way that served the country's best interest. And that interest rested in the continuation of Iran's pragmatic entente with Israel.

Of course, one man who felt strongly about the Shah's pro-Israel policy was Ayatollah Khomeini. He had denounced the 1970 ceremonies commemorating 2,500 years of Iranian history as an "Israeli plot against Islam." Khomeini recalled that Cyrus had liberated the Jews from their Babylonian captivity, thus "preventing the natural disappearance of elements who would never be satisfied with anything less than world domination." He implied that the Jews were now helping make the commemoration a success as a means of repaying their historical debt to Cyrus the Great. By 1972, thanks to donations from followers in Iran, Iraq, and Lebanon, Khomeini succeeded in putting his financial house in order and could offer stipends to his agents. The Iraqis also allowed Khomeini air time on their radio for attacks on the Shah's regime. By this time, Savak had enough evidence to suggest that Khomeini was engaged in activities against the government and had established ties with the Palestine Liberation Organization. Both his sons, Mostafa and Ahmad, became frequent visitors to Lebanon, where they received political and military training, first at Amal camps in the south and later at an Al-Fatah base near Beirut. On at least two occasions Arafat met with Khomeini in Najaf during official visits to Iraq. According to one source, the meeting led to an arrangement under which a number of Khomeini's students would be trained under the auspices of the PLO. The first 12, including three women, were dispatched in 1972 and after "graduating" returned to Iran in 1974.[34] Realizing the destructive potential of Khomeini to Iran and his ties to radical elements in the Arab world, General Nassiri decided to arrange for Khomeini's assassination. Unfortunately for General Nassiri (General Nassiri was one of the first high-ranking officials of the Iranian Armed Forces executed upon direct orders from Khomeini after the Ayatollah's return to Iran in 1979), he changed his mind when he was advised by the Shah and by mullahs cooperating with Savak to "forget about the troublemaker,"[35] This fatal decision by the Shah and his advisors not to contain Khomeini would cost them dearly and derail Israeli-Iranian relations, which had gathered momentum during the period from 1968 through 1973.

NOTES

1. *Financial Times*, June 3, 1969, p. 9.

2. Avner Yaniv, *Deterrence without the Bomb: The Politics of Israel Strategy* (Lexington, MA: D. C. Heath, 1987), p. 157.

3. Arthur Goldschmidt, *A Concise History of the Middle East* (Boulder: Westview Press, 1983), p. 289.

4. Ibid.

5. Ibid., p. 291.

6. Ibid., p. 292.

7. Richard Deacon, *The Israeli Secret Service* (London: Hamilton, 1977), p. 259.

8. Michael Brecher, *Decisions in Israel's Foreign Policy* (New Haven: Yale University Press, 1975), p. 446.

9. Yitzhak Rabin, "The Jordanian Crisis of September 1970," in *Israel in the Middle East*, ed. Itamar Rabinovich and Jehuda Reinharz (Oxford: Oxford University Press, 1984), pp. 232–34.

10. Cited in R. K. Ramazani, *The United States and Iran: Patterns of Influence* (New York: Praeger, 1982), p. 43.

11. Ibid.

12. William Griffith, "Iran's Foreign Policy in the Pahlavi Era," in *Iran under the Pahlavis*, ed. George Lenzcowski (Stanford: Hoover Institution Press, 1978), pp. 378–80.

13. Ibid., p. 377.

14. Conversation with former Iranian official, Washington, D.C., 1988.

15. Amir Taheri, *The Spirit of Allah* (Bethesda, MD: Adler & Adler, 1986), p. 165.

16. Documents of the United States Embassy in Tehran, Volume 47, 1979, p. 52.

17. Shahram Chubin, "Iran's Foreign Policy 1960–1976: An Overview," in *Twentieth Century Iran*, ed. Hossein Amirsadeghi (London: William Heinemann Ltd., 1977), p. 201.

18. Yaniv, p. 157.

19. Documents of the United States Embassy in Tehran, Volume 11, 1979, p. 52.

20. Documents of the United States Embassy in Tehran, Volume 36, 1979, p. 44.

21. *Financial Times*, p. 9.

22. Ibid.

23. Conversation with former U.S. Ambassador to Iran Armin Meyer, Washington, D.C., 1987.

24. Documents of the United States Embassy in Tehran, Volume 25, 1979, p. 49.

25. Documents of the United States Embassy in Tehran, Volume 36, 1979, pp. 19–20.

26. Ibid., p. 29.

27. Ibid., p. 30.

28. Documents of the United States Embassy in Tehran, Volume 11, 1979, p. 51.

29. Conversation with former Iranian official, Washington, D.C., 1987.

30. Deacon, p. 260.

31. Conversation with Shmuel Segev, Israel, 1988.

32. *Kayahan* (Weekly International Edition), December 11, 1973.

33. Documents of the United States Embassy in Tehran, Volume 36, 1979, pp. 52–53.

34. Taheri, pp. 165–66.

35. Ibid., p. 169.

5

Iran's Arab Option:
1974-1978

In his detailed study of Israeli-Iranian relations, Marvin Weinbaum explains Iran's foreign policy after the October War with remarkable cogency and foresight:

> Any speculation on the future of Irano-Israeli relations must take into account the twin desiderata of Iran's contemporary foreign policy: to assure territorial integrity through military deterrence, and to foster and safeguard the nation's industrial growth. Both aims find a central focus in the Persian Gulf region, where Iran's armed forces shield its oil resources and expanding markets can absorb Iranian products. Indiscreet ties with Israel could compromise Iranian salesmanship in the [Persian] Gulf and accentuate Arab sectarian and ethnic feelings against Tehran.
>
> The magnanimity in aid with which Iran now woos several Arab states has not as yet forced a compromise of tested policies or traditional allies. Nor have Iran's flirtations with former enemies overcome its fears of Soviet adventurism and Arab fickleness. Marxist plots remain an obsession for the Shah, and fraternity with the Arabs may turn on the longevity of individual leaders. Since Iran has already paid for its awkward entente with Israel and can count its dividends, there is no immediate cause to drop the depreciated insurance Israel provides.[1]

Between 1974 and 1978 Iran balanced two seemingly opposed goals: ending its estrangement with the Arab world and continuing relations with Israel. This duality of interests was primarily a response to what the Shah perceived as the best means to safeguard Iran's emerging military and economic power. And further, an end to the Arab-Israeli conflict could diminish pressure from Arab and radical groups throughout the Middle East. This required a simultaneous move toward military and economic self-reliance and the creation of an environment conducive to regional stability. Israel still played an important role in the Shah's strategy, for Israeli technical expertise could provide the Imperial Iranian Armed Forces with the weapons systems capable of defending Iran against traditional foes like Iraq. Furthermore, the Shah could use his close working relationship with Israeli decision makers and his awareness of Iran' strategic utility for Israel to impress upon the Jewish state the need to make peace with its Arab neighbors.

By the mid-1970s the international system was undergoing a major transformation. The emergence of a multipolar world and the ascendency of North-South issues led to a fluid and multiple web of coalitions that varied according to issue and area, involving states as partners on one question and adversaries on another. The rough strategic equivalence between the United States and Soviet Union led the superpowers to pursue parallel policies of disengagement from global affairs. Although both the Soviet Union and the United States continued their selective commitments to Middle Eastern states, their actions were being increasingly characterized by vacillation and uncertainty, for, of all the zones of instability from which they could take advantage, none was more entangled and difficult than the Middle East.

From 1974 through 1978, several developments set in motion certain significant changes within the Middle East. The first of these was Sadat's decision to reorient Egypt's position in the Arab-Israeli conflict (1974 Separation of Forces Agreement; 1975 interim Sinai Agreement; 1979 Camp David Accords). Although at first it appeared that in opposition to Egypt's peacemaking with Israel a new, reactive Arab cohesion might be forged, this did not happen.[2] This was because of a second development that would undermine Arab cohesion after 1974, namely, the subordination of pan-Arabism to the imperatives of national interest.

Syria, for example, adopted a more pragmatic approach by entering into an agreement with Israel over the Golan Heights in May 1974. This pragmatism also helps explain why Assad, in order to maintain Syria's influence in Lebanon, sent in tanks and troops to attack Lebanese Muslims and the PLO, battering them into submission by the early fall of 1976. The Lebanese Civil War of 1975–1976 is but one example of how subregional or localized issues diverted attention from the core issue of the Arab-Israeli conflict, thus further hastening the fragmentation of the Arab core.

As the 1970s progressed, splits in the Arab world weakened the PLO's ability to galvanize the Arab core against Israel. Individual Arab governments took a more active role in manipulating the Palestinian resistance for their own narrower self-interest. For example, Saudi Arabia and the Arab states of the Persian Gulf, which had large numbers of Palestinians in their labor forces, imposed rigid controls on their political activity. Syria, too, significantly reduced the freedom of action of its large refugee population. The PLO was additionally weakened by internal dissension over matters of strategy and objectives (the formation of the Rejection Front in 1974) and by external interferences by certain Arab states in its internal affairs, manifestly in the Lebanese Civil War of 1975, and by serious conflicts with Syria (1976–1977), Egypt (1977 onward), and Iraq (1978).[3]

Finally, economic developments in the Middle East brought about major changes in Middle East politics by altering the distribution of capability within the regional system. As the financial power of the oil-rich Arab states of the Persian Gulf increased, the distribution of power gradually shifted from radicalism toward conservatism and moderation.

Thus, from 1974 through 1978, the elements that had kept the Middle Eastern system focused on the Arab-Israeli conflict and Arab unity weakened considerably. Not all states thought of "driving the Zionist entity into the sea," and those that still did were busy elsewhere. The fragmentation of the Middle East system, with its most fundamental characteristic being a profusion of conflicts and issues unrelated to the Arab-Israeli conflict, provided Iran with an opportunity to consolidate her gains, and Israel an opportunity to reassess its foreign policy priorities in the wake of the demoralizing October War.

IMPLICATIONS OF THE YOM KIPPUR WAR

The October War showed that the Israeli ability to deter the Arabs from war was not absolute, thus, exposing the limits of Israeli deterrence.[4] In the political debates surrounding Israel's relationship with its neighbors after 1974, security issues loomed large. The development of a strategy that would safeguard Israel's security, however, was not an easy task. Indeed, as Israeli scholar Avner Yaniv suggests, Israel's strategic thought changed after 1974, and Israel entered into what he terms "the era of complexity":

> The weight of decisions that had to be taken, the scope of the domestic and international political canvas that had to be surveyed when critical decisions were made, the frequency with which irreversible decisions were called for, the esoteric complexity of the technology of weapons systems, the tense and fractured domestic political background against which policy had to be promulgated — all these together rendered the making of Israeli strategy [after 1974] a truly gigantic task. In a way, the agenda was almost extensive enough for a world power. The resources, however, were those of a small, psychologically exhausted country.[5]

The most important component of this strategy — and one that would become a major factor in Israeli-Iranian relations — was the decision to provide Israel with a nuclear option. Confronted with the colossal transfer of arms by Western sources to the Arab states after the quadrupling of oil prices in 1974, Moshe Dayan argued that Israel invest in its security within the bounds of its economic capacity. He argued that it was not in Israel's best interest to maintain a balance of conventional forces with all the Arab states. Israel could not control their armament programs. Furthermore, Dayan realized that even if Israel could counter an increase in the Arab conventional forces this build-up would not necessarily ensure Israel's security. Dayan emphasized that "quality and imaginative solutions can preserve [Israel's] edge over Arab quantity, not the current [under the Rabin-Allon-Peres team during 1974–1977] attempt to compete with our adversaries quantitatively."[6] Although in emphasizing quality over quantity, Dayan did not mention the use of a nuclear option, his comments suggested that he advocated a return to what

Yaniv calls a neo-Ben Gurionist concept consisting of three parts:

1. To disconnect the growth of Israel's conventional capabilities from the growth of Arab conventional capabilities and to fix it within a rigid framework based on the growth of Israel's gross national product.
2. To ensure Israel's ability to deter the combined threat of an Arab assault by a last-resort nuclear capability.
3. To draw the attention of the Jewish state's adversaries to Israel's new national security formula without the need to literally "go public" with the bomb.[7]

While Israel did not publicly reveal its decision to develop nuclear weapons or abandon its commitment to deterrence without the bomb, Israel's intentions were discussed in private with the Shah. In an interview with the Kuwaiti correspondent of *al-Siyasah* in August 1975, the Shah seemed to be echoing Dayan's concern over the economic burden if Israel entered an arms race with the Arabs: "There are 100 million Arabs who can use their oil wealth to industrialize and arm themselves . . . Israel can not bear such a burden. Until when can it devote so much money to arms purchases?"[8]

However, while Israel's new deterrence policy and presumably its willingness to place this deterrence at the service of the Shah would enter into Iran's strategic calculus, political developments in Israel would change the Shah's attitude toward Israel. What the Shah did not anticipate was the mobilization of Israeli public opinion behind the Likud Party. Israel's confidence in the superiority of its own army and air force was severely shaken after the October War, and there was widespread dissatisfaction with the Labor Party government. On May 17, 1977, when the elections for the ninth Knesset took place, the Likud, under Menachem Begin, captured the largest block of seats.

David Ben Gurion described Menachem Begin in a letter to the Israeli poet, Haim Gouri in 1963 as a dangerous man who in his zeal to control the historical Land of Israel would kill all its Arab population. Although Menachem Begin did not turn out to be the fanatic that Ben Gurion had described, after Begin's election, the ideological component in the debate about Israel's borders moved center stage. To foreign observers including the Shah Israel's intransigence in resolving the Palestinian problem was frustrating, particularly in view of its rapprochement with Egypt and the return of the Sinai Peninsula. But as Hebrew University professor Shlomo Avineri points out, deep-seated ideological reasons that go beyond the legitimate security concerns regarding the West Bank and Gaza help explain Israel's dichotomous behavior.[9] On the one hand, there is the "territorial" school, basically identifiable with the Likud bloc and its allies. According to this school, Israel should hold as much territory as possible of the historical Land of Israel. An Israel encompassing more of the land of Israel is a more Jewish state. It follows therefore that one is more of a Zionist if one claims Judea and Samaria as parts of the Jewish patrimony; conversely, by expressing a willingness to compromise over Judea and Samaria, one is, as Avineri points out, in some fundamental way unfaithful to one's own Zionist credo. Because the territorial school is very clearly focused on the historical Land of Israel, it does not advocate indiscriminate territorial aggrandizement. This helps explain why the territorialist government of Menachem Begin had no basic ideological problem in giving up all of Sinai at Camp David: it was not considered part of the historical Land of Israel. Begin conducted negotiations with Egypt exclusively in the pragmatic spirit of seeking practical security guarantees for Israel.

Avineri calls the other school, identified with Labor, as the "sociological" school. According to this school, the most important consideration for Israel should be the internal structure of its society, not the extent of its territory. For members of this camp, a territorially larger Israel (by incorporating the West Bank and Gaza) would be less Jewish and less Zionist than a smaller Israel because it would encompass more Palestinian Arabs. Avineri points out that an Israel controlling the West Bank and Gaza would constitute a country whose population would be 60 percent Jewish and 40 percent Arab: such a country would be less Jewish than a smaller and more compact Israel (more or less within the pre-1967 borders, plus East Jerusalem) with merely 15 percent

Arabs. According to the sociological school, the territorial approach is a recipe for catastrophe, for with the extra territory comes a fundamental change in the sociological and demographic nature of Israeli society.

The election of Begin on a territorialist platform, therefore, was a disappointment for the Shah. Iran's relations with Israel were established and flourished under the leadership of the Labor Party, with whom the Shah and his advisors had a good working relationship. The geopolitical and economic views of men like Dayan and Rabin were very similar to those of their Iranian counterparts.

IRAN AND THE ARAB OPTION

It was therefore inevitable that the Shah's conviction that an Arab-Israeli rapprochement, which would add security and stability to the region, would collide with Israel's foreign policy under Begin. Begin's intransigence in dealing with Sadat led the Iranian monarch to prod Israel toward conciliation with the Arabs:

> It's clear to me that President Sadat has less of a complex about peace than anyone else, including the Israelis. He needs it and it is an imperative of his foreign policy. I wish Israel had fewer complexes. Everyone accepts that they are there — permanently. Now they must gamble on peace. And that means [U.N. Resolution] 242, peace treaties in return for evacuation of occupied territories. The alternative is war.[10]

The Shah saw Begin as a hardliner who would jeopardize Sadat's peace plans. He threatened to curtail Iran's military cooperation with Israel if Begin did not show more "flexibility." It is not surprising then that after Begin's election, Moshe Dayan flew to Tehran to assure the Iranian monarch that the peace process would move forward. Dayan continued to meet with his Iranian counterparts and made the same point. The following top secret minutes of a meeting held between Moshe Dayan and General Toufanian in Tel Aviv, dated July 18, 1977, are insightful in this regard:

> General Dayan stated that Israel wants peace, however, without any preconditions and without any but's and if's. General Dayan

stated that Israel is seeking a negotiated peace, beneficial to all parties concerned. General Dayan continued to say that he cannot promise that peace will indeed be reached, but that it is the intention of the present Government of Israel to exhaust all reasonable venues to that end. General Dayan continued to state that all points are open to negotiations, and that Israel is prepared to sit down with her Arab neighbours without any preconditions. General Dayan emphasized, however, that Israel will not negotiate with the PLO and will not agree to a PLO State being established. General Dayan emphasized that Israel is not seeking to gain time, under false pretences. Indeed, Israel is endeavoring to reach a peaceful solution and even if this will be unobtainable in total Israel would even be willing to agree to anything close to that, should the Arabs be reluctant to go the whole way.

General Toufanian remarked that it is his feeling that this is exactly the policy which His Imperial Majesty is advocating. The general continued to say that once His Imperial Majesty will be assured that this is the policy pursued by the present Israel Government, he will order the General to go ahead full speed with our mutual projects, and that cooperation between the two countries would be further developed and deepened.[11]

In February 1978, Begin visited Iran. His meeting with the Shah centered on the suspension of peace talks between Israel and Egypt. The Shah explained to Begin that Sadat, by making a unilateral decision to make peace with Israel, had put himself in a very vulnerable position within the Arab world and that it was important that Begin appreciate Sadat's vulnerability. Whether by design or by accident, the Shah's quest for stability in the region had turned him into an intermediary, and it appears that he played an instrumental role in bringing Israel and Egypt together. This fact may be gleaned from the following letter from William Sullivan, U.S. ambassador to Iran, to Amir Abbas Hoveyda, minister of the Imperial Court, before Begin's visit to Iran, asking that the Shah impress upon the Israeli leader the importance of a resolution of the Arab-Israeli conflict:

Enclosed is a brief account of the outcome of Foreign Minister Dayan's recent visit to Washington, which I would appreciate your bringing to His Imperial Majesty the Shahanshah Aryamehr's attention. We are most appreciative to His Majesty for the continuing exchange on this matter. . . . Israelis have expressed unhappiness with our recent references to "withdrawal on all fronts" under UN Res. 242. . . . From our recent exchanges with the Israelis, it is apparent that Begin is not yet prepared to accept the principle of withdrawal from the West Bank, understandable in view of his long-held ideological commitments, but of crucial importance if there is to be a successful solution to the problem and any prospect of a peace settlement. We believe this will be the most difficult decision for the Israelis to face in the coming weeks. We are certain that His Majesty will recognize the significance of this particular point and look forward to hearing the results of His Majesty's meeting with the important visitor expected later this week.[12]

Although Iran's desire to see a settlement of the Arab-Israeli dispute came into sharper focus after Begin's election, as early as April 1974, according to secret U.S. Department of State briefing papers, Iran was pressing the United States to pressure Israel into making peace with its Arab neighbors:

The Shah feels the U.S. should make every effort to bring about an early resolution of the Arab-Israeli situation. He is on record as opposing the Judaization of Jerusalem and supporting Israeli withdrawal from all occupied Arab territories and restoring the legitimate rights of the Palestinians.[13]

ISRAEL AND ITS STANDOFF
WITH THE UNITED STATES

While Iran was asking for U.S. cooperation in resolving the Arab-Israeli conflict, critics of Kissinger's step-by-step approach to a Middle East settlement were arguing that it had exhausted itself. The Republican administration of President Ford, therefore, turned to the idea of a comprehensive solution that would include the Palestinian issue in developing a solution. Beginning with the premise that a just and durable peace in the Middle East was a central objective of the United States, the administration argued that the legitimate interests of the Palestinian Arabs had to be taken into account in the negotiation of an Arab-Israeli peace. In fact, the administration identified the Palestinian dimension of the Arab-Israeli conflict as the heart of the issue: "Final resolution of the [Arab-Israeli] problem will not be possible until agreement is reached defining a just and permanent status for the Arab peoples who consider themselves Palestinians."[14]

Although the United States redefined its approach to the Arab-Israeli conflict in the aftermath of the October War, it did offer incentives for Israel. The United States seemed to be telling Israel that in return for its withdrawal from the territories occupied in 1967 the United States would be willing to guarantee Israel's security. In view of the tremendous help Israel had received from the United States during the October War and the importance of U.S. military and economic aid, it was not surprising that the idea of a formal alliance with the United States became increasingly attractive to Israel's policy makers. Even Moshe Dayan, who was the most ardent supporter of self-reliance, reached the conclusion that if the United States were to offer a "firm, binding and long-term defense treaty," he for one would view it as a "cardinal achievement." This clearly reflected a sober realization that Israel had become so critically dependent on the United States that the question was no longer whether to enter into an alliance with the United States but, rather, under what terms.[15]

However, the terms of the U.S. pledge to guarantee the security of Israel had two major problems. Labor Party decision makers saw that the United States had stood by Israel during the October War despite the absence of any formal alliance, while Israel retained the occupied territories. Therefore, as long as Israel was able to make its relationship with the United States an increasingly binding one, a formal alliance under unfavorable terms was not necessary. The Likud and the territorialists took a straightforward hard line. They opposed the ceding of the territories, either in return for a formal alliance with the United States or as part of a peace package with the Arabs.

Relations with the United States gradually improved from 1974 through 1978, and the United States contributed to Israel's conventional deterrence strategy without a formal alliance. This did not resolve the fundamental problem of Israel's security predicament: in the absence of a binding and long-term formal alliance with the United States, and in view of the anarchic nature of the international and Middle East environment, Israel throughout its history has been compelled to take care of its security unilaterally. Indeed, it can be argued that Israel's conduct since 1948, including its cultivation of closer ties to Iran, has been to a large extent in response to the inherent dangers that this unruly regional and international system poses. The period from 1974 through 1978, therefore, was no exception: the need to develop a nuclear option, "intransigence" over the issue of exchanging territories for peace, the build-up of its conventional forces, and guarantees from the United States as an insurance policy against external aggression were all in response to the challenges of the Jewish state's security imperatives — a response that would affect her relations with Iran.

IRAN'S SEARCH FOR STRATEGIC STABILITY

The basic political and strategic consideration that influenced Iran's policy was the direct intersection of the Arab-Israeli conflict with the United States-Soviet Union conflict of interest over the Middle East. After 1974, the fragmentation of the Arab core coincided with an informal coalition of relatively moderate forces in the Arab world. The Shah viewed this combination as the best means to realize the overriding Iranian goal of creating a regional environment favorable to a greater degree of security and stability. Therefore, the Shah's increasing concern with the perceived intransigence of Israel in the peacemaking process was rooted in his fear that the breakdown of negotiations and the outbreak of another Arab-Israeli war would, more than any other single factor, radicalize and polarize the Middle East and revive Soviet influence.[16] This point, and its linkage to the security of the Persian Gulf, is clearly reflected in the following U.S. Department of State document, dated April 1974:

> The Shah takes a close interest in our detente with the USSR and the possibility that it might free Soviet resources for the Middle East. The Shah believes Soviet activity in the Middle East indicates a continuing use of proxies such a Iraq and South Yemen to accomplish Soviet foreign policy goals. The Shah remains concerned by the potential for instability — and Soviet exploitation of it — in neighboring countries. He is concerned about radical movements in the Persian Gulf; Iraqi hostility toward Iran; and separatist activity in Pakistan's frontier provinces near his borders. He recognizes the need for, and has been seeking, improved relations and cooperation with the more moderate Arab governments, in order to

help them prevent the kind of radicalization that could threaten Iran's Persian Gulf life-line to the outside world. Establishing this cooperation is not easy because of long-standing Arab wariness toward Iran.[17]

Another powerful motive that spurred the Shah's interest in ending Iran's estrangement within the Arab world was to retain his country's leadership role in OPEC. The success of Iran's expensive, but necessary, military procurement policy was to a large extent dependent on increased oil revenues, which in turn hinged on the degree to which Iran could impose her hawkish pricing policy on the Arab members of OPEC. Therefore, the cooperation with Saudi Arabia, for example, in a common front on oil pricing required a detente in Arab-Iranian relations that would extend beyond OPEC agreements.

Therefore, in an attempt to buttress the moderate alternative in the Arab world and to win the passive assent of Arab leaders to Iran's hegemony in OPEC and the Persian Gulf — a foreign policy goal beyond the scope of Israel and Israeli-Iranian relations — the Shah embarked on his plan of exercising Iran's Arab option by first paying a visit to his friend Anwar Sadat in January 1975:

> Egypt can help smooth over the suspicions and rivalries that still jeopardize Iran's relations with [the Arab states]. President Sadat is in a strong position to mediate in the potentially explosive dispute with Iraq over the Kurdish war. After his talks with the Shah, President Sadat is expected later this month to visit Baghdad where Egypt's relations are on the mend. It would be the most concrete achievement of this stately toing and froing if President Sadat were able to persuade two such long-standing enemies to draw in their horns. Accommodation between Iran and Iraq, accompanied by reassurances that Baghdad will not subsequently divert its energies to a revolutionary crusade in the [Persian] Gulf, is the sine qua non of stability in this area.[18]

The Shah's cultivation of closer ties with Egypt were based on his belief that "Egypt is to the Arabs what the United States is to Europe." The Iranian Monarch understood the pivotal role of Egypt and the weight that country could bring to bear on other Arab states in the settlement of the Arab-Israeli dispute. Furthermore, Egypt could serve as the springboard from which Iran could launch its campaign of rapprochement with the Arab world. Over and beyond the strategic logic of Iranian-Egyptian relations, which would henceforth serve as the linchpin of Iran's Arab option, it was the bonds of personal friendship between Anwar Sadat and Mohammad Reza Shah Pahlavi that drew the two countries closer together. It is not surprising, therefore, that when President Sadat asked the Shah to purchase $50 million worth of ammunition from Egypt for budgetary reasons, the Iranian monarch obliged. And when Egypt's Soviet-made Antonov 12 transport aircraft were unable to carry the cargo to Tehran, Sadat asked the Shah to lobby the United States for the delivery of 12 C-130 Hercules to Egypt. Indeed, the bonds of friendship were so deep that the Shah was the first person with whom Sadat discussed his decision to go to Jerusalem: he told the monarch's envoy to Cairo to "tell my brother, Mohammad Reza Shah, that Egypt is dying of poverty, if I go to Israel, the United States will give me the money I need to save Egypt."[19]

While the Shah stood by Sadat, so too did the Egyptian president stand by the Shah when Khomeini was about to descend on Iran. Sadat called the Shah's personal envoy to discuss with him a plan to assassinate Khomeini in Paris. The Egyptian president proposed sending a paid assassin with a delegation from the Al-Azhar Mosque who were going to Paris to "pay their respects" to Khomeini. That same night, the Shah's envoy sent a "For His Majesty's Eyes Only" cable to the Shah's residence. Four days later, Hosni Mubarak called the Shah's envoy to his office and showed him the exact copy of the cable he had sent to the Shah published in a French newspaper! The only person between the cable and the Shah was the chief of the Imperial Inspectorate, the enigmatic General Hossein Fardoust, a boyhood friend of the Shah, who reported only to the monarch himself.[20] When Richard Helms, former U.S. ambassador to Iran and CIA director, visited the ailing monarch at Cornell University Medical Center in New York, the deposed monarch, with tears in his eyes told him, "I don't understand Fardoust. I treated him as a brother. Why did he turn against me?"[21]

Iran's support and friendship with Egypt soon led to more cordial Iran-Arab relations. In December 1975, the Shah hosted a visit from President Assad of Syria. Realizing that Iran's relations with the Arab world as a whole would be constrained by the dynamics of inter-Arab politics, the Shah's courtship of Assad was, in part, to appease the Syrian leader and prevent him from jeopardizing Iran's rapprochement with Iraq. Toward this end, the government of Iran extended $150 million to Syria. During the course of their meeting, Assad downplayed the activities of Khomeini supporters in Zaynabia (a Shiite holy shrine where Khomeini's messages were put onto cassettes by Shiite activists) and Musa Sadr's assistance to Khomeini's followers in Lebanon.[22] However, he did promise the Iranian monarch that in the event that either the Shiites in Zaynabia or Musa Sadr became too powerful, he would curtail their activities.

Such an occasion did arise. At the end of 1977, Assad asked for a meeting with the Shah's representative in Beirut. Assad began by saying, "Imagine this table to be Iraq. Why don't you and I shake hands from under the table and allow Syria to provide military assistance to the Kurds in Iraq?" In return, Assad promised to close down Zaynabia, which by late 1977 had become an important asset to Khomeini. When asked about the fate of Musa Sadr, Assad responded, "He will no longer play a role in Lebanon."

When the Syrian offer was brought to the Shah's attention he remarked, "So they want to kill Sayyed Musa [Sadr]." And on the issue of Syrian assistance to the Kurds via Iran's Khuzistan province, the Shah added, "You know that our policy is to abide by the Algiers Accord, but if Syria wants to provide the Kurds with weapons, tell them (the Syrians) we will close our eyes." When the first shipment of arms for the Kurds arrived, however, it was turned back, and Syrian demands for an explanation were left unanswered. Assad then took a belligerent stance toward Iran and resumed his assistance to the Shah's opponents.[23] Assad could have easily sent weapons to the Kurdish rebels from his own territory because the Kurds are located in northern Iraq, which is closer to the Syrian border than the Iranian one. His attempt to have shipments routed from Iran through Khuzistan province might have been a ploy to deliver arms to Khomeini supporters in that heavily Shiite area. Thus it may be that the arms were turned back by the Iranian authorities deliberately.

Of all the developments in Iranian foreign policy from 1974 through 1978, the Shah's 1975 rapprochement with Iraq was the most significant and came as a complete surprise to both Israel and the United States. By late 1974, the Kurdish situation had, from the point of view of Iran, become critical. With the help of Soviet weapons, the Iraqi army had inflicted heavy losses on the Kurdish rebels, but Iranian artillery fire from across the border had also inflicted serious casualties on the Iraqis. In a CENTO meeting before the 1975 Irano-Iraqi agreement, General Nassiri told the Iranian delegation that "the British have informed us that Hasan al-Bakr will soon be replaced by Saddam Hussein, someone His Majesty can strike a deal with should he so desire."[24]

Whether prompted by a change in Iraqi leadership or not, the Shah's motivation for ending Iran's war of attrition with Iraq was based on two reasons. First, the Shah realized that he was faced with the choice of increasing support to the Kurds, which might have meant the use of Iranian ground troops, if he wished to attain a military victory.[25] Second, the importance of securing the shipping lanes through which Iran's oil traveled, which had by 1975 extended Iran's security perimeter from the Persian Gulf to the Gulf of Oman and the Indian Ocean, necessitated the creation of a favorable regional environment. In other words, Iran was inclined to shape its policies toward Iraq — and indirectly toward Israel — with a view to its effect on the environment that engulfed not only the Arab-Israeli zones, but also the sea lanes of the Persian Gulf, the Gulf of Oman, and the Indian Ocean. On March 5, 1975, the Shah signed an agreement at an OPEC summit meeting in Algiers with Saddam Hussein. The main provisions of this unilateral decision by the Shah were that Iran would abandon support of the Kurdish rebellion in return for Iraq's abandoning support of subversive movements against Iran in the Persian Gulf and granting to Iran the thalweg boundary (deepest channel of the river) for the whole length of the Shatt-al Arab.

Judging from the perceptions of the Israelis as reflected in their press, it appears that they saw Iran's exercise of its Arab option in the same light as did the Shah. For example, during the Shah's visit to Jordan and Egypt in 1974 and January 1975, the Jerusalem *Post* soberly assessed these historic visits in the context of the Shah's "apparent determination to build up his country as a major Middle East power wielding a greater influence in the area and the Israeli-Arab conflict through closer cooperation with the Arabs." Even more to the point, the Mapam *Al Hamishmar* commented that if "the Shah's efforts are aimed at establishing a bloc based on Egypt-Iran-Saudi Arabia, this new arrangement of forces should not worry Israel (though there may be a cooling off of relations with Jerusalem). It should have a moderating effect on Soviet influence and strengthen the political option in the region."[26]

Although Israel could understand the logic of an Iran-Iraq rapprochement, it also could not fail to realize that it ran contrary to Israel's own vested interest in continued instability in Iranian-Arab relations. Immediately after returning from Algiers, the Shah ordered the Kurdish border be closed and that Mossad's station chief be informed. When the news was given to the Israeli, he was incredulous. The Algiers Accord was a tremendous loss for Israel. Yitzhak Rabin flew to Tehran for an explanation from the Shah. From the Israeli vantage point, by not informing Israel of his decision to enter into a peace agreement with Iraq, the Shah had created the impression that links with the Jewish state had become more expedient than imperative. Indeed, the closure of the Iran-Iraq border to the Kurdish rebels fighting the Baathist regime of Baghdad was a severe blow to Israel because it lost access to that area of Iraq. This raised in Israeli minds an important question: had the conventional strategic logic that Israel provides a diversion for a potentially expansive and aggressive Arab nationalism lost its appeal for Iran?

The Shah's reply to Israel's ambassador, Uri Lubrani, was that "Iran will be attacked by Iraq, and the question is not if but when." He then went on to assure the Israeli envoy that the Algiers Agreement reflected his need to "buy time" and his desire to defuse an extremely combustible issue of potential conflict. The Shah fully realized and confided to United States Ambassador Richard Helms that "neither Iran nor Israel wants to be alone in a sea of Arabs." This perception of Iranian-Arab relations was grounded on the Shah's basic premise that the dynamic of Arab nationalism required a competition in establishing their "nationalist" and "anti-Zionist" credentials, leaving little stability to be expected in political investments in Arab goodwill toward Iran. The Iranian monarch saw the endemic problem in Iranian-Arab relations as being the internal dynamic of Arab politics. This tended to escalate nationalist and anti-Zionist rhetoric by the externalization of their energies (e.g., attacks on Iraq from Damascus and the People's Democratic Republic of the Yemen for selling out "Arab land" after its Algiers Agreement with Iran).[27] Iran's Arab option, therefore, which was a main feature of her foreign policy from 1974 through 1978, was by no means a "tilt" toward the Arab position in the Arab-Israeli conflict. It was, instead, a response based on the need to extend Iran's security perimeter.

While Iran's cold war with the Arab world was thawing, Iran's relations with the Soviet Union remained static and cold during the period from 1974 through 1978. The Shah saw the major threat to Iran's national security interests to be Soviet involvement in regional conflicts as well as Soviet interference in the internal affairs of Iran by supporting terrorist organizations like the Fedayeen Khalgh and the Mojahedeen Khalgh. Soviet assistance to rebels in the Gulf of Oman, Soviet ties to Libya (which had been encouraging terrorism within Iran), the Soviets strong ties to Iraq (which by 1976 possessed very advanced aircraft of Soviet manufacture such as MiG-21s and MiG-23s), her naval build-up in the Indian Ocean, a missile reloading facility in Berbera (Somalia), and her influence in the People's Democratic Republic of Yemen and on the Indian subcontinent were of concern to Iran. The following confidential documents from the United States Embassy in Tehran, covering the period from 1974 through 1977, reflect the extent of Soviet involvement in Iran and the nature of Iranian-Soviet relations:

> June 2, 1974
>
> According to intelligence records: 67 of the Soviets assigned to Iran are known or suspect KGB or GRU intelligence officers. These officers are scattered for cover purposes throughout the various Soviet establishments in Iran. The figure of 67 intelligence officers is a very conservative one.
>
> October 18, 1976
>
> I took the opportunity to outline the public record on the deterioration of Soviet-Iran relations, including this morning's article in the *Tehran Journal* on Soviet arms sales to Iraq, and asked

his reaction. Kazankin (Soviet embassy second secretary) described Soviet-Iran relations as "neither good nor bad." He suggested that economic ties continued and said the present visit of Soviet Minister of Commerce would result in a new five-year economic agreement at "approximately double" the present level of Soviet-Iran trade. Under questioning, Kazankin admitted the Russians were being highly critical of Iran's arms deal with the U.S. and asked me why I thought Iran needed sophisticated arms. I replied that the Iranians thought they needed the arms to protect themselves against Iraq, which was receiving sophisticated Soviet weaponry. Kazankin volunteered no response and slid to another subject.

December 14, 1977

Kazankin took particular pains to probe repeatedly about the recent spate of demonstrations, speeches, etc. I suggested mildly that he might be able to tell me, since it was being charged that these demonstrations were inspired by foreign powers. In his most pious, injured voice, he denied any links with the demonstrations or demonstrators, insisting that they were simply "the will of the people" ... Kazankin continued fishing as to whether we knew about any officers arrested for espionage.[28]

The reason for Kazankin's curiosity concerning the latter point was to determine the fate of one of their paid agents, General Mogharrebi of the Imperial Iranian Armed Forces. After a nine-month investigation, in December 1977, Savak's bureau of counterespionage identified General Mogharrebi as a Soviet agent, and he was tried on December 15, 1977, for selling top secret information to the Soviets.

If relations with the Soviet Union were characterized by deep-seated mistrust and outright fear, Iran's relations with the United States from 1974 through 1978 were complex, entangled, and interdependent while remaining amicable. By 1974, Iran had moved from being a consumer of security — "the policed of the Persian Gulf" — to becoming a partial producer of security — "the policeman of the Persian Gulf," thus, corroborating the Shah's dictum that "the more powerful a nation becomes, the more responsible."[29] Nonetheless, in order to carry out his efforts to police Iran's enlarged security perimeter, the Shah required either a stronger formal alliance with the United States or a massive transfer of sophisticated arms. The Shah cultivated closer ties to the United States but also emphasized the development of his armed forces. He viewed international relations in strategic terms, and the underlying premise of both these strategies was the contribution they would make to Iran's deterrence capability. The Shah explained his policy to Israel's envoy Uri Lubrani: "An Iran-Iraq war will be a regional conflict and since the United States won't intervene in regional conflicts, I have to fend for myself." He then went on to say, "but, Soviet involvement will bring the United States into Iran, that is why we allowed the American spy stations on our border with the Soviet Union."[30]

By allowing Washington to move the Central Intelligence Agency's strategic weapons monitoring system from Turkey, where it was closed after the U.S. embargo in 1974, to Iran, the Shah had enhanced Iran's deterrence posture tremendously. The by-product of the United States' deepened reliance on the highly secret listening posts (to monitor Soviet ballistic missile launches and to eavesdrop on radio conversations by Soviet military aircraft, tanks, and field units) was to increase Iran's ability to influence U.S. policy behavior on the second aspect of the Shah's deterrence strategy, namely, the purchase of advanced weapons systems in order, as the Shah put it, "to fend for ourselves." During the period from 1973 through 1977, the value of military purchase agreements between the two countries amounted to over $11 billion and included the delivery of F-4, F-5, and F-14 aircraft, Hawk missiles, and naval vessels. The arms build-up was in line with Iran's intention of eventually assuring her own defense in a wider security perimeter. On the political level, it was seen as an indicator of Iran's resolve, as an investment in a commodity that was more fungible than oil-power.[31] The Shah, therefore, viewed Iran's arms acquisition as the acid test of U.S. commitment to Iran and to his regime.

The election of Jimmy Carter as president of the United States in November 1976 came as a blow to the Shah. Iran's ambassador to London wrote in his diary on August 8 that the Shah "felt that Jimmy Carter may have 'Kennedy-type pretensions' and would prefer to see Ford re-elected." Carter had adopted two principal campaign themes that worried the Shah: the reduction of U.S. arms sales and human rights, both of which could become sources of friction in United States-Iranian relations. Moreover, given the fact that the Shah had always had more success with Republicans than Democrats, he had reason to view the change in administration with special concern.[32] Indeed, he was right. Some members of the new administration believed that there was a "need for fundamental change in Iran."[33] This new policy position is borne out in the following classified Department of State "Annual Policy and Resource Assessment for Iran" dated April 5, 1977:

> 1. Two of Iran's basic policies most directly shaped by its proximity to the Soviet Union and its assessment of Soviet intentions are its military modernization program and repression of internal communist activity. These are also two policies most likely to be brought into question by the new Administration's emphasis on limiting transfer of conventional arms and on human rights. Lack of agreement in either area is certain to influence adversely the measure of success we have in furthering our other interests in Iran and, to some degree, in the region.[34]

By the end of 1978, however, U.S. fortunes in Iran looked bleak. Terrorists, including Islamic fundamentalists who were freed from prison in order to appease the Carter administration's human rights policy, continued to engage in acts of violence against military and civilian targets including the Jewish Immigration Agency in Tehran. In July 1978 Uri Lubrani wrote a gloomy prognosis expressing his view that the Shah would not survive for more than two or three months. His assessment, according to the last U.S. ambassador to Tehran, William Sullivan, was based on the fact that "the Israelis enjoyed an information network that was second to none" in Tehran as a result of the "large colony of eighty thousand Jews in Iran who penetrated into almost every aspect of Iranian life."[35] Although Lubrani's report was passed on to Washington, according to Gary Sick, who was the principal White House aide for Iran under Carter, it was never reported to the White House. Indeed, "Lubrani later stated publicly that he discussed his concerns with Ambassador Sullivan, but Lubrani's analysis was not mentioned in embassy reports or during Sullivan's consultations in Washington during the summer of 1978,"[36] This was not the only instance when William Sullivan failed to convey important information to Washington about events in Iran. In January 1978, a Congressional delegation visited Iran, and their agenda included a lunch with General Toufanian. In his meeting with the U.S. senators, General Toufanian argued that "our country is in danger, and your human rights policies will turn Iran into Lebanon and Tehran into Beirut." He tried to impress upon the delegation that applying Western democratic standards to Iran's traditional society was not prudent, and that U.S. insistence that the regime's leftist and religious opponents be freed from prison would spell disaster for Iran. Ambassador Sullivan's confidential memorandum to Washington, however, read as follows:

> General Toufanian described Iranian procurement process, Ambassador outlined general security assistance situation relating to Iran, and United States Army Mission Headquarters (ARMISH)/Military Advisory Group (MAAG) reviewed in-country US management of the Iranian program.[37]

In *Mission to Tehran*, General Robert Huyser outlines how Sullivan advocated the Shah's departure, failed to brief Huyser about his meeting with opposition figures, railed against the Carter administration, and supported Khomeini as he prepared to return to Iran from exile.[38] In a meeting with a former Iranian official in California after the establishment of an Islamic Republic in Iran, General Huyser remarked, "I don't know who Sullivan was working for."[39] Although differences of opinion among U.S. policy makers influenced events in Iran, the point is that after a meeting between the Shah and Ambassador Sullivan and British Ambassador Sir Anthony Parsons, the Iranian monarch told General Toufanian: "They (ie., the United States and Britain) have decided our fate. I have to leave my country."

Meanwhile, the Shah's foreign and domestic supporters were urging him to take a tougher stand, unaware that the Iranian monarch was dying of cancer and under the influence of medication. In the summer of 1978, Bashir Gemayel, leader of the Lebanese Phalange, apparently prompted by an Israeli request, apprehended key opposition figures. They included Mostafa Chamran and Ibrahim Yazdi (who would later form the nucleus of the Islamic Revolutionary Guards), Mohammad Montazeri, Ayatollah Montazari's son (he was trained in PLO camps and subsequently won notoriety as

"Ayatollah Ringo" for his gun-toting antics), and Sadegh Ghotbzadeh. They were to be flown on a Falcon aircraft to Oman and handed over to Iranian authorities. At the last minute, the new chief of Savak, General Nasser Moghadam, ordered the plane back to Lebanon.[40] Whatever his reasons for allowing Khomeini's key advisors to go free, the mild-mannered and highly cultured General Moghadam was executed upon direct orders from Khomeini despite assurances to his wife to the contrary. While the new chief of Savak was vacillating, Savak's bureau of internal security had written a memorandum to the Shah urging him to allow the assassination of Khomeini. The Shah's response, which he wrote on the same memorandum, was to "leave Khomeini alone, he is a British agent."[41]

For many U.S. policy makers, the most pressing question to emerge from this debacle was "who lost Iran?" A quick glance at the course of action, or lack thereof, taken by the Shah, his advisors, his opponents, and the people of Iran, however, suggests an equally important question to ask, "did Iran lose itself?" Whatever the answer, the loss of Iran to Khomeini's Islamic fundamentalism was as much a surprise to the United States as it was to Israel, which, despite its superior intelligence on Iran, was unable to attach an exact time to the Shah's downfall.

PREMISE OF IRAN'S ISRAEL CONNECTION

Indeed, when Uri Lubrani came to Iran as Israel's envoy in 1973, his most pressing task was not to discover when the Shah would fall, but to determine when the Iranian monarch would meet with him to discuss the broad outline of Israeli-Iranian relations:

> I viewed the meetings between the Israeli leaders and the Shah as important. In the first years of my service in Tehran, I was not given the opportunity of meeting him face to face. Only three and a half years after my arrival in Tehran, was the dam opened and I given the opportunity to meet him.[42]

During the course of his meeting with Uri Lubrani, the Shah offered four reasons why Iran maintained "an alliance with Israel."[43] First, he said that "Israel occupies Iraq's attention and is considered the lightning rod of Arab hearts." In other words, from the Shah's perspective, Iran's alliance with Israel would serve as a strategic decoy in order to divert Arab attention and resources away from Iran. The Shah believed that his Israeli connection would provide a deterrence to Arab regimes because it would create the impression that if an Arab state were to attack Iran, Israel would take advantage of this pretext to strike Iraq's western flank. The Shah believed he could count on the Israelis — the alliance with Israel had met Iran's expectation throughout the 1950s, 1960s, and well into the 1970s — and he believed that tacit, rather than formal, diplomatic relations were the best policy to keep the Arabs guessing about the consequences of an attack on Iran. From the Israeli point of view, such an influence on the Arab strategic calculus could not be too readily assumed. The absence of a formal and public dimension in Israel's relations with Iran implied the continued existence in the Israeli mind of an irreducible residue of doubt, particularly in view of Iran's adoption of an Arab option after 1974: if there were another war between Israel and the Arabs, would Iran do anything to help? According to Yaniv, few Israeli policy makers entertained any illusions about that.[44]

The Shah's second reason for Iran's cultivation of closer ties to the Jewish state was that "Israel is a country that has the developed technology we need. Its know-how is complementary to ours." Indeed, on his return visit to the Ghazvin Plain in January 1974, the Shah was visibly moved by the progress the region had made since the joint Israeli-Iranian effort to redevelop the area had begun in 1962 after the earthquake. And when the director of the Ghazvin Plain Development Organization informed the Shah that his technicians were trained in Israel, the Iranian monarch responded by saying, "This is what Israeli know-how will do for us." And as he commandeered his helicopter for a second aerial look over the rejuvenated Ghazvin Plain he turned to his entourage and said, "This is what I want for my country."[45]

Iran's cultivation of closer ties to Israel for technical purposes was not confined to agricultural projects; Iran's strategic agenda for the 1970s and beyond required her to shop for Israel's military expertise as well. The climax of military cooperation between Israel and Iran was Shimon Peres's 1977 visit to Tehran for talks with the Shah. The outcome was a secret $1 billion oil-for-arms agreement that covered a number of military projects, the most important of which was the development of a missile system capable of carrying nuclear warheads. Israeli scholar, Aaron Klieman, explains the underlying rationale for such a move in terms of strengthening not only the recipient country's force posture but also its military-industrial base. For Iran, Israel's technical military assistance afforded a chance to escape from the dangers of high cost and political risk of an arms build-up. Israeli assistance in the production of basic weapons and the incorporation of marginal improvements was a cheap, simple, and effective way by which Iran could avoid the problems created by the overly sophisticated hardware offered by the larger suppliers, which absorbed precious funds but did not improve military preparedness. By such means as licensing, comanufacture, and similar joint ventures, Iran could pursue "indigenous arms production in order not to become dependent on foreign military supply nor to link itself irrevocably to one of the superpowers."[46]

Although the Shah was very knowledgeable in technical military matters, all arms purchases decisions were left to the energetic General Toufanian. Toufanian was respected by his U.S. and Israeli counterparts as a soldier and as a capable manager. Toufanian ran his own large ordnance factory in Tehran. He was one of a handful of individuals in the upper ranks of the Shah's personal advisors and had the total support and trust of his commander-in-chief.

It is not surprising, therefore, that when in 1974 the Israelis asked General Toufanian whether he was interested in seeing films of Syrian-Israeli aerial dogfights taken during the October War, he enthusiastically accepted. After reviewing the films, he came to the conclusion that Israel's air superiority was because its aircraft was modified to carry machine guns. After returning to Iran, he ordered that machine guns be installed on the Iranian Air Force's F-4 Phantoms in order to enhance their performance. The Israelis' adding a structure onto the exhaust system of their fighter jets to counter Arab heat sensor missiles also interested General Toufanian. In view of the costs of modifying Iran's F-4s to carry a similar structure versus the cost of losing an F-4 to a heat-seeking missile, the Israeli option made economic and military sense and was adopted.

The Shah and General Toufanian strongly believed that Iran's procurement and military modernization programs had to be geared to the country's plans for rapid industrialization. The use of Israeli know-how had to be in line with this fundamental objective. The plan to manufacture Iranian-made versions of Israel's 120 mm mortars and 155 mm self-propelled guns inside Iran is a case in point:

> General Dayan asked General Toufanian abut his plans concerning the "Salagad" Mortar project. General Toufanian responded by saying that this is indeed a project in which His Imperial Majesty is interested. The General added that during Zablodowitz's [director general of Soltam, an Israeli company] recent visit to Tehran, progress had been made concerning the envisaged mortar factory and that a contract covering this project is to be signed within three months. The General added that following his discussions with Mr. Zablodowitz, he has conveyed to His Imperial Majesty Zablodowitz's proposal that an Iranian team make a thorough assessment concerning the 155 mm. gun. According to the proposal, this team should go to Israel, Germany and Sweden in order to study the progress made on this gun and report to His Imperial Majesty. The General added that he is well aware of the fact that the 155 mm. gun in Israel is by far advanced and that the German and Swedish guns are not yet in production and will possibly also be inferior to the Israeli gun, the latter gun will be chosen.[47]

After careful studies by engineers of the Imperial Iranian Armed Forces and a site survey by Israeli and Iranian experts, an area south of Isfahan was chosen for the construction of a factory and a contract for the production of 60 mm, 81 mm, 120 mm, and 160 mm mortars and 155 mm self-propelled guns was finalized. By 1979 the project was in its final phase, and General Toufanian had agreed to give the marketing rights of any 155 mm gun over and above the requirements of Iran's armed forces to Zablodowitz. In line with Iran's policy of strengthening Pakistan's military capabilities to counter India's military superiority, General Toufanian proposed to President Zia that the guns on Pakistan's tanks be changed to the 155 mm guns that were being built in Isfahan. In the summer of

1978, a Pakistani delegation visited the Iranian army's testing center at Asadabad for demonstrations and agreed to purchase the 155 mm guns. Events in Iran soon put an end to Iran's first entree into international arms sales.

The relationship between Iran and Israel had another important rationale, which was also touched upon in the Shah's conversation with Lubrani: "Israel is a good and stable market for Iranian oil." In June 1974, a high-ranking Israeli delegation came to Tehran to negotiate the purchase of Iranian crude. The following confidential memorandum from the U.S. Embassy in Tehran details the meeting:

> In conversation with Embassy officials on June 11, Moshe Bitan, Managing Director of Paz Oil Company, stated that he had just returned from Tehran where he headed an Israeli team negotiating purchase of crude oil. He said that agreement had been reached for 2 million tons, which would be imported over the second half of 1974, at a price of 93% of posted price, ie. about $11 per barrel. He added that the Government of Iran (GOI) is trying to negotiate compensation from Iranians for "overcharging" for a 2 million tons of crude imported during the first half of 1974 at an auction price of $16.53. Bitan did not seem to think there was much chance Iran would agree to compensation, which would require political decisions at the highest levels. . . . Bitan said he was not privy to GOI considerations of possible disposition of Abu Rodeis oil fields. He did say that Israel refining capacity would not be affected by the loss of Sinai crude. Although the refinery at Ashdod had been configurated with the relatively easy Abu Rodeis oil in mind, a shift to lighter crude input could be accommodated.[48]

By 1975, international political developments came to affect Sinai oil. As part of an interim agreement with Cairo, in September, Israel agreed to give Egypt the Sinai oil fields. Israel's agreement, however, was prompted by Prime Minister Rabin's visit to Tehran in the spring of 1975.[49] The purpose of Rabin's visit was to obtain a personal assurance from the Shah that Iranian crude would be substituted for the oil from the Sinai fields. Rabin had grown distrustful of the Shah because Israel was not informed of Iran's peace treaty with Iraq. Without a personal guarantee, Rabin was afraid that Israel's total production could drop precipitously to the 700 bpd of crude produced within its old borders.

By 1976, Israel became almost wholly dependent on imports to meet its domestic consumption needs of almost

150,000 barrels per day. Iran, in turn, became the supplier of approximately 75 percent of those needs, with Mexico supplying the rest. This point, and Iran's desire to keep her oil sales to Israel a secret, are captured in the following confidential memorandum from the U.S. Embassy in Tehran dated November 17, 1976:

> Reliable information on the destination of Iranian oil exports is generally difficult to obtain, but this is particularly the case when the destination is Israel. Iranian officials, very conscious of the possibility of needlessly antagonizing their Arab partners in OPEC, will normally not discuss oil exports to Israel. Nevertheless, information from a variety of sources indicates that at least 75 percent of current Israeli domestic consumption of approximately 50,000 barrels per day is supplied by Iran (ie. 112,000 bpd). Moreover, the only oil that flows through the Trans-Israel Pipeline (Tipline) which runs northward from the Gulf of Aqaba to the Mediterranean port of Ashkelon, is from Iran. During 1976, something on the order of 350,000 barrels per day of Iranian crude oil is thought to have been trans-shipped through Tipline for customers in Europe and beyond.[50]

In an effort to free itself from dependence on Iran, Israel actively sought new suppliers. Those efforts were stimulated by briefings from Uri Lubrani about increased instability in Iran. Israel moved quietly to stockpile a six-month reserve (four million tons) of oil in Negev desert storage facilities. At Lubrani's urging, long-term supply arrangements were established with Mexico, Nigeria, Gabon, and the North Sea producers before the Shah's departure from Iran in January 1979.

Although the sale of Iranian oil to Israel was motivated in part by political considerations, the underlying premise was its contribution to Iran's foreign exchange reserves. The same motive applied to Israel. Despite the various political and strategic goals that both Iran and Israel pursued, some observers have said the "whole Iranian escapade boiled down to little more than a promising commercial opportunity."[51]

But there were important diplomatic reasons for the friendship. According to the Iranian monarch, the fourth reason for maintaining Iran's Israeli connection was that "Israel has the United States as a supporter. Therefore, Iran needs the good offices of Israel to explain itself to the United States." The election of Jimmy Carter on a platform that emphasized human rights and limiting the sale of conventional weapons provided a context for the Iranian government to ask Israel to lobby on its behalf. On January 20, 1977, a meeting was held in Israel between members of a high-level delegation from the Iranian Foreign Ministry and Israeli officials including Yigal Allon. The Iranians asked that "Israel use its influence in the American media to stop the attacks on the Iranian government." The U.S. media, however, continued to report what it saw as a rapidly deteriorating situation in Iran, regardless of any influence the "Jewish lobby" may have had. Iranian ideas of the power of U.S. Jews was overblown. Nevertheless, the notion that the Jewish lobby could sway Congressional and public opinion was so powerful among the Iranian leadership that General Toufanian asked the Israeli military attache to Iran, General I. Segev, to ask Uri Lubrani (who had by September 1978 been replaced by Joseph Hermelin as the new representative to Iran) to return to Tehran for consultations. General Toufanian requested that Lubrani plead Iran's case with the Carter administration and members of Congress in order to let them know that "our country is being destroyed." Lubrani obliged, and a meeting was arranged in Washington, D.C., with high-level administration officials. The meeting did not take place because Iran's ambassador to Washington, Ardeshir Zahedi, failed to appear.[52]

This was not the only time that Uri Lubrani intervened on behalf of the regime in Tehran. Fully aware of the Shah's belief that Israel could sway public opinion in the United States, Lubrani had suggested to Iranian officials in 1976 that Iran organize a public relations campaign. The idea for the proposed campaign was handled by Shlomo Argov, then deputy director-general of the Israeli Foreign Ministry. He mobilized the services of Daniel Yankelovich, the well-known New York public relations expert, but the campaign had little effect.[53] For Israel, simply explaining Iran's complex strategic, political, economic, and cultural make-up to the U.S. public and the Congress was a difficult task. However, to the Shah and his advisors, it appeared easy, particularly because such an effort was viewed as a logical extension of Israel's "special relationship" with Washington. The failure to appreciate the impossibility of swaying U.S. public opinion is borne out in the Shah's last meeting with Lubrani on November 11, 1978. According to Lubrani, the Shah was very disappointed at the Carter administration for not appreciating the danger that Khomeini posed to Iran and bitter about the attacks in the U.S. media against him and his regime. The Shah failed to appreciate, however, that the Iranian people, not the U.S. people, would decide his fate.

ISRAEL AND IRAN AND THE
FIGHT AGAINST TERRORISM

Israeli-Iranian relations were held together by other threads during this period. One was the collaboration and exchange of information between Mossad and Savak on terrorism. An issue of particular importance was Iranian terrorists trained in PLO camps. Although the Israeli position of not negotiating with the PLO was well known, the most revealing statement of the Iranian attitude toward the Palestinians was made by the Shah in an interview with the Beirut weekly *al-Hawadis* on December 13, 1974:

> We have stood and we still stand at the side of the Palestinians, despite the fact that some groups of the resistance trained Iranian saboteurs to infiltrate our territory, kill people, and blow up various installations. We know how to discriminate between the justness of the Palestinian question and the wrongdoing directed against us by some Palestinians. What I fear is that Palestinians may allow international circumstances to make their cause a tool of Soviet strategy.[54]

That Iranian terrorists might be somehow connected to the Soviet Union, Libya, or the PLO raised the level of anxiety among Iranian government officials and members of the intelligence community. Therefore, cooperation with Mossad in order to keep a close watch over terrorist groups like the Fedayeen Khalgh and Mojahedeen Khalgh took on added significance for Savak. Iran's intelligence services were fortunate that some of the Israeli Embassy's new staff that had arrived in Tehran with Uri Lubrani were capable intelligence officers. The following secret memorandum from the U.S. Embassy on "Background Information on the Israeli Trade Mission" in Tehran is revealing in this regard:

Arieh Levin, formerly named Lova Lewin, born circa 1927 in Iran, is suspected Intelligence officer.... Abraham Lunz, aka Rami Luncz, born February 1931 in Tiberias, was Director of Naval Intelligence, IDF-Navy since 1971. Described as highly intelligent and capable line officer, experience in communications and electronics. Lunz and his Deputy, Moshe Moussa Levi, were both known personally and professionally to Defense Attache's Office Tel Aviv as outstanding intel officers.... Lt. Col. Moshe Moussa Levi was Foreign Liaison Officer at IDF Hqs prior to Tehran assignment in 1974. In August 1966 one Major Levy (possibly identifiable) was reportedly assisting Iranian instructor at newly-established intelligence school; apparently helped arrange training schedules and organize instructional material. This man, in Iran on loan, was then commander of the "Direct Secret Collection Agency." Lt. Col. Levi was disillusioned when he first assumed his current post, because of lack of work. However, he soon created tasks for himself, including developing info on the Iranian order of battle.[55]

With memories of the 1972 massacre of Israeli athletes at the Munich Olympics fresh in their minds, a major challenge for Savak officials was the protection of Israeli athletes invited to Tehran to participate in the 1974 Asian Games. One month before the opening ceremonies were to take place at Aryamehr Stadium, the Imperial Iranian Air Force's Intelligence Unit warned Savak concerning one of their cadets, Mohammad Baradaran Khosrowshahi. After following Khosrowshahi for several days, Savak raided his safe-house and arrested him along with six other colleagues. Their interrogation led to the arrest of 70 members of the Fedayeen Khalgh at another safe-house. This, in turn, led the security services to a man called Habib Baradaran Khosrowshahi, who was an employee of the National Organization for Physical Fitness and responsible for the building at the Aryamehr Stadium. When Savak officials arrested him at his office, he first denied involvement with the Fedayeen Khalgh, but after interrogation, he admitted that he and four other members of the Fedayeen Khalgh who were posing as workmen had placed bombs in the stands and in the foreign dignitaries box. Their goal was to detonate the bombs during the opening ceremonies. Hundreds of innocent people, including the Israelis, would have been killed.

Savak relayed the information to Israel. To ensure their security, the Israeli athletes came to Tehran and settled in their dormitories a day before their scheduled arrival. Security around their dormitories was tightened, and only 30 non-Israeli passes were issued to their premises. Thus, a massacre by the Fedayeen Khalgh, which would have been potentially more deadly than the Munich tragedy, was prevented by Savak.

MAINTAINING THE ALLIANCE

During the period from 1974 through 1978 foreign ministers of both Iran and Israel were also working in close cooperation to prevent such issue as the Algiers Accord between Iran and Iraq, the possibility of suspending oil shipments to Israel, and the Arab-Israeli conflict from harming Israeli-Iranian relations. While Prime Minister Rabin's 1975 visit to Tehran after the Iran-Iraq Algiers accord left Israelis assured that Iran's reason for making peace with Iraq was simply to buy time, Foreign Minister Yigal Allon's 1976 visit was to get a guarantee from the Iranian monarch that Iran would not suspend oil shipments to Israel. Uri Lubrani's account of Allon's August 1976 visit is not only substantive, but offers a unique perspective into the nature of Israeli-Iranian relations and Israeli perceptions of Iran's key decision makers:

> The absence of the Iranian foreign minister from the reception committee at the airport was not accidental. The foreign minister, [Abbas Ali] Khalatbari, was well known, and it was not desirable for questions to be asked about his presence at the airport. Furthermore, Nasiri was always the host for Israeli personalities. Khalatbari was an experienced diplomat of the old school, educated and brought up in the West, a graduate of French universities, who had climbed up through the ranks of the Foreign Ministry. It would be best to describe him as the Shah's faithful retainer in the sphere of foreign policy. . . .
> Prime Minister Hoveyda was waiting for Allon in his luxurious office. He had already managed to fill himself in on the talks Allon had held with the Shah and the Foreign Minister. Right from the outset of the meeting, a feeling of intimacy was created between Allon and Amir Abbas Hoveyda, who was born in Acre. He moved up through the ranks of the Iranian bureaucracy after he began his service in the Foreign Ministry. He was then appointed to a senior post in the national oil company of Iran and finally became Prime Minister. Hoveyda was a highly educated man and at home with

Western culture. He had a good command of English, French, German, and Arabic. Hoveyda would follow events in the world not only in the political and economic sectors but was also conversant with trends in English, American, and French literature. Hoveyda was not an Arab sympathizer. The talk moved on to affairs of culture and economics, and there was a feeling that it could have gone on and on. But Allon had to leave on the El Al plane, and it was clear that he and Hoveyda regretted having to part.[56]

Hoveyda and Khalatbari were two of Iran's premier statesmen and public servants. They were executed upon direct orders from Khomeini in 1979. Included in their lengthy list of "crimes" was their association with "agents of Zionism."

As he had promised, in March 1977, Iranian Foreign Minister Khalatbari visited Israel and met with Prime Minister Yitzhak Rabin, Foreign Minister Yigal Allon, and Yitzhak Hoffi, director of Mossad. This time, it was the Iranian foreign minister who had come to get assurances from the Israelis about their position on the Arab-Israeli conflict. Yitzhak Rabin, in his opening remarks, explained that Dr. Khalatbari's visit to Israel, as the first foreign minister of Iran to do so since the inception of relations between the two countries, demonstrated the foresight and concern the Shah had for the problems of the Middle East and the world. He then went on to explain that after his discussions with U.S. officials concerning Israeli-Arab relations before Dr. Khalatbari's visit, Israel and the United States had developed a coordinated and parallel strategy based on strengthening Israel and diminishing Soviet influence in the Middle East. The Americans agreed that no Arab country would make peace with a weak Israel. Furthermore, the Soviets would not gain from stability in the region, and that was why they encouraged the Arabs not to make peace with Israel. U.S. diplomacy, therefore, would attempt to diminish Soviet influence in the Middle East in order to create a favorable environment for peacemaking efforts of the moderate Arab states.

Although Khalatbari did not agree with Rabin on the first point, Khalatbari did agree that a settlement of the Arab-Israeli dispute, irrespective of the formula, would be a severe blow to Soviet influence in the Middle East. His talks with Yigal Allon turned to the Palestinian question and Sadat's visit to Tehran:

Allon: Recently the Egyptian President paid a visit to Iran. I would welcome your comments in this regard.

Khalatbari: During his stay a number of issues were discussed. It was interesting however that he was not too vociferous when it came to the issue of Palestinian rights and the PLO.

Allon: President Sadat in a recent conference in Cairo displayed tremendous emotion on the Palestinian issue. However, your comments seem to suggest that President Sadat has a more rational view of the topic. I would not doubt that the Egyptians talk about the Palestinian issue differently when they are outside their country as opposed to when they are inside.

Khalatbari: What do you think of a Palestinian state on the West Bank and the Gaza strip. I believe you agree with it in principle?

Allon: We consider the establishment of such a state as the first step toward the destruction of Israel and have emphasized a number of times that the Palestinian problem can only be solved in the framework of a Federation with Jordan.[57]

The Iranian Foreign Minister was attempting in diplomatic language to impress upon his Israeli counterpart the need to address the Palestinian issue directly and to include the Palestinians in direct negotiations for a permanent settlement of the Arab-Israeli conflict. This idea was not new; Khalatbari had discussed it with Yasser Arafat in Bangkok as early as 1974. However, at that time, due to Savak's overwhelming evidence of ties between Arafat and Iranian terrorist organizations, he abandoned the idea of an Iranian initiative on behalf of the PLO. Top-ranking Savak officials rightly argued that a rapprochement with the PLO would almost certainly jeopardize Iran's deep-seated relations with Israel.

Foreign Minister Khalatbari's talks with Yitzhak Hoffi centered on the changing political climate in the Horn of Africa. By the time of Khalatbari's visit to Israel, Emperor Haili Selassie had been overthrown by the Marxist forces of Mengistu Meriam. Both Iran and Israel had established good relations with the deposed Ethiopian ruler and shared a common interest in preventing a complete or hostile communist control of the Horn of Africa, which bordered the Red Sea. Iran's shipments of oil to Israel and Western Europe passed through this waterway. Despite its Marxist orientation, however, Israel had resumed relations with Ethiopia, although secretly, when the Mengistu regime sought Israeli military advice and assistance.[58] Meanwhile, Iran viewed the Mengistu regime as Marxist and a danger to her security interests in the Horn of Africa. In view of the strategic importance of that region for both Iran and Israel, General Dayan, on a number of occasions, asked the Iranian envoy to Tel Aviv "to tell His Majesty and Foreign Minister Khalatbari not to look at Ethiopia as a communist state. Tell your Ambassador to Ethiopia to contact our man there. Mengistu is on our side."[59] During Kalatbari's meeting with General Hoffi, the importance of a coordinated policy toward the Horn of Africa was discussed.

By the end of his visit to Israel, Foreign Minister Khalatbari was convinced, despite his reservations over Israel's position in the Arab-Israeli problem, that "Iran needs Israel as a fulcrum." Although he realized that the stability of Iran's extended security perimeter required a resolution of the Arab-Israeli conflict, he also recognized that its protection against hostile forces such as the Soviets or radical Arab states, necessitated the inclusion of Israel as an element of Iran's deterrence calculus.

While Iran's foreign minister was discussing these issues in Israel, Israel's foreign minister, Moshe Dayan, was shuttling between Tehran and Tel Aviv in an attempt to temper Iran's Arab option by assuring the Shah that Israel was ready to make peace. This was not Dayan's first or even second visit to Iran. The two men had met when Dayan was minister of agriculture and Israel was providing assistance "for the development of several branches of farming in Iran.... The Shah was interested in raising the standards and output of Iran's farmers."[60]

Dayan's last visit to Iran followed immediately after Sadat's historic visit to Israel in November 1977. The purpose of Dayan's trip was to give the Shah a firsthand report on the Egyptian president's talks and to express his views on the prospects for peace. His first question, however, was whether the Shah would agree to an official announcement of Dayan's arrival. The Iranian monarch turned down Dayan's request, arguing that he could not afford to make such news public. The Shah also rejected Dayan's proposal to raise their respective countries' diplomatic missions to the status of official embassies flying the Iranian and Israeli flags. He noted that the Palestinians and supporters of the PLO enjoyed considerable influence over the Islamic leaders in Iran. "The problem of my country," he explained, "is the religious fanaticism among the masses of the people. If it were not for that, Iran would today be as advanced as a European country and not subject to the influence of the religious leaders who prevent progress and development." He spoke in the same vein about the problem of Jerusalem. According to Dayan, the Shah did not share the position of the Saudi Arabians who viewed the issues of Palestine and the State of Israel from a Moslem viewpoint. Sadat, he argued, should ignore the Arab rejectionist states and others who are opposed to his peace efforts. The meeting between the two statesmen ended with a warning from the Shah that Russia did not favor peace in the Middle East and would do all in her power to sabotage it. It was to this end, he pointed out, that the Soviets were arming Iraq and Syria. "Israel would do well," the Shah told Dayan, "to take into account that these countries, at the initiative and backing of Soviet Russia, would again make war on Israel [and Iran]."[61]

Dayan's remarks are interesting in two respects. First, it is evident that the Shah's desire that Iran not be publicly associated with Israel was a concession to a strong and influential domestic constituency, apart from external considerations of not wanting to antagonize the Arab countries. Second, and closely related to the first point, is that Israel was fully aware of this Iranian dilemma, and, in order to make it difficult — and even impossible — for Iran to exercise its Arab option, pressed the Shah for de jure recognition whenever an opportunity presented itself.

Israel had tried such maneuvers before, most recently when Sadat arrived at Ben Gurion Airport. Accordingly, an official invitation was sent to the chief of Iran's mission in Tel Aviv asking him to be the first official to greet President Sadat as he got off his plane. The Israeli officials insisted that because the Iranian envoy was from a friendly Muslim country, it would be very appropriate for him to be the first in line to welcome the Egyptian president. With the eyes of the world on this historic visit, Iran could ill afford international headlines reading "Iranian Ambassador to Israel Greets President Sadat," thus presenting Iran with a fait accompli.

Iran's envoy politely declined the invitation, citing as his reasons the inappropriateness of such a diplomatic move and the damage it would do to Israeli-Iranian relations.[62]

OPERATION FLOWER: RESPONDING TO A SECURITY PREDICAMENT

Another factor drawing Iran and Israel together during this period was Operation Flower, a joint, top-secret missile project. Although various intervening factors entered into the Israeli-Iranian decision to cooperate in the development of a missile system capable of launching a nuclear attack, the fundamental reason was an underlying security dilemma mutual to both countries that stemmed from the anarchic nature of their regional environment. The Shah explained Iran's predicament in response to a question from *Newsweek* in November 1977:

> Q. You are still frequently accused of having "la folie des grandeurs" in your arms purchases. With scheduled deliveries, you will have more hardware than France, Britain or West Germany. Are you trying to achieve a sort of self-sufficiency because of what you perceive to be U.S. unreliability?
>
> The Shah of Iran: It's not only U.S. unreliability as we witnessed in Vietnam, Cambodia, Laos and during the India-Pakistan wars. It's also U.N. impotency. We have settled our differences with Iraq, but their military buildup continues. And I wonder how many of your editorial writers and congressmen realize that Iraq has more planes, tanks, and guns than we do [even] ground-to-ground SCUD missiles. Nor are we just another state. Look at our borders. What would happen if what remains of Pakistan were to disintegrate? *If we don't assume [our own] security in the region, who will do it?*[63]

Israel felt the same need. The rationale behind the need for self-reliance was explained by Ezer Weizman in a meeting he had with General Toufanian to discuss the Flower Project. The strength of Israel to deter its adversaries, Weizman advised, rested upon its ability to become economically and industrially independent. Then, after citing Israel's various achievements in developing its own tank and the Kfir fighter plane, he posed an important question to General Toufanian: "Are we going to team together and do things [independently] or not?"[64]

Israeli and Iranian decision makers reached the conclusion that the survival of Israel and Iran would be a function of their own resources, particularly military resources. Indeed, the basic premise of the Israeli-Iranian missile project was a strong sense of beleaguerment and the determination to be prepared for a wide range of contingencies that could have spawned in the anarchic environment in which both nations found themselves.

Although the missile project seems to have been part of Israel's nuclear program, it represented for Iran a means of conventional deterrence designed to change the strategic calculus, the order of strategic preference, and the political intentions of her adversaries. The Shah felt a nuclear deterrent was unnecessary and even dangerous for Iran. Indeed, when a high-ranking Savak official presented his memorandum of conversation with Uri Lubrani in which the latter proposed joint nuclear projects, the Shah wrote back, "this memorandum should be destroyed."[65] The cardinal point of the Shah's national policy was not to have nuclear weapons:

> Q. Israel is known to have military nuclear capabilities, although they deny it publicly. What are your intentions in this field?
> The Shah of Iran: So far, non-nuclear. Against whom should we have such weapons? My immediate neighbors will try to manage and cope with conventional weapons. As for the U.S.S.R., it's utterly ridiculous to arm yourself with two or three nuclear devices against all their megatons.[66]

Indeed, the immediate reason for Iran to participate in Operation Flower was the Soviet delivery of SCUD missiles to Iraq. These missiles could have wreaked havoc on Iran's military installations and population centers. The United States refused to sell Iran comparable Pershing missiles, arguing that the potential nuclear capability of these missiles was ill suited for Iran's needs. And when the U.S. ambassador, William Sullivan, was approached in order to get Washington's approval of Iran's decision to develop its own missile system, he responded, "I will not allow American parts to be used for this project."[67]

Presumably the United States was not aware of this joint Israeli-Iranian missile project. In an interview with the New York *Times* in 1986, Gary Sick said that he was surprised to learn that "two countries closely allied with the United States were conducting joint military operations without talking to us about them." And Harold Saunders, former Assistant Secretary of State for Near Eastern Affairs, in an interview with the same newspaper said that while "Israel built a lot of things for the Iranians that we did not know about," it surprised him that "the Israelis would have brought the Iranians into the development of a missile that may have been part of their nuclear program. If that is the case, I am surprised that we did not know about it."[68] However, Colonel Entezami of the Imperial Iranian Air Force who was assigned to monitor the landing of the missile (a surface-to-surface ballistic missile capable of carrying a warhead of 750 kilograms up to 120 miles) into the Negev Desert after its firing witnessed two U.S. helicopters flying over the site, leaving the question of the extent of U.S. knowledge of the joint Israeli-Iranian nuclear missile project open to interpretation.

The following minutes of the July 18, 1977, meeting between General Toufanian and his Israeli counterparts not only demonstrate the significance of the Flower Project to both Iran and Israel; they also offer a rare glimpse at how the agreement on one of the Middle East's best-kept secrets was finalized:

> Gen. Weizman: The last thing we want and the last thing we need is war. You must remember that Egypt, Jordan, Syria, are all around us, they possess now over 5000 tanks and over 1300 fighting airplanes. Iraq can move in 48 hours with quite a force. Saudi Arabia is buying a lot of arms. Libya is an arsenal of weapons. And I don't want to go into high strategy but you only have to look at the map and see what happens to a small country like ours if we go all the way back to the old borders without real security . . . I hope we will prove to the world that what we want is really peace and quiet. One of our great generals is now the Minister of Agriculture, General Sharon. He is growing vegetables instead of shooting at the enemy. This is a great advance towards peace.
>
> Gen. Toufanian: You know, in principle, we think peace is in the interest of everyone. We realize the difficulty . . . I think we are the only two countries in the region that can depend on each

other. Because look at Pakistan. And Iraq, we know what they are doing, an arsenal of Russia. You have two Russian arsenals — Gaddafi and Iraq. And we have Iraq as an arsenal of Russia, and not only an arsenal. They want to come to the Persian Gulf. . . . We are obliged to develop some type of deterrent force.

Gen. Weizman: You must have a ground-to-ground missile. A country like yours, with F-14s, with so many F-4s, with the problems surrounding you, [must have] a good missile force, a clever and wise one. You will see the missile tomorrow.[69]

Because Iran was reluctant to have direct military ties with Israel over the missile, when General Toufanian returned to Tehran an oil-for-arms deal was arranged such that the missiles would be shipped to Sirjan in central Iran through a Swiss front company for assembly and testing. At Sirjan, a runway capable of handling 747 jets was to be constructed to bring in the missiles. A testing range was to be located near Rafsanjan, from where the Israeli-Iranian missile could be fired 300 miles north into Iran's Lut Desert and south into the Gulf of Oman. Iran made its first contribution toward the missile project in 1978 by shipping $260 million worth of oil from Kharg Island to Israel. For Iran, the missile project was also a means for rural development of the areas around central Iran, and by 1979 3,000 housing units had already been constructed for workers who were to be employed by the Imperial Iranian Armed Forces.

For Israel, the missile project offered three added advantages beyond its strategic value. Having spent millions on developing earlier missile systems, the cooperation with Iran provided desperately needed financing in order to improve the accuracy of such missiles as the Jericho. As Aaron Klieman notes in this book, *Israel's Global Reach*, coproduction and other mutually beneficial arrangements help in finding badly needed investment capital for Israel's own military projects.[70] A second advantage for Israel was that Iran could offer a site for long-range testing beyond the watchful eyes of its enemies. Finally, Israel hoped to temper Iran's Arab option by integrating itself into Iran's arms procurement policy.

The agreement that Shimon Peres signed with the Shah in April 1977 included, in addition to the Flower Project, another top-secret project involving electronic countermeasures

(ECM). Installing Israeli-made ECMs onto Iran's F-4s and F-14s was necessary to protect them from antiaircraft missiles that the Soviets had provided Iraq. Commander of the Imperial Iranian Air Force, General Gholam Reza Rab'ii was dispatched to discuss the project with the Israeli Aircraft Industry Ltd. Another high-ranking official to visit Israel was Admiral K. M. Habibollahi, commander of the Imperial Iranian Navy. In addition to talks concerning the purchase of chaff dispensers for Iran's naval fleet, the minute of his meeting with Admiral Barkai, commander of the Israeli navy, indicate that a number of other topics were discussed as well:

> Group A.   Subjects existing in the Israel Navy that may be of interest to the Imperial Iranian Navy which Admiral Barkai offered to open for inspection.
> 1.   Range tables for 76 mm. gun.
> 2.   Inspection of Israel Naval School.
>
> Group B.   This group of subjects includes a list of equipment that has already been developed by the Israel Navy and is currently being fitted into our ships. These subjects could be inspected by the Imperial Iranian Navy specialists and eventually, after due staff work, be purchased from our industry as cooperation between the two navies develops:
> 1.   360 degrees Thermal Radar for use in ships and airplanes.
> 2.   Conversion of existing airplanes in the Imperial Iranian Navy into Maritime Control airplanes, using the concept of the Israel Navy.
>
> Group C.   This group of subjects includes items that are in various stages of R & D. Admiral Barkai strongly emphasized the importance he attaches to this equipment and the cost effectiveness of transforming these projects into joint projects. Cooperation in these subjects would enhance the existing ties between the two navies.
> 1.   An acoustic self-defense system for submarines that would include the capability to jam and deceive enemy sonars, to jam and deceive enemy torpedoes and to release anti-torpedo decoys.
> 2.   Enhancing the Flower Project to enable it to be launched from submarines.[71]

As is apparent from these minutes, one of Israel's primary reasons for wanting a joint naval cooperation program with the Imperial Iranian Navy was to obtain Iranian financing for some of its important strategic objectives. For example, the advantage of launching a Flower missile from a submarine (in 1977 Israel had acquired three British-made Vickers submarines) would be to extend its range, thus enabling Israel to launch a nuclear attack against such cities as Tripoli, Damascus, or Baghdad from the Mediterranean.

Iran's desire for naval cooperation with Israel was based on her need to protect the shipping lanes extending from the Persian Gulf to the Gulf of Oman and into the Indian Ocean, which she saw as being threatened by India and Iraq. This anxiety was clearly expressed by General Toufanian in his July 1977 meeting in Tel Aviv. At that meeting he raised the question of whether the Israelis had any knowledge of a joint French-Indian project for the development of a surface-to-surface missile with a 600 kilogram warhead. While the Israelis were aware of a joint French-Iraqi nuclear reactor project, they had no information on any French-Indian venture but agreed to research the subject and report back to General Toufanian who was keenly aware of Iran's need to maintain its military effectiveness in the Indian Ocean.

Thus, although during the period from 1974 through 1978 Iran exercised its Arab option hoping to establish peace in the Middle East, her military cooperation with Israel, a function of shared security imperatives, suggests that Iran — and Israel — realized that military force remained the ultimate arbiter of the destiny of nations. For two states, subjected to recurrent pressures from hostile enemies and located in a combustible region of the world, the attractions of increased military self-reliance were all but irresistible. Additionally, for the Shah of Iran, an adequate defense was seen as a prerequisite for safeguarding his country's domestic development, not, as his opponents argued, a diversion from, or alternative to health, education, and welfare expenditures.[72] The Iraqi missiles that fell on Iran during the recent Iran-Iraq war, killing innocent people and destroying the country's industrial base, are a clear reminder that in the final analysis, the Shah was right about this issue and his critics and opponents were wrong.

ISRAEL AND THE IRANIAN
JEWISH COMMUNITY

In addition to providing capital for its defense projects, Israel had other reasons for cultivating close relations with Iran during the period. The demographic component of Israeli foreign policy was reactivated as concern over the Jewish community in Iran heightened. The following letter from the U.S. Embassy in Tel Aviv to the U.S. Embassy in Tehran dated April 30, 1976, explains the situation of Iranian Jews:

> Ovadia Danon will be coming to Tehran in the near future on assignment with the Jewish Agency. He told us that Israeli leaders are somewhat concerned about the Jewish community in Iran; he described that community to us as being wealthy but becoming increasingly Persian. The community has been generally supportive of Israel but not as helpful as would be desired. Danon's job will be essentially one which is concerned with cultural affairs and Jewish traditions, as he described it to us, but we believe his primary purpose is to do what he can to strengthen the ties between the Jewish community there [in Iran] and Israel. For your information we also believe he may be somewhat involved with Israeli intelligence activities.[73]

When weighed against Ambassador Lubrani's decision to diversify Israel's oil imports at a time when he sensed some trouble looming ahead in Iran, Danon's mission comes into sharper focus: on the one hand, to obtain information from the well-informed Jewish community in Iran concerning the strength of the religious opposition and, on the other hand, to assure the community of Israel's assistance in case the internal situation deteriorated and they needed to leave Iran on short notice. The level of Israeli anxiety over Iran's internal situation and its consequences for the Jewish community increased as a number of anti-Israeli articles surfaced in the Iranian press:

> Fariborz Atapour, a prominent Iranian journalist, is the Israeli mission's favorite villain. About 18 months ago (September 1975) Shani (First Secretary, Israeli Mission) gathered a number of Atapour's anti-Israeli writings and complained to the Foreign Ministry. They promised to restrain Atapour but did not do so until Shani had repeated his demarche every two weeks for the next

three months. In the process, Shani learned that Atapour had taken considerable amount of money from the Syrian government and indeed was regarded by his colleagues as being very much a "man on the take."

Shani said newspaper reports of an attempt by two terrorists to shoot their way into the Jewish Agency were only semi-correct. There were two men involved and both were killed. The Iranians believe the pair were fanatical right-wing Moslims who may have been casing the Jewish Agency for future action.[74]

By the time Lubrani sent his report to Jerusalem (June 1978) predicting the demise of the Pahlavi regime, the Jewish community in Iran had become aware of the impending danger as well. According to the U.S. Embassy in Tehran, a number of Iranian Jews inquired about immigration to the United States. When asked why they wished to leave Iran, they replied that for members of a religious minority the future looked grim. In Shiraz, where the Jewish community numbered approximately 10,000, religious intolerance by Shiite fundamentalists was such that they circulated a petition demanding Jewish employees of the Nemazi Hospital be fired. However, a substantial group of Iran's 90,000 Jewish community had not made up their minds whether to leave Iran. For them there appeared "no alternative but to ride out Iran's social and political crises and hope for the best."[75]

THE BREAKUP OF THE ALLIANCE

For Iran's Jewish community, however, hope turned to despair. By the end of 1978, Iran was in turmoil, and the Shah was under pressure to leave Iran. With the breakdown of law and order after the Shah's departure, General Segev, Israel's military attache, called General Toufanian in desperation, telling him that "the Palestinians are about to take over our mission." This time, however, the Iranian General could not help. "I'm sorry, General," he replied, "but I am unable to assist you." And with this conversation, 30 years of Israeli-Iranian friendship and cooperation came to an abrupt end.

Relations between the two countries were deep and diverse, based on a persistent, resilient, and durable convergence of geopolitical, military, and economic interests. On the one hand, Iran cultivated closer ties to Israel to counter

Arab radicalism and Soviet influence, to obtain Israeli know-how for economic and military development, to sell her oil, and to explain herself to the United States at times when Iran's security interests were not fully appreciated in Washington. On the other hand, Israel's cultivation of closer ties to Iran stemmed from the demographic component of its foreign policy, which stressed the importance of world Jewry, and the strategic component, which was encapsulated in the Periphery Doctrine predicated on a common fear of hostile Arab intentions.

With the establishment of an Islamic republic in Iran, the Israeli Embassy in Tehran was given to the Palestinians who had served as Khomeini's fifth column in the critical days leading to his return from exile. And with a foreign policy predicated on the slogan, "Neither East nor West, [only] Islamic Republic," there appeared little room for Israel in an Iran under Khomeini. Thus, while the United States was being vilified as the "Great Satan," Israel had assumed the mantle of "Little Satan." The Israeli-Iranian connection had finally come to an abrupt end — or had it?

NOTES

1. Marvin Weinbaum, "Iran and Israel: The Discreet Entente," *Orbis* 15 (Winter 1975): 1085–87.

2. Tareq Ismael, *International Relations of the Contemporary Middle East* (Syracuse: Syracuse University Press, 1986), p. 57. Ismael notes that in opposition to Egypt's peace treaty with Israel, at the 1978 Ninth Arab Summit Conference in Baghdad, 20 Arab League members condemned Sadat's policies and took action against Egypt.

3. Ibid., p. 58.

4. Avner Yaniv, *Deterrence without the Bomb: The Politics of Israel Strategy* (Lexington, MA: D. C. Heath, 1987), p. 189.

5. Ibid., pp. 190–91.

6. See Yaniv, p. 195.

7. Ibid.

8. R. K. Ramazani, "Iran and the Arab-Israeli Conflict," *Middle East Journal* 32 (Autumn 1978): 421.

9. See Shlomo Avineri, "Ideology and Israeli Foreign Policy," *Jerusalem Quarterly* 37 (Winter 1986): 4–6.

10. Arnaud de Borchgrave, "The Shah on War and Peace," *Newsweek*, November 14, 1977, p. 69.

11. Documents of the United States Embassy in Tehran, Volume 19, 1979, pp. 1–3.

12. Documents of the United States Embassy in Tehran, Volume 11, 1979, pp. 62–63.

13. Documents of the United States Embassy in Tehran, Volume 8, 1979, p. 60.

14. Harold Saunders, "United States and the Palestinian Issue," in *Israel in the Middle East,* ed. Itamar Rabinovich and Jehuda Reinharz (Oxford: Oxford University Press, 1984), p. 316.

15. Yaniv, p. 215.

16. Ramazani, p. 428.

17. Documents of the United States Embassy in Tehran, Volume 8, 1979, p. 65.

18. "End of an Estrangement," *Financial Times,* January 8, 1975, p. 5.

19. Interview with former Iranian official, Washington, D.C., 1987.

20. General Fardoust was the only high-ranking official who had pursued his entire training with Britain's MI-5 and MI-6. By authority vested in him by the Shah, General Fardoust was in touch with MI-5 and MI-6 officials of the British Embassy in Tehran.

21. Conversation with Richard Helms, Washington, D.C., 1987.

22. Musa Sadr was initially hired by Savak to build a base for himself in Lebanon and to strengthen the Shiite community in that country against the influence of the Sunnis and the PLO. The maverick clergyman, however, turned against the Shah toward the late 1970s.

23. The plot to kill Musa Sadr was conceived by the Syrian and the Libyan governments who saw his activities in Lebanon as a menace. Toward this end, Libya invited Sadr to attend an annual religious ceremony in Tripoli. Hafez Assad encouraged Sadr to go to Libya in order to "patch things up" with Qaddafi and, therefore, obtain some financial assistance from the Libyan strongman. Knowing that Musa Sadr would be eliminated in Libya, Hafez Assad approached Iran, which by then had suspected Sadr of being a double-agent, to allow him to supply the Kurdish rebels in Iraq in return for getting rid of Musa Sadr.

   According to an interview with the Shah's envoy to Egypt, Sadat explained that in 1978 the Soviet Union became aware of a British plot to assist Musa Sadr in establishing an Islamic republic in Iran (at that time Sadr's popularity exceeded that of Khomeini's). In view of Soviet anxieties over the establishment of an Islamic republic on their southern flank, they asked the Syrians to assassinate the Shiite leader.

24. Interview with former Iranian official, Washington, D.C., 1987.

25. William Griffith, "Iran's Foreign Policy in the Pahlavi Era," in *Iran under the Pahlavis,* ed. George Lenzcowski (Stanford: Hoover Institution Press, 1978), p. 381.

26. Ramazani, p. 422.

27. Shahram Chubin, "Iran's Foreign Policy 1960–1976: An Overview," in *Twentieth Century Iran,* ed. Hossein Amirsadeghi (London: William Heinemann, 1977), p. 201.

28. Documents of the United States Embassy in Tehran, Volume 47, 1979, pp. 60–88.

29.   Shahram Chubin, "Iran's Defense and Foreign Policy," in *Iran in the 1980s*, ed. Abbas Amirie and Hamilton Twitchell (Tehran: Institute for International Political and Economic Studies, 1978), p. 326.

30.   Interview with Uri Lubrani, Israel, 1988.

31.   Chubin, "Iran's Foreign Policy 1960–1976: An Overview," p. 218.

32.   Gary Sick, *All Fall Down: America's Tragic Encounter with Iran* (New York: Random House, 1985), p. 22.

33.   Conversation with Donald McHenry, Washington, D.C., 1985.

34.   Documents of the United States Embassy in Tehran, Volume 8, 1979, pp. 158–63.

35.   William Sullivan, *Mission to Iran* (New York: Norton, 1981), p. 62.

36.   Sick, p. 37

37.   Documents of the United States Embassy in Tehran, Volume 12, 1979, p. 23.

38.   See Robert Huyser, *Mission to Tehran* (New York: Harper and Row), 1986.

39.   Interview with former Iranian official, Washington, D.C., 1987.

40.   Interview with former Iranian official, Los Angeles, 1987.

41.   Interview with former Iranian official, San Francisco, 1988.

42.   Uri Lubrani, "The Iranian-Israeli Relationship," in *Israel in the Middle East*, ed. Itamar Rabinovich and Jehuda Reinharz (Oxford: Oxford University Press, 1984), p. 342.

43.   Interview with Uri Lubrani, Israel, 1988.

44.   Yaniv, p. 159.

45.   Interview with former Iranian official, Washington, D.C., 1988.

46.   Aaron Klieman, *Israel's Global Reach: Arms Sales as Diplomacy* (New York: Pergamon-Bassey's, 1985), pp. 128–29.

47.   Documents of the United States Embassy in Tehran, Volume 19, 1979, p. 13.

48.   Documents of the United States Embassy in Tehran, Volume 36, 1979, p. 55.

49.   Interview with Shmuel Segev, Israel, 1988.

50.   Documents of the United States Embassy in Tehran, Volume 36, 1979, p. 61.

51.   Yaniv, p. 158.

52.   Interview with former Iranian official, Washington, D.C., 1987.

53.   Benjamin Beit-Hallahmi, *The Israeli Connection* (New York: Pantheon Books, 1987), p. 11.

54.   Ramazani, p. 427.

55.   Documents of the United States Embassy in Tehran, Volume 11, 1979, pp. 59–60.

56.   Lubrani, pp. 342–47.

57.   *Kayhan*, Shahrivar 1, 1358 (August 1979), p. 8.

58.   Yaniv, p. 222.

59.   Interview with former Iranian official, San Jose, 1988.

60.   Moshe Dayan, *Breakthrough* (New York: Alfred Knopf, 1981), p. 32.

61.   Ibid., pp. 106–07.

62. Interview with former Iranian official, San Jose, 1988.

63. de Borchgrave, p. 70.

64. Documents of the United States Embassy in Tehran, Volume 19, 1979, p. 4.

65. Interview with former Iranian official, Los Angeles, 1987.

66. de Borchgrave, p. 71.

67. Interview with former Iranian official, Washington, D.C., 1987.

68. "Israelis' Secret Records Tell of Missile Deal with Shah," New York *Times*, April 1, 1986, p. 2.

69. Documents of the United States Embassy in Tehran, Volume 19, 1979, pp. 1–19.

70. Klieman, p. 129.

71. Documents of the United States Embassy in Tehran, Volume 19, 1979, pp. 62–64.

72. Chubin, "Iran's Defense and Foreign Policy," p. 315.

73. Documents of the United States Embassy in Tehran, Volume 11, 1979, p. 54.

74. Ibid., p. 56.

75. Documents of the United States Embassy in Tehran, Volume 37, 1979, p. 23.

6

Israel and the
Khomeini Regime

A little over a year after the establishment of an Islamic republic in Iran, reports of arms transfers to that country surfaced in the international press with little fanfare. But when it was discovered that it was Israel that was selling weapons to the Ayatollah Khomeini, the transfers not only captured the headlines but also were highlighted in a widely publicized Congressional hearing in 1987. The following is a sample of reports from various sources detailing the sale of Israeli weapons to Iran since 1980:

> According to the *London Observer* Israel's arms sales to Iran total $500 million annually. In a 1980 agreement, Israel sold Iran ammunition and spare parts for Chieftain tanks and US-made F-4 Phantom aircraft. . . . In 1981, Yaacov Nimrodi, an intimate of leaders across the Israeli political spectrum, sold the Iranian defense ministry $135,842,000 worth of Hawk anti-aircraft missiles, 155 mm. mortars, ammunition, and other weapons. Nimrodi, Iranian officials, and a brother of Syrian President Assad made a deal to ship 40 truckloads of weapons a day from Israel to Iran, via Syria and Turkey. A 707 had been carrying loads of 1,250 TOW missiles from Israel to Iran via Malaga, Spain.[1]
>
> Israel has secretly agreed to supply Iran with arms and ammunition worth about $50 million which it seized from arsenals of the Palestine Liberation Organization in Lebanon. . . . Other intelligence sources reckon that Israel had previously sent supplies worth more than $150 million to Iran.[2]
>
> Israel handled most of its sales through Faroukh Azzizi, an Iranian arms merchant who lives in Athens. Azzizi purchased US-made TOW missiles from Israel in November 1982. The shipment went to Amsterdam before reaching Tehran.[3]

An Israeli-owned company sold Iran Sidewinder air-to-air missiles, radar equipment, 40,000 mortar rounds, 400,000 rounds of machine-gun and other ammunition, 1000 field telephones and 200 telephone scramblers. The invoices were date-stamped Jan. 6, 1983.[4]

In clandestine deals with Iran, Israel continues to supply ammunition for 155 millimeter artillery, 109 millimeter recoilless rifles, and parts for Iranian F-4 fighter aircraft.[5]

The House majority leader said today that Israel, acting with the approval of the United States, had shipped Iran 2008 TOW anti-tank missiles and at least 235 Hawk anti-aircraft missiles, a quantity of weapons much greater than previously acknowledged.[6]

One of the most baffling questions to arise from the Iran-Contra affair is Israel's seemingly paradoxical role in helping to strengthen a regime that vilifies it as the "Little Satan" and promises its would-be martyrs that the next stop after "conquering Baghdad" is the "liberation of Jerusalem." On the surface such a decision defies logic, but not when tested against historical precedents, such as the 1959 sale of military items to West Germany in the wake of the European Jewry's destruction at the hands of Nazi Germany. Israel's pragmatic approach to weapons transfers is best expressed by Ben Gurion, in his defense of the 1959 sale, when he told the Knesset:

In anything having to do with foreign affairs we ask ourselves one simple question: "what is good for Israel?" And if it is good, then all my emotions and Jewish instincts, all my Jewish as well as human pride tell me: "do whatever is best for Israel and what is required for its security."[7]

Twenty years later, Ben Gurion's directive loomed over Israel's decision makers with a sense of urgency, as a major pillar of "the Old Man's" peripheral policy was swept aside by the rising tide of Islamic fundamentalism. Tel Aviv's link to Tehran seemed to have been permanently severed. When the Shah left Iran, Khomeini inherited the world's sixth largest army, foreign currency reserves of nearly $26 billion, an oil industry earning $105 million a day, a GNP ranking of thirteenth in the world, and the Shah's legacy of close relations with Israel. While accepting the bulk of his inheritance, Khomeini did not agree to a continuation of relations with Israel and put an abrupt end to this legacy. He emphasized his rejection of the Shah's policy by transferring the Israeli mission to the PLO. In many respects, relations between the two countries were the same as they were in 1948: an Iran under the influence of anti-Israel clerics and an isolated Israel. What, then, accounts for the Israeli-Iranian nexus since 1979?

The basic premise of this chapter is that the simultaneous convergence of Israel's human, economic, and geopolitical interests in Iran, on the one hand, and Khomeini's ideological crusade against the "enemies of Islam," on the other, help explain the durable, yet asymmetrical, links between Israel and the Khomeini regime.

ISRAEL AND THE AYATOLLAHS:
THE LOGIC BEHIND THE CONNECTION

Just as in 1948, the immediate reason for Israel's cultivation of closer ties to the Khomeini regime stemmed from the demographic component of Israel's foreign policy, namely, concern for the safety and welfare of Iran's 90,000 Jewish community. Nowhere in the modern Islamic world had Jews enjoyed more freedom and influence than in Iran under the Pahlavi dynasty. At the height of their prosperity under the Shah, like many other religious minorities, they maintained their own schools, synagogues and social institutions.[9] This situation changed with the Shah's departure from Iran on January 16, 1979.

Uri Lubrani notes that after the fall of the Shah, Israel was faced with several problems. In addition to the loss of Iranian oil and concern over the future of Israeli-Iranian relations, Israel was faced with a third, and more immediate problem: the welfare of Iranian-Jews.[10] However, before Israel could address the issue of the indigenous Jewish population, it was imperative that its embassy personnel leave Iran before being lynched by Khomeini's militia. The 33 Israelis who remained in Iran, including Joseph Hermelin (Israeli representative to Iran) sought protection at a temporary safe-house provided by Ibrahim Yazdi, a close confidant of Khomeini — most probably at the request of the U.S.

government.[11] Then came the call for help to William Sullivan, the U.S. ambassador to Iran:

> I received a telephone call from my Israeli colleague, who had literally gone underground with his staff after his building had been taken over by the Fedayeen and given as a gift to the PLO. Since El Al aircraft could no longer come to Iran, he pleaded with me to take his people on one of our planes as soon as possible. He told me he had thirty-two officials and could get them all to the airport within two hours of the moment I gave him notice that the plane was ready. This posed something of a problem, since it meant bumping thirty-two Americans off the airlift, but, under the circumstances, I judged the Israeli danger to be greater than our own. Accordingly, I arranged space for thirty-two people on one of our flights and through a complicated series of signals got the word to the Israelis. With typical efficient discipline, they rounded up their people and arrived at the airport in good time and in good order for departure. There was only one complication. They had thirty-three rather than thirty-two, but one American citizen readily volunteered to cede his position and let all of them go. They left with considerable relief, and I received a nice message of thanks from Foreign Minister Moshe Dayan.[12]

While Israeli personnel were being secretly airlifted out of Iran, Iranian Jews were making preparations to leave their homeland, as harassment and persecution by the new regime increased. Before coming back to Iran from exile abroad, Khomeini had assured the Jewish community that Iranian-Jews would not be harmed. However, this promise was broken when, in April 1979, Habib Elghanian, president of Iran's Jewish community, was executed. At least five other Jewish leaders suffered a similar fate in the following months. The following documents obtained from the U.S. Embassy in Tehran highlight the plight of this besieged community after January 1979:

> January 8, 1979
>
> According to the Israeli mission here, some 8–10,000 Jews have left the country, leaving a community of 70,000 or so. Representatives of the Israeli mission tend to emphasize in their conversation the elements of danger which are leading Jews to emigrate.
>
> May 11, 1979
>
> A prominent member of the Los Angeles Jewish community, Osias G. Goren, has called assistant secretary Derian about the rapidly deteriorating status of Tehran Jewish community. The Los Angeles

community has reports from Tehran, following Elghanian execution, that many members of Tehran Jewish community [are] being picked up and entire community is in danger. Appeal to assistant secretary was for immediate United States Government action.... We have received from White House, Congress, and the public, statements of intense concern about status of Iranian Jewish community.

May 25, 1979

We have had several conversations with Israeli officials about situation of Jews in Iran.... Kotlowitz said that he was afraid that the Elghanian execution was not an individual case and that other Jews are being held as hostages. Shani, who spent two years at the Israeli mission in Iran, said that he feared not so much further executions as a general deterioration of the position of the Jewish community.[13]

To Israeli decision makers Khomeini's passionate hatred of Israel clearly had extended to Iran's Jewish community, and their plight became an important consideration in Israeli policy toward Iran. With the severance of diplomatic relations, however, Israel's policy options were severely limited. The government of Israel was faced with a dilemma. On the one hand, it could not put pressure on the Khomeini regime to end its persecution of Iranian-Jews for fear of antagonizing the clerics even more. On the other hand, a passive policy would not remove the danger that the Jewish community was facing with each passing day. An answer developed late in the year. The U.S. arms embargo against Iran in November 1979 forced the Khomeini regime to start looking for desperately needed spare parts for its U.S.-made weapons. Ben Gurion's defense of the 1959 arms transfer to West Germany could now be invoked with poignancy: if selling arms to Khomeini would help Iranian Jews escape that country then Israeli leaders felt such a course had to be taken. A tacit agreement was made with the Islamic republic: in exchange for spare parts, Iranian-Jews would be allowed to leave Iran.

The government of Israel has been reticent about its efforts to rescue Iranian-Jews, but the Austrian foreign minister told reporters at a United Nations luncheon on October 2, 1987, that Iran had been secretly permitting thousands of Iranian-Jews to leave the country through Pakistan. They were then flown to Austria and allowed to immigrate to the United States and Israel. He added that the immigrants crossed the Iranian border in buses, without any opposition from local authorities. The Jewish exodus intensified in 1983 when about 2,000 Jews leaving a Tehran synagogue at the end of Friday night prayers were stopped by Khomeini's Revolutionary Guards and taken by bus to prison, where according to the *London Economist* they spent a terrifying night.[14] The Austrian government reported that since 1983, when this incident took place, 5,100 Iranian-Jews came through Austria and that the flow increased sharply, to 1,483, in the first eight months of 1987.[15] It is estimated that since the government of Israel started providing the Khomeini regime with arms in 1980, 55,000 Iranian-Jews have been permitted to leave Iran.

Although the government of Israel denies any arms-for-Iranian-Jews deal with Iran and emphasizes instead the strategic considerations of the Iran-Iraq war, privately they acknowledge that selling weapons to Khomeini is implicitly connected to the plight of Iranian-Jews.[16] This position is consistent with Israeli arms transfers to the Kurdish rebels who were fighting the Iraqi army in the 1970s. That policy had its strategic dimension, but it also entailed a demographic component, which led to the exodus of 8,000 Iraqi-Jews from that country.

In addition to the demographic factor, Israel has sold weapons to the Khomeini regime for an economic reason. Israel's arms exports play a significant role in the country's economy, making up 20 percent of total exports and accounting for 60,000 jobs — one-fifth of the total Jewish work force in the manufacturing sector.[17]

This economic rationale is clearly enunciated by Israeli scholar Aaron Klieman. To remain viable the Israeli economy must be oriented toward industrialization and foreign trade. Total exports are spearheaded by industrial products. Industrial exports, in turn, are dominated by three sectors — metals, electronics, and aerospace equipment. Each of these includes defense-related items. Therefore, defense output has become a critical factor in the growth of industrial as well as total exports, hence, of the economy as a whole. In short, Israel's weapons transfers go far beyond political, defense, strategic, and security concerns. Economic trade, industrial growth, and scientific development are vitally affected by the degree of success in finding outlets for military products. Thus, finding markets for Israel's defense exports has evolved from what might once have been considered economic opportunity to an economic necessity. "A figure of somewhere near $1 billion in defense export earnings," Klieman concludes, "is not to be scoffed at in the context of Israel's [economy]."[18]

Limitations imposed on an academic and an outsider make it difficult to obtain exact figures for Israel's arms transfers to the Khomeini regime, but there is no doubt that they have contributed to its international balance of payments. According to intelligence sources, for example, from 1979 to October 1982, Israel supplied Iran with $150 million worth of weapons.[19] Even as late as the summer of 1986, unconfirmed reports received by U.S. intelligence sources indicated that the Israelis had negotiated to sell up to $750 million in arms to Iran, a package including U.S.-made TOW antitank missiles, Israeli Gabriel air-to-surface missiles, F-4 and F-5 aircraft engine parts, tanks, and jeeps.[20] Furthermore, in view of Iran's cash flow problems, it is quite possible that barter deals, similar to the one arranged for the Flower Project, may have been arranged whereby Israel would receive Iranian oil in exchange for arms. This was indeed what Amiran Nir, an advisor to Shimon Peres, suggested to Iranian officials on his secret trip to Iran in May 1986, when Colonel Oliver North and his Iranian counterparts could not agree on the method of payment by Iran. According to the Tower Commission Report, Nir asked whether it might be agreed that "since the U.S. Government cannot deliver without advance payment and Iran cannot pay in advance, we will examine mid-term financial arrangement possibilities, such as oil deals." The advantage of an arms-for-oil arrangement for Israel is that it relieves aggregate international balance of payments pressures by financing some of its oil import bill.

Apart from the demographic and economic rationale, a third reason for the sale of weapons to Iran was to keep channels to moderates in the Khomeini regime open, with the ultimate aim of overthrowing Khomeini. This policy was clearly outlined by Uri Lubrani in a seminar held at Tel Aviv University on December 4, 1986:

> I maintain that we are witnessing the decline of Khomeini's revolution. . . . The Iranian people are beginning to feel dissatisfied and frustrated. . . . We Israelis must relate to the problem of Iran on

two levels, which, at first glance, seem to contradict each other. The first level is the confrontation between Israeli troops and the Iranian death emissaries. These emissaries have been responsible for the kidnapping and murder of IDF soldiers and Lebanese fighters taking part in the long struggle against terror on Israel's northern border and in the Lebanese security zone. . . . The second level on which we must relate to Iran is the long-term strategic level, which stems from geopolitical logic. Our long-term policy should not be aimed against the Ayatollah Khomeini and his band of clerics who are in power today. It should be an attempt to relate to the Iranian people, to take into account its sensitivities, culture and history, particularly those periods in Iran's history that converge with ours. Israel should relate to Khomeini's frightening revolution as if it were a passing phenomenon, a subject for scholarly research for many years to come. We must span the circle of enmity surrounding us and make our way to the heart of the Iran that will arise from the embers of the cruel revolution. I want Israel to keep its options open, even the option of approach to Iran.[21]

The cornerstone of Israel's policy toward Iran since 1979 is captured by Lubrani's remarks; namely, the distinction between Iran the geopolitical entity and its regime. Official Israeli policy has been to view the Khomeini phenomenon as a parenthesis in Iran's history. Therefore, the idea of selling weapons is to keep the lines of communication between Tehran and Tel Aviv open until Islamic fundamentalism loses steam and is ultimately replaced by moderates. For example, in 1981 and 1982, Israeli Defense Minister Ariel Sharon repeatedly pressed the Reagan administration for permission to sell some of its stock of U.S.-made arms to Iran's military with the idea of gaining influence with moderate Iranian military officers. According to a U.S. official, "his thesis was, we'll cozy up to some of these army generals because they're the ones that'll knock off these madmen."[22] This Israeli line was offered a public audience on February 8, 1982, on a BBC *Panorama* program shown on Israeli state television. One of the participants, David Kimche, then director-general of the Israeli Foreign Office, spoke about the need to supply equipment to the Iranian military, as well as the need to keep the Iranian military strong. Lubrani, who was also a panelist, recommended a military coup against the Khomeini regime. He explained that Tehran could be taken by 100 tanks and that Israel was eager for a coup without delay but that the United States was slow in reaching a decision.[23] And in October 1987, Lubrani's boss, Defense Minister Yitzhak Rabin, summarized the policy of his government toward Iran as such:

> Iran today is a bitter enemy of Israel in its philosophy. I believe that as long as Khomeini is in power there is no hope for any change. But at the same time, allow me to say that for 28 of 37 years Iran was a friend of Israel. If it could work for 28 years ... why couldn't it once this crazy idea of Shiite fundamentalism is gone?[24]

The fundamental assumption behind Israel's arms-for-Iranian moderates policy was that the Khomeini regime could either be overthrown or that it would somehow disappear. In either case, it was important for Israel to establish links with elements within the Iranian system as an insurance policy for the future of Isareli-Iranian relations. Unfortunately for Israel — and the United States, as the testimony of those involved in the Iran-Contra affair demonstrated — as long as hardliners remain in power, moderates are not likely to show their true colors.

The last and most important rationale of Israel's sale of arms to Iran was an extension of the third, which distinguished between Iran's geopolitical importance and its regime. Thus, while Israel's policy of establishing links with the Iranian nation, particularly its military, was done with an eye toward the future, the geopolitical importance of Iran to Israel took on added significance with the advent of the Iran-Iraq war, which increased the strategic utility of Iran for Israel tremendously.

Almost 30 years after Ben Gurion put his doctrine of the peripheral pact into practice by inviting the Shah of Iran to join Israel in preventing the establishment of an Arab Middle East allied with Moscow, Israel's Defense Minister Yitzhak Rabin explained in reference to a question concerning the sale of arms to Khomeini's Islamic republic Iran's strategic utility:

> What is good for Israel is a no win situation in the Iran-Iraq war. This is in Israel's strategic interest and the political mileage that Israel has gotten out of it has been invaluable. The peripheral pact [with Iran under the Shah] only neutralized the Arab inner circle, but did not strategically diminish the threat. Whereas with the Iran-Iraq war, a balance of threat has been created for Israel.[25]

Rabin's explanation of why Israel sold weapons to Iran captures the essence of the fundamental durability that goes to the heart of Israel's pragmatic entente with Iran. This durability transcends any ideological, historical, or cultural affinity and is based, rather, on the age-old principle of balance of power. By tying down Iraq's army around the Shatt-al-Arab waterway and its northeastern borders, Iran has fulfilled its ultimate role not only as a balancer but also as a periphery state. Iran effectively removed the threat of the Arab Eastern front against Israel and kept Baghdad distracted from the anti-Israel resistance front. As *Ha'aretz* columnist Abraham Schweitzer put it: "Iran is important in and of itself, as it sits in the rear of our potential enemies. If and when the [Persian] Gulf war ends, Iraq will always have to watch its eastern flank."[26] Yitzhak Shamir's explanation for Israel's contacts with Iran, as expressed during his February 1987 visit to the United States, was even more straightforward. While recognizing the ideological and cultural differences between the two states, Shamir argued that Iran's strategic utility for Israel rested in that country's continuing war with Iraq, an Arab enemy state.[27] Involved elsewhere, Iraq was precluded from joining any military Arab coalition against Israel.

From a regional perspective, providing military assistance to Iran in her war against Iraq has also contributed to Israel's security by drawing a wedge within the Arab zone. Since its outbreak, the Iran-Iraq war has caused important rifts in the Arab world. Syria and Libya support Iran while all other Arab countries to a lesser or greater degree support Iraq. Thus, since 1980, two of Israel's most vociferous enemies — Syria and Libya — worked to undermine another of Israel's traditional enemies, Iraq. Furthermore, the challenge of the Iran-Iraq war caused some Arab states to form their own alliance systems. For example, in 1981, Saudi Arabia, Kuwait, Oman, Bahrain, Qatar, and the United Arab Emirates formed the Gulf Cooperation Council to protect themselves against the spillover effects of the Iran-Iraq war. One effect of Israel's support of Iran in its war against Iraq has been that it has helped diminish the importance of the Arab-Israeli conflict in the Middle East affairs by concentrating Arab military and financial resources away from Israel and toward the Persian Gulf war. In short, in its search for security Israel responded pragmatically and used whatever resources it had available to keep a balance of power between Iran and Iraq by siding with Iran.

THE IRAN-CONTRA AFFAIR: THE ISRAELI LINK

Thus, while U.S. Secretary of State George Shultz traced the origins of the Iran-Contra affair to Israel, which he inaccurately said "suckered" the United States into the initial arms sales to Iran in 1985, Iran-Contra was only a side effect of Israeli policy. The rationale behind Israel's role in Iran-Contra was based on four points: an on-going interest in the safety and welfare of Iran's Jewish community, the economic incentives introduced by Iran's desperate need for arms, the desire to maintain ties to Iran's military establishment, and the desire to fuel the Iran-Iraq war, thus diverting Arab resources and energies to the conflict in the Persian Gulf and away from Israel. In practical terms Israel may have had an interest in the United States pursuing an arms-for-Iran initiative, but to suggest, as Lt. Colonel Oliver North does in his testimony on July 14, 1987, that the United States was lured into the Iran arms deal is unconvincing:

> Sen. McClure: If I understand your testimony to this point, the United States was approached by representatives, first from Israel and then from Iran, suggesting that we open a dialogue with elements inside Iran looking towards the time when there would be a different regime and a different relationship between the United States and that new regime in Iran, am I correct?
>
> Lt. Col. North: Yes, and to assist in furthering that change of regime.
>
> Sen. McClure: And I — I would submit from my own standpoint that any administration that was given any hint that that was possible and did not pursue that opportunity would be derelict, not because we like Khomeini, because obviously we do not. We're not seeking to deal with Khomeini; we're seeking to find a way to deal with a different government in Iran than the one that exists there now, recognizing the importance of that country geostrategically and also economically because of the importance of oil to the world's economy. Am I correct?
>
> Lt. Col. North: Yes sir.
>
> Sen. McClure: Now, to the Israelis, a failure of this policy would not be nearly so damaging would it? More or less, the risks of

failure on the Israeli scale of cost-benefit was far less important to them than it was apparent would be to us.

Lt. Col. North: I could agree to that.

Sen. McClure: I go through that not because I have any disrespect for the Israelis, but I do wonder why it was that US policymakers walked in step with Israeli policy and didn't respond to what were apparent inducements being offered by them at a time when the risks to them were much less than the risks to us.[28]

While Senator McClure's last point highlights the risks involved for the United States in pursuing Israel's agenda as it concerned Iran, within Israel there were those who advocated a hands-off policy toward Iran, arguing that Israel's arms sales to Iran were based on an obsolete strategic doctrine, namely, the peripheral policy. Proponents of this school argued that in the past, the inner circle of Nasser's Egypt, Baathist Syria and Iraq, and Qaddafi's Libya represented the revolutionary forces while on the periphery, Iran was a supporter of the status quo. Since 1979, however, Iran has been an advocate of revolutionary change whereas the inner circle has shifted toward a more moderate stance. Iraq, for example, has moved closer to the United States and has moderated its position regarding Israel since the Iran-Iraq war began. The gravest threat to Israel, therefore, emanates from the periphery and could reach Israel either directly or through Lebanon. As Israel Defense Force Chief of Intelligence General Amnon Shachak envisions it, Tehran, if victorious in its war against Iraq, plans "to export the Islamic revolution to all states in the region and to destabilize their regimes." Abba Eban, chairman of the Knesset Defense and Foreign Affairs Committee, went even further when he said, "The greatest danger to Israel is the Khomeinist threat; I wouldn't sell Iran a broken typewriter."[29]

These critics point to Iran's anti-Israel role in Lebanon, particularly the suicide truck bomb attack on the Israeli military headquarters in Tyre that killed 29 Israeli soldiers in 1983. Another example of Iran's anti-Israel campaign in Lebanon was Hezbollah's penetration of Jazin to break the Israeli security zone in southern Lebanon on direct orders from Tehran in 1987.[30] The critics stress that these incidents are by no means isolated but rather reflect Tehran's determination to "eradicate Israel." Thus, one day after the Israeli invasion of Lebanon, the commander of the Islamic Revolutionary Guard Corps, Colonel Sayyed Shirazi, revealed to his Syrian counterparts that Iran was planning "a religious war [jihad] against the Zionist entity" in coordination with the Iranian Supreme Defense Council. Later, Iran's Prime Minister, Mir Hossein Musavi, unfurled the banner of "victory to Al-Quds [Jerusalem]" in asking his cabinet to approve a budget for the war against Israel. He was also the first official of the Khomeini regime to say that Palestine was "a part of the Islamic homeland."[31]

The critics of Israel's arms-for-Iran policy charge that in the final analysis, Iran's Islamization of the Arab-Israeli conflict — rise of Islamic fundamentalism alongside Palestinian nationalism in the West Bank and Gaza, on the one hand — and its politicization of Lebanon's Shiite community through Islamic Amal, Hezbollah, and Islamic Jihad, on the other hand — pose a greater danger to Israel's security than its Arab neighbors.

THE KHOMEINI REGIME: THE PRAGMATISM BEHIND THE FANATICISM

Thus, while the proponents of arms sales to Iran emphasize the geopolitical importance of that country as a balance against Israel's Arab enemies (the theory being my enemy's enemy is my friend), opponents stress the inherent hostility of Iran toward Israel (my enemy's enemy is also my enemy). Tehran's view of Israel has been more straightforward. The Islamic republic has viewed its contacts — as opposed to relations — with Israel as more expedient than imperative. Nonetheless, it accepted the necessity of dealing with "Little Satan."

One example of how this durable, yet asymmetrical, nexus developed occurred immediately after the outbreak of the Iran-Iraq war when Israel's military attache to Paris, realizing Iran's desperate need for weapons and resorting to a time-honored Israeli tactic, told an Iranian official to "put down all your military requirements on an Islamic Republic of Iran letterhead and I will deliver them to you."[32] In exchange for the U.S.-made spare parts and Israeli arms that he was going to deliver, the Israeli military attache asked that direct contacts between his government and officials of the Khomeini regime be established. Although the request for direct contacts was denied, the Israeli offer to provide much-needed weapons was accepted. Officials of Iran, whose foreign policy slogan reads, "neither east nor west only Islamic Republic," practiced policy according to a slightly different slogan, "neither east nor west, sometimes Israel, when it serves our interest best." The first glimpse of the full extent of this pragmatic entente was revealed when, on July 25, 1981, an Argentinian plane loaded with spare parts for M-68 tanks and large quantities of ammunition was shot down over the Soviet Republic of Armenia. The plane, which flew regularly between Cyprus and Iran, originated from Israel. Meanwhile, according to a September 22, 1983, document of the French intelligence service (D.G.S.E.), contacts between Israel and Iran's embassy in Paris unfolded as follows:

> The Iranian embassy in Paris is engaged in talks with representatives of Israel for the purchase of spare parts for aircraft from that country. In order to protect the secrecy of these talks, they are being held at the Swiss embassy in Paris, which operates as a liaison [between the embassies of Israel and Iran]. The spare parts are sent to the Swiss embassy in Paris, which is then flown to Iran on Air France. Payment for the deliveries is also handled by the Swiss.[33]

How does one explain this contradictory behavior of the Iranian government? In his authoritative book on the Khomeini regime's foreign policy, R. K. Ramazani argues that "both the challenge of revolutionary Iran and the response of other Middle Eastern states to Iran's challenge are multidimensional." Therefore, he argues, "an exclusive emphasis on the military, ideological, or political aspects of these phenomena will not adequately explain them."[34]

One way of putting the Iran-Israel relation in this multidimensional perspective is to examine Iran's Syria connection, which provides interesting parallels. Although Iran and Syria profess irreconcilable ideologies — Iran's Shiite fundamentalism versus Syria's secular pan-Arabism — they have found some common ground with regard to a variety of regional issues, most notably the Iran-Iraq war. Consequently, since September 1980, when the Iran-Iraq war started, there has been limited cooperation along the Tehran-Damascus axis. Immediately following Iraq's invasion of Iran, Tehran decided that despite Syria's secular pan-Arab orientation, an alliance with Syria presented Iran with a realistic chance to tilt the balance of power, which was overwhelmingly in Iraq's favor. Thus, in an effort to save the "glorious Islamic revolution," Iranian decision makers took the pragmatic approach and allied themselves with the Baathists of Syria.

However, the commonality of interest ended at this point, for despite the fact that Khomeini and Hafiz Assad harbored a common enmity toward Saddam Hussein, it is safe to assume that Assad did not share Khomeini's interest in seeing an Iranian-installed Islamic republic in Iraq. Second, while Assad cooperated with Iranian Revolutionary Guardsmen, mullahs, and volunteers in Lebanon for a brief time between 1982 and 1985 (against Israel and U.S. involvement), he resented their continued intrusion and did not find the extremist Khomeini-supported Islamic Amal of Hussein Musawi nor the Hezbollah faction palatable. Khomeini's policy toward Lebanon was largely determined by his Islamic vision whereas Syria perceived its huge investment in Lebanon as crucial to its own political stability, its ability to determine Palestinian politics, and its overall standing in the Arab world. And finally, in spite of their similar anti-Israel rhetoric, Khomeini and Assad differed over the acceptable method of resolving the Arab-Israeli problem. The Islamic republic's goal of "eradicating the Zionist entity" collided head-on with Syria's principal objective, the recovery of the Golan Heights.[35] In short, Iran's alliance with Syria was at most a pragmatic response to the acute security imperative she faced after the Iraqi invasion.

When viewed against the backdrop of Iran's Syria connection, the Iranian relationship with Israel since 1979 comes into sharper focus. Although Tehran has been one of the most implacable enemies of Israel, it has not refused Israel's offer of military assistance, especially when such assistance has coincided with acute security problems. Thus, as was the case with Syria, Iran responded with unswerving pragmatism to her security imperatives following Iraq's invasion and purchased U.S.-made Israeli arms. In short, the

Islamic republic's ideological crusade against Israel has at times been constrained by its need to procure weapons for its war with Iraq.

In fact, Iran has chosen the pragmatic course on other occasions as well. Iran's initial response to the July 20, 1987, United Nations Resolution 598 — calling for an immediate cease-fire between Iran and Iraq and withdrawal of all forces to internationally recognized boundaries — was negative, arguing that it had been formulated and adopted by the United States with the intention of intervention in the Persian Gulf without "consultation from the Islamic Republic of Iran." Iran argued that it reflected "the Iraqi formula for the resolution of the conflict."[36] However, a little less than a year after rejecting it, Ayatollah Khomeini accepted Resolution 598, describing his move as "worse than drinking snake venom." He explained his rationale in blunt terms: without a cease-fire the Islamic republic would not survive. Herein lies the rationale for purchasing arms from Israel. Although it might be considered "worse than drinking snake venom," if it contributed to the viability of the Islamic republic, it would be acceptable. The Islamic republic is not above pragmatism, but it adopts a pragmatic approach when its survival is at stake.

Israel's military assistance to Iran has won it only limited leverage in Tehran. Of necessity, as Ramazani notes, Israel has adopted several approaches to threats from Iran. Thus, while Israel has been supplying Iran with arms, it has not hesitated to use force to protect itself against Khomeini's anti-Israel drive into Lebanon. For example, in retaliation against the truck bomb attack on the Israeli military headquarters in Tyre in November 1983, Israel mounted two air raids on barracks housing Khomeini's revolutionary guards in the area of Baalbek, killing 23 guardsmen.[37]

A little less than two years after the Iranian "martyrs" at Baalbek were buried, Iran bought 504 TOW antitank missiles from Israel for use in her war against Iraq. This incident in particular, and Israeli-Iranian relations in general, suggests that since the establishment of an Islamic theocracy in Iran the dynamics of these relations may best be characterized in terms of a pendulum swinging between Islam and realpolitik. At times when the pendulum has swung toward Islamic ideology, Israeli-Iranian relations have been marked by hostility and outright conflict (e.g., in Lebanon). At times when the pendulum has swung toward realpolitik and common security imperatives (e.g., enmity toward Iraq), the Tehran-Tel Aviv axis has proved to be an important element of the Middle Eastern power configuration. This confirms the Arab saying that "necessity should not be condemned."

CEASE-FIRE IN THE PERSIAN GULF

The important question now is, with Iran's acceptance of UN Resolution 598 and a cease-fire in the Persian Gulf war, in which direction will the pendulum of Israeli-Iranian relations swing. Because Iran has agreed only to a cease-fire and because the conflict has not been conclusively settled, it is too early to draw any conclusions. The cease-fire is only the first clause in UN Security Council Resolution 598. Other clauses in the resolution are a mutual withdrawal of all forces to internationally recognized boundaries without delay, the release and repatriation of prisoners of war, and the establishment of an impartial body to inquire into responsibility for the conflict in order to demand indemnification for war damages.[38] These clauses will remain a constant source of friction between Iran and Iraq, and, as long as they are not resolved, the two countries will continue to maintain forces along their borders. Therefore, despite the cease-fire between Iran and Iraq, the Persian Gulf war is not officially over, and the basic terms of Israeli-Iranian relations has changed very little since the outbreak of hostilities. From a policy standpoint, this means that Israel will continue its dual policy toward Iran: to find channels to Khomeini's heirs such as the "pragmatic" speaker of the Majlis, Hashemi-Rafsanjani, while checking the Islamic republic's activities in Lebanon in support of radical Shiite factions. Israeli reaction to Iran's acceptance of UN Resolution 598 seems to confirm this reality. Prime Minister Shamir reiterated this Israeli position in an interview with *La Vanguardia*. He pointed out that while there have been some points of common interest, there are no relations between Iran and Israel. "The Republic of Iran," Shamir emphasized, "is governed by Muslim fanatics. This entirely alters the situation [despite the cease-fire]. Its aspirations to export Islamic fanaticism threatens not only Israel but also Egypt, Jordan and even Syria."[39]

Yaacov Nimrodi, the former Isareli military attache to Iran who masterminded the initial Israeli — and U.S. — overtures to the Khomeini regime, takes Prime Minister Shamir's point a step further. He maintains that with Iran's acceptance of a cease-fire the "Iraqi option" is no longer relevant. "Israeli policymakers," he points out, "should give thought to the changes taking place in the land of the ayatollahs and persevere in seeking channels leading to dialogue and affinity."[40] This effort to reexamine ties with Iran and to reestablish a deeper Israeli-Iranian connection is not without a caveat, which was expressed by Defense Minister Rabin in an interview following Iran's acceptance of UN Resolution 598. Mr. Rabin pointed out that "as far as Iran is concerned, one of the more interesting tests of the sincerity of its move would be checking the effect it will have on its ties with Hezballah and that organization's strength."[41]

If statements emanating from Iran are any indication of the direction it seeks in terms of relations with Israel, it would appear that Israel can hope for little in terms of Tehran's continued involvement in Lebanon. This policy statement appeared in an article, "New Policies after the Cease-fire," in the government-controlled newspaper *Keyhan*:

> There is a passage in the imam's [Ayatollah Khomeini] hajj message which should always be remembered by our government officials: "Whether we like or not, the Zionists ... will be after us to sully our religious dignity and our ideological identity." [Therefore] until such time as Zionism believes in the slogan, "from the Nile to the Euphrates" ... we too are ready to liberate the collective Islamic energy throughout the world. We will not rest until the world engulfers are destroyed. This is the basic and vital philosophy of the revolution and nothing else.[42]

Indeed, following the assassination of officials of the Amal movement, the Islamic republic's foreign ministry announced on September 23 (1988) that "Lebanon is at the forefront of an anti-Zionist struggle, safeguarding this stronghold from Zionist plots is the duty of all regional progressive and Muslim forces."[43]

Although the extent to which a cease-fire in the Iran-Iraq war will constitute a new phase in the direction of Isareli-Iranian relations is still unclear, the weight of available evidence suggests that the general contours of Israel's relations with the clerical regime in Tehran and the latter's virulent anti-Israel stance remain unchanged. The key question that remains to be addressed is to what extent will the current impasse become a permanent feature of Isareli-Iranian relations.

NOTES

1. Jane Hunter, "Israeli Arms Sales to Iran," *The Washington Report on Middle East Affairs* (November 1986): 2–3.

2. "Iran and Iraq," *Economist Foreign Report*, October 28, 1982, p. 1.

3. Ed Magnuson, "Arms for the Ayatollah," *Time*, July 25, 1983, pp. 26–28.

4. Boston *Globe*, July 17, 1983, p. 4.

5. *CBS Evening News*, June 12, 1984; transcript in *Department of Defense Radio-TV Defense Dialog*, June 13, 1984, p. 5.

6. New York *Times*, November 21, 1986, p. 1.

7. Cited in Aaron Klieman, *Israel's Global Reach: Arms Sales ad Diplomacy* (New York: Pergamon-Bassey's, 1985), p. 99.

8. Round table discussion with Yitzhak Rabin at Tel Aviv University, January 4, 1988.

9. Iranian Jews are descended from the oldest and one of the most illustrious of Jewish diasporas. In 597 B.C. Nebuchadnezzar of Babylon sacked Jerusalem and took with him back to Babylon thousands of the Jewish upper class. Jews fared well in their Babylonian exile. When Cyrus the Great conquered Babylon in 539 he issued an edict the following year permitting the Jews to return to Jerusalem. Some accepted the offer under the leadership of Zerubbabel. Many Jews remained, yet throughout the age these Iranian-Jews kept their Jewish identity. The measure of sophistication and culture of Persian Jewry can be appreciated by the fact that parts of the Bible (the books of Ezra, Daniel, Nehemiah, Ester, and sections of Chronicles) were written in Persia. Ezra, for example, was a Persian Jewish priest-scribe who collected and integrated the ancient scrolls of the Torah into an organized whole. On the first day of 444 B.C., the completed Torah was publicly read before an assembled audience in Jerusalem. See "In Zerubbabel's Footsteps," *Economist*, February 13, 1987.

10. Interview with Uri Lubrani, Israel, 1988.

11. Interview with former Iranian official, Los Angeles, 1988.

12. William H. Sullivan, *Mission to Iran* (New York: Norton, 1981), pp. 270–71.

13. Documents of the United States Embassy in Tehran, Volume 37, 1979, pp. 25–32.

14. "In Zerubbabel's Footsteps," *Economist*, February 13, 1987.

15. Washington *Post*, March 10, 1987, p. 1.

16. Interviews with Arieh Levin, Israel Foreign Ministry, and Joseph Alpher, Jaffee Center for Strategic Studies, Israel, 1988.

17. "Selling Defense," *The Israel Economist*, July 1984, p. 21.

18. Klieman, pp. 55–65.

19. "Iran and Israel," *Economist Foreign Report*, October 28, 1982, p. 2.

20. Washington *Post*, November 6, 1987, p. A32.

21. Uri Lubrani, "Open Options," *New Outlook*, January/February, 1987, pp. 12–13.

22. Washington *Post*, August 16, 1987, p. A26.

23. Benjamin Beit-Hallahmi, *The Israeli Connection* (New York: Pantheon Books, 1987), p. 13.

24. Washington *Post*, October 29, 1987, p. A38.

25. Round table discussion with Yitzhak Rabin at Tel Aviv University, January 4, 1988.

26. Cited in Joseph Alpher, "Arms for the Ayatollahs," *Moment*, May 1987, p. 16.

27. Beit-Hallahmi, p. 14.

28. *Taking the Stand: The Testimony of Lieutenant Colonel Oliver North* (New York: Pocket Books, 1987), pp. 681–88.

29. Alpher, p. 17.

30. Round table discussion with Yitzhak Rabin at Tel Aviv University, January 4, 1988.

31. R. K. Ramazani, *Revolutionary Iran* (Baltimore: Johns Hopkins University Press, 1986), p. 156.

32. Pierre Pean, *La Menace* (Paris: Fayard, 1987), p. 22.

33. Ibid.

34. Ramazani, *Revolutionary Iran*, p. 3.

35. Ibid., p. 245.

36. For Iran's complete response to UN Resolution 598 see Majid Khadduri, *The Gulf War* (New York: Oxford University Press, 1988), pp. 219–22.

37. Ramazani, *Revolutionary Iran*, p. 157.

38. For the complete text of United Nations Security Council Resolution 598, see Khadduri, *The Gulf War*, pp. 215–16.

39. See FBIS/NES, September 7, 1988, vol. 88, no. 173.

40. Jerusalem *Post International Edition*, August 27, 1988, p. 7.

41. FBIS/NES, July 10, 1988, vol. 88, no. 139.

42. FBIS/NES, August 23, 1988, vol. 88, no. 163.

43. FBIS/NES, September 27, 1988, vol. 88, no. 187.

7

The Future of
Israeli-Iranian Relations

This study explains the story of Israeli-Iranian relations in terms of a conceptual framework organized into seven categories: the anarchic nature of the international and regional environment; the demographic component of Israel's foreign policy; the need to contain Soviet and Sunni Arab hegemony of the Middle East; Israel's technical assistance to Iran and the sale of Iranian oil to Israel; Israel's special relationship with Washington; Iran-Arab and Arab-Israeli relations; and the nature of the regime in Iran. This conceptual framework provides a valuable tool to understand the dynamic of the Tehran-Tel Aviv axis and its future direction.

ANARCHIC NATURE OF THE INTERNATIONAL
AND REGIONAL ENVIRONMENT

From our examination of the period between 1948 and 1988, we have seen that regardless of who rules in Tehran or Tel Aviv, both Israel and Iran exist in a hostile geopolitical environment. Both states in their search to respond to this security predicament have over the years found common ground for the establishment of a pragmatic entente. As Israeli scholar Avner Yaniv writes:

> It is difficult to ignore the strength and fundamental durability of the Israeli connection with Iran. The root of this connection [is] neither history, nor ideology, nor indeed, any cultural affinity.

> Whatever the regime, the response of [Iran and Israel] to the age-old
> rules of balance-of-power game — in itself a variant of what might
> be called deterrence diplomacy — keeps leading them into each
> other's embrace. The mutual interest may be limited, but it has been
> real enough all along.[1]

The fundamental challenges of the international and regional
setting that Iran and Israel find themselves locked into, which
led and continues to lead both states in one another's
direction, will constitute an enduring feature of any analysis of
future Israeli-Iranian relations.

DEMOGRAPHIC COMPONENT OF
ISRAEL'S FOREIGN POLICY

Concern for the safety and welfare of all Jews worldwide is
a matter of national vocation for the state of Israel. Although
this issue has entered into Israeli foreign policy calculations
intermittently and only on occasion involves Iran, it will draw
Israel into a close relationship with Iran when the need arises.
Thus, even though no more than 25,000 Iranian-Jews live in
Iran today; should the Islamic republic renew its campaign of
terror against this vulnerable minority, Israel would have
reason to intensify its efforts to entice Iran, by every means
available, including the shipment of arms, to allow them to
immigrate to Israel.

CONTAINMENT OF SOVIET AND SUNNI-ARAB
HEGEMONY OF THE MIDDLE EAST

Iran's effort, both now and in the past, to promote her
broader goals in the Persian Gulf and in the Arab world, to
assert her regional role, and to gain recognition for that role
has been challenged by Sunni-Arab states unilaterally or in
concert with the Soviet Union. This challenge is permanent;
therefore, the goal of challenging it transcends the nature of
the regime in Tehran.

In the past, the Shah perceived these goals as being best
served by strengthening status quo forces against reactionary
powers. His alliance with Israel, therefore, was to enable him
to create as congenial a regional environment as possible for

Iran's security and other interests, which were being threatened by the Soviet Union and Arab radicalism. Thus, for 30 years, the Shah's strategic thought intersected with Israel's peripheral policy, which was designed to contain and neutralize the Soviet-Arab encirclement of Israel.

Despite the change of regime in Tehran, the challenge of Arab hegemony — particularly in the Persian Gulf — continued unabated and manifested itself in the crudest form when Iraq invaded Iran in September 1980. In order to keep itself alive and defend Iran's territorial integrity the Khomeini regime established military links with Israel. This pragmatism, however, has been tempered by the Islamic republic's vision of its regional goals, namely, the strengthening of Islamic and other revolutionary forces in the region.[2] To a certain extent, the Islamization of the region does not appear to be in tandem with Israel's orientation of a status quo foreign policy. Rather, it is in direct conflict with Israel's attempts to bolster the moderate elements in the region for peace with Israel. Iran sees Israel as the major obstacle to the Islamization of the Middle East, and it views the Sunni-Arab states in the same light. From Shiite Iran's perspective, pan-Arabism and pan-Islamism represent "deviations from the true path."[3]

In addition to its ideological objections to Sunni-Arab hegemony, Iran has territorial goals that conflict with those of Sunni Iraq. The Islamic regime has insisted on using the 1975 Algiers Accord between the Shah and Saddam Hussein, an agreement establishing the thalweg as the border between Iran and Iraq along the Shatt-al-Arab, as the basis for a settlement of its war with Iraq: "We will in no way allow the 1975 accord be undermined even at the expense of the resumption of the war."[4] In this respect, Islamic Iran's perceptions of the vital importance of the Persian Gulf and preventing Arab hegemony over it are remarkably similar to those in the past.

As in the past, should the regime in Tehran, whatever its future make-up, feel that it cannot unilaterally contain Soviet or Sunni-Arab hegemony over what it perceives to be its vital strategic, economic, and political interests, it will reactivate its Israeli connection in whatever form necessary. In the final analysis then, although it is very difficult to imagine the Islamic republic befriending Israel, any serious outside threat to its existence may trigger an Israeli link to protect the Islamic republic from, as they will phrase it, "Soviet atheists and enemies of Shiism."

TRADE IN TECHNICAL ASSISTANCE AND OIL

The Shah of Iran was willing to solicit Israeli expertise in agriculture and military technology in order to develop his country and raise the standard of living. In exchange Iran supplied Israel with crude oil. The clerical regime's agenda and hostility toward Israel preclude any such arrangement. The following policy statement that appeared in *Keyhan* after the cease-fire with Iraq echoes this situation:

> One area that must be watched most urgently and of necessity by the country's officials is the regime's foreign relations and diplomacy, especially with regard to trade and economic relations. . . . Now, after the establishment of a cease-fire, we have to implement new plans and programs that will not violate the fine, steadfast aspirations of the revolution. . . . Our war against the world aggressors [United States and Israel] is no longer a military one, but an economic and cultural one. . . . To face history's tricksters, we too must have tricks up our sleeves. We must not give points without first taking them. Giving and getting points must never compromise the revolution's principles.[5]

In view of this dogma-driven agenda of traditionalists in Iran today, one may safely conclude that the prospects for any future Israeli technical assistance to Iran or the sale of Iranian oil to Israel, which was an important variable in Israeli-Iranian relations under the secular rule of Mohammad Reza Shah Pahlavi, are highly unlikely.

ISRAEL'S SPECIAL RELATIONSHIP WITH WASHINGTON

An implicit reason for Iran's Israel connection was the Shah's determination that his country's economic, military, and geopolitical agenda receive support in the United States. The Shah was well aware of the special relationship between Washington and Tel Aviv and did not hesitate to invoke

Iran's close ties to Israel in order to win executive and legislative approval for economic or military assistance to Iran. It is precisely this association with the United States that has led Khomeini to bestow upon Israel the title "Little Satan." Tehran views the Washington-Tel Aviv axis as a "conspiracy against Islam" and an attempt to exploit the "oppressed masses." The argument is that as long as the clerical regime stays in power, its need to explain itself to the United States by cultivating closer ties to Israel is a moot point, for the Islamic republic, unlike Iran under the Shah, has no agenda to defend in the United States.

IRAN-ARAB AND ARAB-ISRAELI RELATIONS

A major determinant of the strengths and weaknesses of Israeli-Iranian relations has been Iran's relations with the Arab world, on the one hand, and the extent to which the Arab-Israeli conflict has narrowed or widened Iran's distance from the Arab world, on the other hand.

Historically, the interaction of five factors has determined the underlying characteristics of Iranian-Arab relations: ethnic and religious differences; competing nationalisms; territorial disputes; ideological differences; and Iran's links to Israel.[6]

One of the most divisive factors in Iranian-Arab relations has been the combination of ethnic particularism — Iran's insistence on retaining its distinct Persian culture — and religious particularism — Iran's embrace of Shiism. As such, Iran is perceived by most Arabs as a Persian/Shiite entity, a fact that transcends the nature of the regime in Tehran.

Arab nationalist/irredentist ambitions against Iran, as symbolized by Arab efforts to change the name of the Persian Gulf to the Arabian Gulf and claims to the Iranian province of Khuzestan (called Arabistan by the Arabs), are another factor limiting the extent of Iranian-Arab amity. This factor is also independent of who rules in Tehran. In the past, Tehran's response to the challenge of Arab nationalism was perceived as a manifestation of Persian imperialism; today it is viewed as Shiite expansionism.

A number of active and latent territorial disputes between Iran and the Arab states continue to strain these relations (e.g., disputes over the three Persian Gulf islands of Abu Musa and the Greater and Lesser Tunbs). The most pressing and costly has been that over the Shatt-al-Arab waterway dividing Iran and Iraq. As in the past, Iranian insistence on using the 1975 Algiers Accord as the basis for settling this territorial dispute is reflective of an underlying truism that territorial disputes with Arab states will continue to plague Iranian-Arab relations regardless of who rules in Tehran.

Ideological differences between Iran and the Arab states stem from a seemingly perpetual clash within the Middle East between forces of change and those of the status quo. Arab enmity toward Iran during the reign of the Shah emanated form such radical states as Egypt (under Nasser), Syria, Iraq, and Libya. Today, the conservative, status quo oriented Arab states such as Saudi Arabia and Jordan are hostile to Iran. As long as the Middle East remains fractured by ideological disputes, Iranian-Arab relations will be burdened by ideological differences.

The fifth source of tension in Iranian-Arab relations has been Iran's Israeli connection. Whereas in the past, a majority of the Arab states viewed the Shah's cultivation of ties to Israel as an act of treason, some Palestinians and other Arabs now view Iran's intransigent stance in its conflict with Iraq as having damaged the Arab cause by diverting Arab energies from a united front against Israel. Although no direct mention is made of the latter pint, the *al-Fajr* commentary on Iran's acceptance of UN Resolution 598 comes very close:

> During these [eight] years, Iran's rulers have reiterated their rejection of all good-offices and Islamic, Arabic, and international efforts to resolve politically their conflict with Iraq. When resolution 598 was issued and Iraq accepted it out of a desire to provide a serious opportunity for a political settlement under UN auspices, Iran's rulers persisted in their customary rejection and escalated their pernicious fight against Iraq and other states of the Arab Gulf.[7]

The foregoing analysis suggests that the underlying forces affecting Iranian-Arab relations have remained remarkably constant irrespective of who rules in Tehran. This constancy, in turn, implies that Iran's national and security imperatives will continue to be at odds with Arab aspirations, particularly in the Persian Gulf. The degree to which Iran's relations with the Arab states affect Israeli-Iranian relations has historically been determined by Arab-Israeli relations. In short, the simultaneous convergence of Iranian-Arab relations with Arab-Israeli relations helps explain the nature and course of Iran's relations with Israel.

When Arab radicalism threatened Iran's interests in the region in the 1960s, the Tehran-Tel Aviv connection was at its zenith. As Iran-Arab relations deteriorated, Israeli-Iranian relations were strengthened by developments in the Arab-Israeli conflict and by the extent to which Israeli victories in its wars before 1973 had weakened the Arab radicals. With the ascendency of moderate elements in the Arab world after 1973 and the Iranian concern that another Arab-Israeli war would destabilize the region, the Shah chose to exercise Iran's Arab option. Although the Arab option was not a tilt toward the Arab position, it signified Iran's determination to impress upon Israeli leadership the need for a peaceful settlement of the Arab-Israeli conflict. More importantly, it signified the need to distinguish between the Arab-Israeli conflict and the Palestinian-Israeli conflict. The Shah and Foreign Minister Khalatbari believed that the crux of the Arab-Israeli dilemma was the Palestinian issue and that a resolution of this issue would bring peace and stability to the region. By resolving the Palestinian problem, the Arab states would be denied their major excuse for not making peace with Israel. It should come as no surprise, therefore, that in their meetings with their Israeli counterparts after the October War Iranian officials pressed the Israelis to recognize the legitimate rights of the Palestinian people. This Iranian position, however, did not turn into an ideological crusade for one basic reason: the Shah viewed Iran's relations with Israel as too valuable to be exchanged for Palestinian rights. From the Shah's perspective, the return on Iran's investment in relations with Israel was greater than the potential return Iran would gain from investing in the goodwill of radical Arab forces.

This viewpoint decreased in importance after the Ayatollah Khomeini took power. While the Khomeini regime's war with Iraq poisoned Iran-Arab relations far more than in the past, Israel's invasion of Lebanon in 1982, its continued occupation of the West Bank and Gaza, and the use of a unified Jerusalem as its capital since 1967 has created a deep-seated rift between Tehran and Tel Aviv. Indeed, the Islamic republic's preoccupation with the "liberation" of Jerusalem was evident at the war front, where signs were put up by the Revolutionary Guards indicating the number of kilometers to "al-Qods" or Jerusalem. Thus, the conflictual nature of the Islamic republic's relations with most Arab states — other than Syria — has not contributed to an improvement in relations with Israel, except for an occasional need to purchase arms.

In terms of the future, therefore, the intersection of Iran's relations with the Arab states and Arab-Israeli relations will set the tone for Israeli-Iranian relations. The situation implies that the contentious nature of Iranian-Arab relations that creates a similarity of interest with Israel might provide a context for an Israeli-Iranian rapprochement. However, the extent to which this similarity of interest contributes to Israeli-Iranian relations will be determined by the nature of the regime in Tehran and its perceptions of the Arab-Israeli conflict.

WHO RULES IRAN: SECULARISTS OR TRADITIONALISTS

Although the foregoing factors have played an important role in Israeli-Iranian relations, the question of who rules Iran has had the most immediate effect on these relations. Thus, Israeli-Iranian relations from 1948 through 1953, a period in which Shiite clerics wielded tremendous influence in Iranian politics, may be characterized as ambivalent whereas relations during the period from 1954 through 1978, when the secularists had control of the country, can be described as accommodative. After the establishment of the Islamic republic, in which all decision making is controlled by Shiite clerics, relations between Iran and Israel have been antagonistic. Quite naturally a major policy debate today in Israel centers on the question of who will rule Iran after Khomeini's death.

Proponents of keeping Israel's Iran option alive, such as Defense Minister Rabin and Uri Lubrani, argue that Khomeini and the Islamic republic are a parenthesis in the history of Iran. Iran and the people of Iran, they argue, are far too important to Israel's strategic interests to be abandoned. The basic premise of the pro-Iran school is that the major threat to Israel's security is its traditional Arab enemies, Libya, Iraq, and Syria. Therefore, it is important to keep the Iran option open. Opponents of the Iran option contend that the Islamic republic is here to stay and that Israel has nothing to gain and everything to lose by courting Iran. Israeli decision makers must "wake up from the peripheral policy" and recognize that Iran is now Israel's foremost enemy.

The idea of exercising Israel's Arab option gained prominence during the course of the Iran-Iraq war. Opponents of the Iran option argued that as long as the war between Iran and Iraq continued, a gradual integration of the Arab zone into Israel's strategic thinking was essential, and they pointed to the Iran-Iraq conflict as an excellent opportunity to cultivate closer ties to Iraq and its moderate Arab supporters. Although cease-fire in the Persian Gulf war has effectively ended any hopes of an Iraqi option, Israeli policy makers have reason to exercise extreme caution in implementing this dangerous policy alternative.[8] As Defense Minister Rabin pointed out after Iran's acceptance of UN Resolution 598:

> Let us not forget: Iraq initiated the war against Iran in 1980. In 1975, the same guy who initiated the war in Iraq, Saddam Husayn, signed an agreement with the Shah of Iran, in which all the oil problems were solved. The rights of navigation at the Persian Gulf were settled. The fact that he had signed an agreement did not prevent him from going to war once he believed that the strategic situation had changed in his favor. The fact that his signature was on the paper did not bother him for more than a few seconds. When he thought he had the advantage, he used force to achieve goals he could not have achieved before.[9]

The choice for Israel about keeping its Iran option alive is problematic. Although the clerical regime has periodically made calls for an Iranian march to "liberate" Jerusalem, in order for Iran to march toward Jerusalem it must pass through Iraq. After ten years of war it is difficult to envision an Iranian-Iraqi partnership against any common enemy.[10] Furthermore, as Prime Minister Shamir pointed out in an interview with *La Vanguardia*, "Iraq's stance toward Israel has always been very hostile. Once Iraqis are free of the war perhaps they will be tempted to form a front against us."[11]

In the final analysis, therefore, Israel's cultivation of closer ties to Iran will, as it has over the past 40 years, be a function of the limits the global and regional setting impose on Israel. To the extent that Iran can add to Israel's security, either in absolute terms or marginally, she will figure prominently in Tel Aviv's strategic thinking — whoever rules in Tehran. From the Iranian perspective, as long as a clerical regime remains in power, there seems little hope of any rapprochement with Israel. Despite arms purchases from Israel, Islamic challenge to Israel appears to be a durable feature of Iran's foreign policy. Although this policy may now change with the death of Khomeini, any successor who wishes to establish his revolutionary credentials must continue Khomeini's legacy, and an integral part of this legacy has been open hostility toward and distrust of Israel.

CONCLUSIONS

Israeli-Iranian relations have fluctuated between the extremes of friendship and outright hostility. During the late 1940s and early 1950s, relations were clearly fragile. From the mid-1950s until the late 1970s, they were stable and cordial. And since 1979, relations between Israel and Iran have been marked by mistrust and hostility. A more differentiated interpretation, based on the main factors leading to both change and continuity in Israeli-Iranian relations as outlined in the previous chapters, leads to three important conclusions:

The character of the regime in Tehran has had the most immediate influence on Israeli-Iranian relations: secularists have welcomed ties to the Jewish state whereas traditionalists have opposed cultivation of closer ties to Israel.

Although the regime in Tehran, whatever its character, is subject to change, the geopolitical predicament that creates a convergence of interest between Israel and Iran is durable.

Israel and Iran, by nature of their geopolitical position — which is a function of the international and regional system — exist dangerously. In other words, each finds the other a potential asset in counterbalancing its more immediate adversaries.

Four of the seven variables that form these conclusions are permanent and impinge on Israeli-Iranian relations with varying degrees irrespective of who rules in Iran: the anarchic nature of the international and regional environment, the demographic component of Israel's foreign policy, the need to contain Soviet and Sunni-Arab hegemony of the Middle East, and the intersection of Iranian-Arab relations on the one hand and Arab-Israeli relations on the other. The picture that emerges of the substantial base for Israeli-Iranian relations is a fairly clear one. The anarchic nature of the international and regional system and the need to contain Soviet and Sunni-Arab hegemony of the Middle East give exceptional support; continued concern for the safety of the Jewish community inside Iran helps; and Iran's contentious relations with the Arab states and the direction of the Arab-Israeli conflict must be rated as more helpful than detrimental. When one moves to the question of who rules in Tehran, however, the picture begins to change. Unlike Iran under the Shah, the establishment of an Islamic republic in Iran has not been favorable to Israeli-Iranian relations. What emerges, therefore, is a picture of ideologically and politically motivated rejection of Israel, combined with a measure of pragmatism.

This situation implies that, in the future, Israeli-Iranian relations will remain a mixture of tactical cooperation over issues pertaining to the survival of Jewish and Iranian statehood tempered by ideologically motivated disagreements — a pragmatic entente responding to the exigencies of survival in the tumultuous politics of the Middle East in particular and the world at large.

NOTES

1. Avner Yaniv, *Deterrence without the Bomb: The Politics of Israel's Strategy* (Lexington, MA: D. C. Heath, 1987), p. 223.

2. Shireen Hunter, "Islamic Iran and the Arab World," *Middle East Insight* 5 (September 1987): 20.

3. The failure of pan-Arabism to integrate the Arab system encouraged the Saudis to cultivate a new identity: pan-Islamism. For a

detailed discussion of pan-Islamism and pan-Arabism, see Abdul-Monem Al-Mashat, "Stress and Disintegration in the Arab World," in *Pan-Arabism and Arab Nationalism: The Continuing Debate*, ed. Tawfic E. Farah (London: Westview Press, 1987), pp. 165–76.

4. Comments by Hojatoleslam Ali Akbar Hashemi-Rafsanjani, Speaker of the Majlis in FBIS/NES, September 21, 1988, vol. 88, no. 183. Also for the full text of the 1975 Algiers Accord see Majid Khadduri, *The Gulf War* (New York: Oxford University Press, 1988), pp. 201–07.

5. FBIS/NES, August 23, 1988, vol. 88, no. 163.

6. For a detailed discussion of Iranian-Arab relations, see Shireen Hunter, "Islamic Iran and the Arab World," *Middle East Insight* 5 (September 1987): 17–25.

7. FBIS/NES, July 21, 1988, vol. 88, no. 140.

8. According to Israeli sources the Iraqi military's most substantial improvement since its war with Iran has been in its air force, which after being restructured, proved its ability to perform long-range raids and precise attacks. The sophisticated means at the disposal of the Iraqi pilots enable the accurate firing of a missile carrying 300 kg of explosives from a range of 30 km to 40 km. This ability, according to Israeli military strategists, presents Israel with a problem that cannot be solved through mere organization. For a discussion of the Iraqi military's potential see FBIS/NES, July 21, 1988, vol. 88, no. 140.

9. FBIS/NES, July 18, 1988, vol. 88, no. 145.

10. For a discussion of Israel's options after the cease-fire in the Persian Gulf see comments by Isareli Defense Minister Yitzhak Rabin in FBIS/NES, July 20, 1988, vol. 88, no. 139.

11. Comments by Prime Minister Yitzhak Shamir in FBIS/NES, September 7, 1988, vol. 88, no. 173.

Bibliography

BOOKS (ENGLISH, FRENCH, PERSIAN)

Amir, Shimeon. *Israel's Development Cooperation with Africa, Asia, and Latin America.* New York: Praeger, 1974.

Amirsadeghi, Hossein, ed. *Twentieth Century Iran.* London: William Heinemann Ltd., 1977.

Art, Robert, and Robert Jervis. *International Politics.* Toronto: Little, Brown and Company, 1985.

Aryanpour, Abbas. *Iranian Influence in Judaism and Christianity.* Tehran: Golshan Press, 1970.

Badeeb, Saeed M. *The Saudi-Egyptian Conflict over North Yemen, 1960–1970.* Bounder, CO: Westview Press, 1986.

Bayne, E. A. *Persian Kingship in Transition.* New York: American Universities Field Staff, Inc., 1968.

Beit-Hallahmi, Benjamin. *The Israeli Connection: Who Israel Arms and Why.* New York: Pantheon Books, 1987.

Bill, James A. *The Eagle and the Lion: The Tragedy of American-Iranian Relations.* New Haven: Yale University Press, 1988.

Brecher, Michael. *The Foreign Policy System of Israel.* New Haven: Yale University Press, 1972.

____. *Decisions in Israel's Foreign Policy.* New Haven: Yale University Press, 1975.

Calvocoressi, Peter. *International Politics since 1945.* New York: Praeger, 1968.

Dayan, Moshe. *Breakthrough.* New York: Knopf, 1981.

Deacon, Richard. *The Israeli Secret Service.* London: Hamilton, 1977.

Goldschmidt, Arthur. *A Concise History of the Middle East.* Boulder, CO: Westview Press, 1983.

Ismael, Tareq Y. *International Relations of the Contemporary Middle East.* Syracuse, NY: Syracuse University Press, 1986.

Klieman, Aaron S. *Israel's Global Reach: Arms Sales as Diplomacy*. New York: Pergamon-Bassey's, 1985.

Lenczowski, George. *The Middle East in World Affairs*. Ithaca, NY: Cornell University Press, 1962.

___, ed. *Iran under the Pahlavis*. Stanford, CA: Hoover Institution Press, 1978.

Lieber, Robert J. *Theory and World Politics*. Cambridge, MA: Winthrop, Little-Brown, 1972.

Morgenthau, Hans J. *Politics among Nations: The Struggle for Power and Peace*. New York; Knopf, 1985.

North, Oliver L. *Taking the Stand: The Testimony of Lieutenant Colonel Oliver L. North*. New York: Pocket Books, 1987.

Pahlavi, Mohammad Reza Shah. *Mission for My Country*. London: Hutchinson Press, 1961.

Pean, Pierre, *La Menace*. Paris: Fayard, 1987.

Peres, Shimon. *David's Sling*. London: Weidenfeld and Nicolson, 1970.

Rabinovich, Itamar, and Jehuda Reinharz, eds. *Israel in the Middle East*. New York: Oxford University Press, 1984.

Ramazani, R. K. *Iran's Foreign Policy, 1941–1973*. Charlottesville, VA: University of Virginia Press, 1975.

___. *Revolutionary Iran*. Baltimore, MD: Johns Hopkins University Press, 1986.

___. *The United States and Iran: The Patterns of Influence*. New York: Praeger, 1982.

Rejwan, Nissim. *The Jews of Iraq*. London: Westview Press, 1985.

Reppa, Robert B. *Israel and Iran: Bilateral Relationships and Effect on the Indian Ocean Basin*. New York: Praeger, 1974.

Shafa, Shojaedin. *Jenayat va Mokafat*, Vol. 3. Paris, 1986.

Sick, Gary. *All Fall Down: America's Tragic Encounter with Iran*. New York: Random House, 1985.

Spykman, Nicholas. *The Geography of Peace*. New York: Harcourt Brace Jovanovich, 1944.

Taheri, Amir. *The Spirit of Allah*. Bethesda, MD: Adler & Adler, 1986.

Waltz, Kenneth. *Theory of International Politics*. New York: Random House, 1979.

Yaniv, Avner. *Deterrence without the Bomb: The Politics of Israeli Strategy*. Lexington, MA: D. C. Heath, 1987.

___. *Dilemmas of Security*. New York: Oxford University Press, 1987.

ARTICLES

Alpher, Joseph. "Arms for the Ayatollahs." *Moment* (May 1987): 15–18.

Avineri, Shlomo. "Ideology and Israel's Foreign Policy." *Jerusalem Quarterly* 37 (1986): 3–13.

Bialer, Uri. "The Iranian Connection in Israel's Foreign Policy, 1948–1951." *Middle East Journal* 39 (Spring 1985): 292–315.

Housego, David. "End of an Estrangement." *Financial Times*, January 8, 1975.

Hunter, Shireen. "Islamic Iran and the Arab World." *Middle East Insight* 5 (September 1987): 17–25.

Jones, J. D. "Growing Importance of a Very Discreet Friendship." *Financial Times*, June 3, 1969.

Levin, Susan. "A Study of Development: Iran." *Near East Report* 10 (January 1966): 1–27.

Lubrani, Uri. "Open Options." *New Outlook* (January/February 1987): 12–13.

Ramazani, R. K. "Iran and the Arab-Israeli Conflict." *Middle East Journal* 32 (Autumn 1978): 413–28.

Rosen, Edward R. "The Effect of Relinquished Sinai Resources on Israel's Energy Situation and Politics." *Middle East Review* (Spring/Summer 1982): 5–11.

Shimoni, Yaacov. "Israel in the Pattern of Middle East Politics." *Middle East Journal* 4 (July 1950): 277–95.

Weinbaum, Marvin G. "Iran and Israel: The Discreet Entente." *Orbis* 18 (Winter 1975): 1070–87.

Weiser, Benjamin. "Behind Israel-Iran Sales, 'Amber' Light from U.S." Washington *Post*, August 16, 1987, p. 7.

THESIS

Shaoul, E. E. "Cultural Values and Foreign Policy Decision Making in Iran: The Case of Iran's Recognition of Israel." Ph.D. dissertation, George Washington University, 1971.

GOVERNMENT DOCUMENTS

Asnad-i Lanah-yi Jasusi (Documents of the United States Embassy in Tehran). Vols. 1–58. Tehran: 1979–1987.

Index

About the Author

SOHRAB SOBHANI is Adjunct Professor of International Relations at Georgetown University.